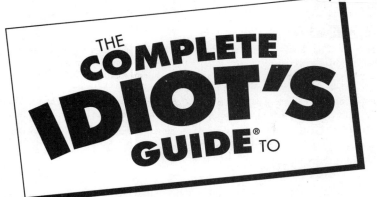

THE COMPLETE IDIOT'S GUIDE TO

Success as a Real Estate Agent

by Marilyn Sullivan

ALPHA

A member of Penguin Group (USA) Inc.

International Standard Book Number: 1-59257-128-x
Library of Congress Catalog Card Number: 2003111794

05   04   8 7   6   5   4

Interpretation of the printing code: The rightmost number of the first series of numbers is the year of the book's printing; the rightmost number of the second series of numbers is the number of the book's printing. For example, a printing code of 03-1 shows that the first printing occurred in 2003.

Printed in the United States of America

Note: This publication contains the opinions and ideas of its author. It is intended to provide helpful and informative material on the subject matter covered. It is sold with the understanding that the author and publisher are not engaged in rendering professional services in the book. If the reader requires personal assistance or advice, a competent professional should be consulted.

The author and publisher specifically disclaim any responsibility for any liability, loss, or risk, personal or otherwise, which is incurred as a consequence, directly or indirectly, of the use and application of any of the contents of this book.

Most Alpha books are available at special quantity discounts for bulk purchases for sales promotions, premiums, fund-raising, or educational use. Special books, or book excerpts, can also be created to fit specific needs.

For details, write: Special Markets, Alpha Books, 375 Hudson Street, New York, NY 10014. To contact the author, e-mail ms@msullivan.com.

Portions of the text in Chapter 2, sections "Personality Profiling" through "Take Your Time," are Copyright © Paul Tieger and Barbara Barron-Tieger, authors of *Do What You Are: Discover the Perfect Career for You Through the Secrets of Personality Type*, and are used herein by permission of Paul Tieger and Barbara Barron-Tieger.

Publisher: *Marie Butler-Knight*
Product Manager: *Phil Kitchel*
Senior Managing Editor: *Jennifer Chisholm*
Senior Acquisitions Editor: *Mike Sanders*
Development Editor: *Ginny Bess Munroe*
Production Editor: *Billy Fields*
Copy Editor: *Michael Dietsch*
Illustrator: *Chris Eliopoulos*
Cover/Book Designer: *Trina Wurst*
Indexer: *Julie Bess*
Layout/Proofreading: *Angela Calvert, Donna Martin*

Contents at a Glance

Contents

Foreword

If you are in the real estate business or considering making real estate sales your career, you need to read this book. Marilyn Sullivan brings a new and refreshing perspective to the real estate profession. As a past president of the National Association of Realtors, I can attest to the fact that the real estate industry is experiencing phenomenal change in the way we do business from the ground floor up. As a result, there is a need for a kind of refurbishing of the way real estate professionals represent and communicate with their clients. Marilyn Sullivan is able to address these issues from many vantage points through her expertise as a real estate broker, lawyer, author, and entrepreneur over the past 25 years.

Marilyn's legal background gives her the tools to define the job of the real estate agent as more of a professional client advocate instead of a salesperson geared toward selling a client on a product. As a broker and lawyer who has analyzed the legal obligation of the real estate agent to her client from both perspectives, she is able to introduce you to a *New Ideal* in the way real estate professionals represent their clients. This important book tutors you in this updated and upgraded model of providing ethics-based, client-first service to clientele. *The New Ideal* as presented in this book is an about-face from salesperson mentality to professional real estate practitioner as the image of the real estate agent evolves with its changing marketplace.

The real estate industry is both rewarded and challenged by technological innovation. The handshake of yesteryear has turned into high-tech methods of conducting business. The business of real estate sales has become so directly linked to the Internet and to a well-organized contacts database, by virtue of its endless stream of people, that technology must be the mainstay of your business. This book shows you how to stay in step with technology and to incorporate it fully into your business, yet still retain the personal touch, which is so important in the real estate business.

Real estate professionals are entrepreneurs in every sense of the word. We work under a company's logo, but we are the owners and operators of our own small businesses. If you come to real estate with an entrepreneurial state of mind, you will have the best chance to achieve maximum success, personal fulfillment, and optimum profit. In this excellent new book, Marilyn coaches you to set your limits high and reach them. Her approach is both practical and philosophical, incorporating high ideals, creative thinking, and practical solutions.

As an innovator of deal-making strategies, Marilyn mentors you to sharpen your creative mindset for forging your own specialties and making deals happen. Home staging is emphasized as a valuable way to advance your listing package and increase the market for residential listings. She also shows you a method of reverse farming whereby your market finds you 24-7 through scrupulous building and indexing of your website.

Marilyn also shares her proven technology-based marketing technique called the *Referral Stream System* to help you build a business that is entirely referral-based. Her *Future Income Stream* strategies will cause you to view your earnings as long-term investments instead of short-term sources of income, transforming you into a profit-earning investor. You will be motivated to adopt an investor state of mind as you are tutored to become a *Top Dog* in your field.

While many other books have been written about how to achieve success as a real estate agent, this book is a treatise on how to practice real estate in a more productive, professional manner. Let me say it one more time; if you are in the real estate business or considering making real estate sales your career, you need to read this book.

Richard Mendenhall

2001 President of the National Association of REALTORS

Introduction

Careers in real estate are appealing to a wider group of people now that the real estate market has earned its reputation as a powerful and reliable sector of our economy. With the real estate market's consistent long-term appreciation and favored tax treatment, real estate as an investment has become enormously attractive, and even more so since interest rates hit all-time lows. When compared with the stock market's dismal performance, the real estate market has taken an enviable leadership position.

The market is not the only aspect of real estate that has experienced influential change. Its workforce has undergone a dramatic shift in the past few years. Not so long ago, a career in real estate sales was the second profession of the homemaker or teacher. In recent years, with the downsizing of corporate America, real estate professionals now include upper management and technology professionals. More and more people are recognizing that the independence afforded the real estate sales professional coupled with the potential for unlimited income make a career in real estate sales quite attractive.

The real estate market's consumer has also transformed as a definitive trend takes place toward moving stock market investments to the real estate market. The real estate investment purchaser is beginning to resemble the weary stock market investor. The residential purchaser, too, has changed as his technological aptitude advances. This new generation of buyers has taken control of their end of the process through utilization of the internet to both search for an agent and for available properties for sale.

These revolutionary changes mark an important crossroads in the real estate industry. No longer will agents write offers on the hoods of cars and bait their clients with sales pitches. Today's agent serves an entirely different consumer and is expected to work faster, smarter, and more efficiently. Mobile technology has replaced the hood of the car, and a more professional client relationship has replaced the old sales routine. Outdated mailers and cold calls no longer create markets, having been replaced by 24-7 web technology and agent specialization. This book addresses the many changes occurring within the real estate industry, and bridges the gap between the real estate industry of yesteryear and the one that is before us now.

A thorough search of the real estate field nationwide brought the publisher to Ms. Sullivan as the ideal candidate to write this innovative book. Review her letter to you inside the front cover and her qualifications inside the back cover of this book. Her 25-year history as an industry leader encompasses technological modernization, entrepreneurial innovation, legal analysis, and integrity-based practice. Without exception, the strategies she has developed and shared in this book make it possible for you to gain momentum no matter where you are in your real estate career.

What You Will Learn in This Book

The Idiot's Guide To Success as a Real Estate Agent is written in six parts. Each one addresses a different aspect of the real estate business.

Part 1, "First Things First," answers your question, "Is real estate for me?" It explores why the real estate profession is luring more and more people through its doors. Although the residential real estate agent is featured throughout this book, the many other career opportunities available to the licensed agent are described with a day in the life of each. This part concludes with a primer on the educational requirements you will need to fulfill prior to obtaining your license and finally, taking the real estate licensing exam itself.

Part 2, "Getting Started," coaches you on making the right choices from the moment you obtain your license. Choosing your first office is a crucial decision since this is where you will develop your style of real estate practice. And, although you will be working under a broker's supervision, you are actually about to become the CEO of your own small business. The business model from which to launch your successful real estate practice includes formulating a concrete small business plan as well as incorporating basic principles of personal and professional power. In this book, you will be coached to adopt an entrepreneurial vision through finding your passion in your work, cultivating and sustaining independent thinking and honing self-discipline as the force that puts it all together. The final step in the small business plan is to build a Power Team that sustains your business and your clientele throughout the rest of your career.

Part 3, "Building an Unbeatable System," provides the stability and competence to give your business a strong foundation. In the real estate world, that means consistent and focused marketing, managing your time, and using technology to the maximum. The many faces of market making are examined, from the old-school handshake to high-tech web-based protocols. The time demons that threaten transactions are identified so you can deal with them in a proactive way. Computer technology with a capital *C* is introduced as a peak platform for your business to serve you and your clients in a powerful way.

Part 4, "Putting It All Together," delivers a new way of practicing real estate through two success-building strategies, the Referral Stream System and the New Ideal. While the Referral Stream System generates your client base and turns your business into a referral-based operation, the New Ideal delivers an upgraded, more professional quality of client service. One system brings clients in the door while the other keeps them after they enter. This part also presents a new perspective on what makes up a winning listing presentation. If any part of this book is the most essential to the creation of your success, this is it.

Part 5, "The Parts of a Transaction," is a primer on real estate practices and principles. It presents the residential real estate transaction from every conceivable perspective: representing the seller or the buyer and preparing and analyzing the transaction documents. Chapters 17 and 18 examine your client relationships from the beginning of a transaction to the very end. The important transaction documents are reviewed from the author's legal-oriented perspective. This part is a mini-legal course that will provide you with a valuable legal resource for the rest of your career.

Part 6, "Becoming a Top Dog," presents the tools and strategies highly successful agents use to move their careers into high gear. These peak performers adopt cutting-edge approaches as they dominate the market through entrepreneurial planning, specialization, and web-based technology. The importance of staging your listings is discussed, beginning at the curb and flowing throughout the home. Top Dogs develop an entrepreneurial state of mind as they plan for Future Income Streams by seeing real estate as a long-term investment instead of a short-term source of income. The Top Dog takes on the image of a profit-earning investor in lieu of a commission-earning salesperson.

The **Glossary** works as a good reference tool for you to access throughout your real estate practice.

Also available from the author on her website, www.msullivan.com, are a number of supplemental tools you may want to avail yourself of in developing and fine-tuning your real estate practice, including:

- A primer on creating your website
- Professional home staging checklist
- List of standard transaction steps
- Agent Red Flag inspection checklist
- Understanding the tax law on sale of a principal residence
- Understanding the tax law on sale of an investment property
- Selling your business as a business opportunity or franchise
- "Maximizing Profit on the Sale of Your Home" seminar agenda
- Sample listing presentation package
- Sample equity-sharing agreement
- FSBOs sample website pages
- Converting commissions to equity interests
- Creating a retirement account pool of investors
- Creating a limited liability company
- Creating a limited partnership
- Seller disclosure instructions
- Offer preparation checklist
- Building *Personal and Professional Power*, Principles 8 through 14
- *Power Team* building checklist
- A primer on self-directed retirement account investment
- A closer look at *The New Ideal*
- *Future Income Streams*, advanced course

See www.msullivan.com for more tools.

Extras

With the hope of making this book easy to read and conveniently organized for finding what you need to succeed as a real estate agent, there are four different types of sidebars that provide additional information. These are explained here.

FYI!

Statistics and other information amplifying important points to give you extra tools and resources.

Real Estate Lingo

Definitions of words or terms for the Real Estate Top Dog's Dictionary, which can also be found in the Glossary.

The Inside Scoop

Insider tips and statistics for use in your career.

Caution

Heads up so you can avoid stumbling blocks others have encountered!

Acknowledgments

My special thanks to Carolina Sullivan for the many hours she lay at my feet or led me on dog walks as the chapters of this book unfolded; to my agents Bob Diforio and Marilyn Allen for making the writing of this book possible; to Mike Sanders, my acquisitions editor, for having faith in my abilities; to Ginny Bess, my development editor, for wise navigation through the manuscript and for her encouragement and support; to Grant Munroe for his technical review; to Carol Coltan and Shannon O'Brien for their talents in refining the manuscript; to the great Spirit above for the creative resources you continually instill in me; to Penguin-Putnam for developing *The Complete Idiot's Guides* as a series of excellent reference books; to Paul and Barbara Tiegers for profiling the personality type for real estate professionals for Chapter 2; to the many Top Dogs who shared their insights and experiences, including Paul Lehman, Melissa Prandi, Maureen McGettigan, Jeff Drawdy, Paul James, and James McKenney, Esq.; to Jim Edmondson for his wisdom; and last but not least, my special thanks to Al Bianchi, Esq., for the many ways in which he has contributed to my success in real estate.

Special Thanks to the Technical Reviewer

The Complete Idiot's Guide to Success as a Real Estate Agent was reviewed by an expert who double-checked the accuracy of what you'll learn here, to help us ensure that this book gives you everything you need to know about succeeding as a real estate agent. Special thanks are extended to Chris Hunter.

Trademarks

All terms mentioned in this book that are known to be or are suspected of being trademarks or service marks have been appropriately capitalized. Alpha Books and Penguin Group (USA) Inc. cannot attest to the accuracy of this information. Use of a term in this book should not be regarded as affecting the validity of any trademark or service mark.

Part 1

First Things First

Although this book is geared toward achieving success as a real estate agent, this first part is for anyone considering becoming an agent. It discusses the reasons why real estate is particularly attractive to people looking for career satisfaction. In fact, with the real estate industry taking its place as a reliable and powerful sector of our economy, there is a clear trend in favor of the profession as a primary career choice.

The real estate field gives its agents a diverse array of specialties from which to make a career choice. The spectrum of careers is featured along with personality profiles that were created just for this book. You will then review a day in the life of each career, so you can take your own personality profile and match it to the real estate career best suited to you. Once you decide that real estate is for you, this part guides you through satisfying the prelicensing educational requirements and taking and passing the licensing exam.

The Attraction of Real Estate

In This Chapter

- ◆ The real estate agent is an entrepreneur
- ◆ A long list of job satisfactions
- ◆ The many roles the agent plays
- ◆ Independence and flexibility mark the real estate profession
- ◆ A potential for great financial reward

Real estate agents are a sneaky bunch. They know they've found utopia, but you'd never know it by speaking with them. People ask, "How do you like what you do?" The agent grimaces, "It's a lot of hard work. There's no rest for the real estate agent." As she walks away, proud to have guarded her secret and her market once again, a smile washes back over her. The truth is the real estate profession confers a bundle of rewards that its members jealously guard.

One reason real estate agents are smiling is that they have discovered a profession that calls to the entrepreneur. It is, so to speak, outside of the traditional career box. Where other careers set very specific criteria for its members, real estate has few. College education? Not required. High school diploma? Not really. Nine to five, five days a week? Nope. Suit and tie? Not for a second. Starter salary with little incremental increases along the way? Definitely not. A boss and the typical working-class hierarchy? Absolutely not. Act a certain way, portray a certain image? No, just be who you are. Respected professional? Yes, especially if you practice according to *The New Ideal* presented in this book. Yes, it can be utopia, but don't let anyone know.

FYI!

Are you too old to make real estate your profession? The average age of real estate agents has increased from age 42 in 1978 to age 52 in 2002. Almost a third of brokers (as opposed to agents) are 60 years old, and 16 percent of brokers are over 60. Only 12 percent of sales agents are under the age of 35, compared to 29 percent in 1978.

Despite the agent's vow to secrecy, real estate has become the number one profession people turn to when their careers prove less than fulfilling. This chapter speaks to the reasons why the real estate profession has emerged as the favored arena for people changing careers. Although the many career options available to the agent are described in Chapter 2, residential sales is featured throughout this book because 80 percent of agents choose to practice in this field.

The Satisfaction of the Job

Now let's take a look at exactly why it is that real estate sales draws people in droves and rewards them so well when they arrive. The factors described at the beginning of this chapter sound like reason enough. No set hours, no boss, and the potential for unlimited pay sound like a terrific offer. The truth is that these are the perks that draw people to the profession, but it's not the factors that keep them. Agents find that there is something more satisfying that lurks behind those big checks at the close of each escrow.

We find that the greatest reward of all is making a difference in our clients' lives. We come to find that our jobs are far more than that of a salesman pitching his product. When we encounter our clients, they are often faced with major life transitions like buying a first home, relocating, getting married, divorcing, starting a business, coping with the death of a loved one, or retiring.

We seem to join their lives in an effort to help them define and obtain property to give them shelter, fill their needs, and provide investment return. No little job, indeed. When it comes right down to it, we discover that our job is to help clients define their most basic core needs and convert them into real estate answers.

It sounds like an impossible job, but we translate our client's needs into rooms and gardens and communities. We help with financial deliberations and transform those assessments into real estate investments. Our role turns out to be one of assisting clients with key life decisions and doing everything possible to make the process seamless, meaningful, and rewarding.

That's why many of us who enter the door of real estate, especially sales, have been through many of our own life transitions and other career portals. We have lived a lot of life and want to mentor others through the process in our work. We usually have a good deal of experience in the belly of life. Although education in its traditional sense isn't required to become an agent, life's extended curriculum of varied experience *is* important if you want to become a successful real estate agent.

> **The Inside Scoop**
>
> The typical agent is a 52-year-old married female, although there is nearly an equal gender split between males and females.

Qualifications for the Job

One of the best advantages of a career in real estate is that it is not bound by the rigid traditional structures that shroud other careers. Real estate is outside of the traditional box, both in terms of its educational requirements and in terms of the practice of the profession itself. Because of these aspects, the real estate career is made for those with an entrepreneurial state of mind.

To qualify for the real estate exam, you are required to complete a certain number of real estate courses. It generally takes two to six months to complete the courses. If you have a college degree or are licensed in a related profession, this time frame is much shorter. Often the real estate licensee is not even required to have a high school diploma.

The facts show, however, that 51 percent of agents have Bachelor's degrees or advanced degrees, 7 percent have no college education, and the rest have some college education. In other words, although the licensing boards do not have high educational standards, agents tend to be well-educated.

In most states there are two levels of real estate agents. The first is an agent or broker associate; the second is a broker. Most people first take the agent's exam and apprentice as an agent for

> **FYI!**
>
> To determine your state's licensing requirements, go to your state regulatory board's website. An Internet search for "(name of your state) real estate commission" or "(name of your state) real estate department" should bring you to the site. Apprenticeship requirements to be eligible for a broker's license also vary by state.

a year or two before taking the broker's exam. Broker licensing is optional, but it is required if you want to work for yourself or employ others. Chapters 4 and 5 describe prelicensing requirements and the licensing exam itself.

The Call to Real Estate

Many of us spend years in training or obtaining educational degrees in one career only to find our way into real estate when boredom sets in. Some people want to do more than the same job everyday in a highly structured environment, and others feel they are ignoring aspects of themselves, such as their interpersonal skills, a passion for their job, and use of their more creative talents. Others find that as they get older, regular jobs carry income ceilings while in real estate income seems to rise with age.

In fact, many agents come to real estate as a second, third, or even fifth profession. A recent survey by the National Association of Realtors revealed that real estate was a first career for only 7 percent of agents. That means that 93 percent of us came from other professions.

In my case, I obtained my law degree, practiced law, and found my passion in real estate after spending years cultivating just one facet of my professional side. Real estate gave me the key to unlock the diversity of my talents and unleash a multifaceted, far more authentic persona.

The same is true of many other professionals dissatisfied with their career choices. Real estate acts like a magnet to those in career transition. The divergent spectrum of roles offered by the real estate career and its liberal working environment make real estate the choice for those who have felt restricted in other professions. Its financial reward is also a factor because the potential money you can make in the real estate field is staggering.

The successful agent finds that he or she often plays the role of decorator, coach, architect, therapist, financial advisor, lawyer, and friend. Real estate is the only profession where you can tap into all aspects of who you are and do it for a living.

The practice of real estate also escapes the traditional working class structure. While the traditional professions are engaged in structured working schedules, real estate has no set hours of operation. Real estate is listed, sold, exchanged, and managed at all times.

FYI!

Real estate encourages you to draw on your life experiences as you mentor your clients through theirs. The person who chooses the field of real estate understands that you can make a living and do what makes you feel good at the same time. In fact, you are almost guaranteed to earn a better living if you enjoy what you do.

The *for sale* sign is always out. Your schedule is earmarked by autonomy and flexibility in determining how and when to render your services.

Real Estate Has No Hierarchy

Real estate professionals are not bound by the traditional choice between self-employment and working for a company. In real estate, you can do both. You join an office within which you work for yourself at your own pace. The office already has a foundation for building your career in place. You just step into the framework and carve out your own niche. Incorporating *floor time* and office meetings is the basis of your schedule, but other than that your schedule is up to your own making.

Real estate also steers clear of the corporate structure that governs most other professions. In a hierarchical structure, centralized power often inhibits creativity in its professionals. The last thing you're supposed to be is your creative, passionate self. The traditional chain of command regulates and instructs its workers. If you step too far from your box, you are pushed back into its confines.

In real estate there are guides, not rules. Office management has very little hold on you because you're making money for them, not the other way around. The result is a far more relaxed environment where there is no real gap between economics and creativity. In real estate, making money and being creative go hand in hand.

Because of these characteristics, people with an entrepreneurial mindset thrive in the real estate industry. Your expertise is derived more from having lived a full life than from years of traditional academia. This high degree of flexibility and autonomy makes real estate the ideal profession for people with an entrepreneurial spirit seeking the ultimate in independence. It also presents the biggest challenge for the undisciplined person.

Real Estate Lingo

Floor time is the rotation of agents to respond to inquiries that come from advertisements and signs. These agents get the walk-in traffic and phone calls to the office where no agent in particular is requested. Now that most agents have direct lines, floor time is fast becoming something of the past.

Caution

Always remember, you make money for your office, not the other way around. New agents often find that they did not stockpile enough funds to get them through their first year in their new career. You should aim at starting your new real estate career with six months of living expenses on hand.

Financial Reward

Another aspect of real estate that attracts consumers and agents alike is its self-sustaining nature. As a natural resource, it is perpetual in its ability to nurture itself under the loving care of Mother Nature. In addition, its consistent appreciation and long-term and short-term tax benefits make it a highly respected commodity and the symbol of the American dream and the icon of inter-generational inheritance.

As agents, we act as its caretaker in our roles as its transfer agents. Our job is to safeguard its tender between purveyors as it travels the chain of supply and demand. When we perform our job, sustainability is built into our profession just as it is built into the earth itself. Its appreciation not only serves our clients, it rewards us with higher commissions and our own personal investments.

Because of these inherent factors, real estate rewards its caretakers' social ability, organization, and determination with the potential for immense financial abundance. When you join the ranks of the real estate entrepreneur, there is no limit to how much you can earn in both money and personal fulfillment. The doors are open, ready for you to reap the limits of your own personal capacity.

Few professions can provide similar rewards without presenting a litany of rules regulating its members' behavior. You can enter the real estate door with just a few months of study, pass the real estate exam, and earn a hardy commission, all in less than six months. There are few other careers where you can net six figures the first year working for yourself and have no set hours and no college degree.

It is not just the commission you earn that marks your success. The financial expertise you gain as an agent is a valuable asset. Not only are you learning how to handle high-stakes deals, but you also learn the tax significance and mathematics of buying and selling properties.

Because of this exposure to a market that continually offers investment opportunities, real estate can become a primary choice of investment, allowing

> **The Inside Scoop**
>
> National median appreciation for 2002 was 6.8 percent. California's appreciation for 2002 was 16 percent, nearly triple the national average. During this same period, the Dow Jones Industrial average dropped 17 percent while the NASDAQ slid 31.5 percent.

> **The Inside Scoop**
>
> The National Association of Realtors reports that the average time agents spent per transaction in 2002 was 20 hours. For an average home price of $160,000 and a commission of 3 percent for just one side of the transaction, the agent earned $240.00 an hour.

you to personally take advantage of its profit potential. Real estate becomes your own thoroughfare to personal and financial abundance, as it sets you up for income streams that will sustain you for the rest of your life. It is no longer just your clients that prosper from your acquired acumen. You step into an investor state of mind as you learn to treat real estate as a profitable long-term investment instead of a short-term source of commission income.

Although this chapter highlights why real estate attracts a wide array of professionals, we will concentrate on the many challenges that face the agent throughout the rest of this book. The profession is not without its downside, but with the concepts presented in this book you will be prepared to encounter them in a confident, empowered manner.

> **The Inside Scoop**
>
> Read any of the *Rich Dad, Poor Dad* books by Robert Kiyosaki. These books will lead you to adopt an investor state of mind through looking for long-term investment as opposed to short-term return.

The Least You Need to Know

- ◆ Real estate is an ideal field for someone who wants to be independent, have a flexible schedule, and enjoy an unlimited income potential.

- ◆ Your career in real estate gives you the ability to become an entrepreneur, develop rewarding client relationships, and ensure future income streams.

- ◆ It can take as little as three months of study to get a real estate agent license.

- ◆ Helping clients with their real estate decisions can be very rewarding in terms of personal satisfaction and financial reward.

Chapter 2

The Spectrum of Careers

In This Chapter

- ◆ Examining the diversity of careers within real estate
- ◆ Profiling your personality
- ◆ Taking your time and determining your passions when choosing a field
- ◆ Dreaming about the niche you can create in real estate

The real estate field gives its licensees a diverse array of specialties from which to make a career choice. For the agent, there is a career for every personality type, from the extreme introvert to the extrovert, and everywhere in between. Like any other career, real estate has its share of distinctive personality traits that mark the successful professionals in each of these specialties.

In Chapter 1, we looked at real estate from more of an intuitive standpoint. What is it about real estate that gives it its glamour and appeal? This chapter describes the spectrum of careers available to you once you are licensed, and the personality type best suited to each career. In the next chapter, we will look at a day in the life of each career professional so that you can see for yourself which field is most attractive to you.

An Overview of Career Choices

Your real estate license allows you to work as …

- ◆ A residential sales agent.
- ◆ A commercial sales agent.
- ◆ A mortgage broker.
- ◆ A property manager.
- ◆ An appraiser.

Later in this chapter, a description of each career is presented along with the ideal personality profile for each. But first, let's profile your personality so you can identify the real estate agent career that fits you best.

FYI!

According to the Tiegers, who wrote *Do What You Are*, the secret of career satisfaction lies in doing what you enjoy most. They say, "A few lucky people discover this secret early in life, but most of us are caught in a kind of psychological wrestling match, torn between what we think we can do and what we (or others) feel we ought to do, and what we think we want to do. Our advice? Concentrate instead on who you are, and the rest will fall into place."

Personality Profiling

The material presented here is based on the excellent work of Paul Tieger and Barbara Barron-Tieger, authors of *Do What You Are: Discover the Perfect Career for You Through the Secrets of Personality Type*. The Personality Type model, which was created by Carl Jung and Isabel Myers, describes four key aspects of personality. The four aspects of Personality Type identify people as being primarily (but not exclusively) either:

- ◆ Extroverts or Introverts
- ◆ Sensors or Intuitives
- ◆ Thinkers or Feelers
- ◆ Judgers or Perceivers

Each person has natural, inborn *preferences* for some processes and characteristics over others. Everyone has the ability to use different parts of their personalities, but their *preferences* reflect their greatest natural strengths and talents. Because Personality Type is clearly linked to career choice, it is possible to predict which types are likely to be more satisfied and successful in different careers.

To identify your type, review the brief lists below and try to determine which one sounds most like you. After you decide on personality characteristics that describe you, look at the profiles based on the same characteristics. This should help you decide which career path is most closely aligned with your personality profile.

Extroverts and Introverts

Extroverts and introverts represent the two different ways people receive and direct their energy.

Extroverts (E) show these characteristics:

- ♦ They are energized by being with people.
- ♦ They often like being the center of attention.
- ♦ They tend to act first, and then think.
- ♦ They talk more than listen.
- ♦ They enjoy a fast pace and lots of variety.

Introverts (I) show these characteristics:

- ♦ They need time alone to "recharge their batteries."
- ♦ They avoid being the center of attention.
- ♦ They think about things before acting.
- ♦ They listen more than talk.
- ♦ They like to focus on one thing at a time.

Are you more of an extrovert or an introvert? _____

Real Estate Lingo

An **extrovert** is a person who directs much of his or her energy to the outer world of people and things. An overwhelming number of real estate sales agents fall into this category.

An **introvert** is a person who focuses his or her energy on the world inside of themselves. They enjoy spending time alone and need this time to 'recharge their batteries.'

Sensors and Intuitives

Sensors and intuitives describe how people take in information.

Sensors (S) show these characteristics:

- They pay attention to facts and details.
- They trust what they experience through their five senses.
- They like new ideas only if they have practical utility.
- They are realistic and value common sense.
- They present information in a step-by-step manner.

Intuitives (N) show these characteristics:

- They pay attention to the big picture.
- They like possibilities and new ideas.
- They value imagination and innovation.
- They like to learn new skills and they get bored quickly.
- They present information in a roundabout manner.

Are you more of a sensor or an intuitive? _____

Thinkers or Feelers

Thinkers and feelers represent the ways that people make decisions.

Thinkers (T) show these characteristics:

- They tend to analyze things impersonally.
- They value logic and objectivity.
- They naturally see flaws and can be critical.
- They value truth more than diplomacy.
- They are often businesslike and assertive.

Feelers (F) show these characteristics:

- ◆ They consider the effect on others of their actions.

- ◆ They value empathy and harmony.

- ◆ They like to please and help others.

- ◆ They are often very sensitive to criticism.

- ◆ They avoid arguments, conflict, and confrontations.

Are you more of a thinker or a feeler? _____

The Inside Scoop

The authors of *Do What You Are* provide good instruction when they say, "Since the right job flows directly out of all the elements of your personality type, you need to spend some time figuring out what makes you tick. By making a conscious effort to discover the 'real you,' you can learn how to focus your natural strengths and inclinations into a career you can love for as long as you choose to work."

Judgers or Perceivers

Judgers and perceivers represent the ways people choose to organize their lives.

Judgers (J) show these characteristics:

- ◆ They are happiest once decisions are made.

- ◆ They have a strong work ethic: work now, play later.

- ◆ They set goals and work toward achieving them.

- ◆ They derive satisfaction from completing tasks.

- ◆ They are organized and take deadlines seriously.

Perceivers (P) show these characteristics:

- ◆ They value spontaneity and like to keep their options open.

- ◆ They have a play ethic: enjoy now, finish job later.

- ◆ They change goals as information changes.

♦ They like starting projects better than finishing them.

♦ They consider deadlines to be "elastic."

Are you more of a judger or a perceiver? _____

Based on these brief descriptions of the different type preferences, record below the four letters that you think represent your Personality Type:

_____ _____ _____ _____

E or I   S or N   T or F   J or P

Caution _____

> This exercise is not a validated test and is only designed to give you a *best-guess estimate* of your Type. To get a more accurate read of your Type, I recommend you take the more complete Personality Type assessment and read the accompanying profiles at www.personalitytype.com.

Next, we will review each of the primary careers available to the real estate agent and discuss some of the ideal personality types for each. Although we use the term *ideal*, in reality all types can and do succeed in all aspects of real estate. But some types are much more naturally suited to, and therefore more likely to succeed in and enjoy, certain real estate careers.

Residential Sales

Ideal personality profile: Extrovert, Sensing, Feeling, Judging (ESFJ); Extrovert, Intuitive, Feeling, Judging (ENFJ); Extrovert, Sensing, Feeling, Perceiving (ESFP); Extrovert, Sensing, Thinking, Judging (ESTJ).

As a residential sales agent, you will help clients buy and sell residential properties, encompassing single family homes, condominiums, and multi-family compounds. You will develop expertise with local communities and their economics, neighborhood statistics, schools, parks, commuting, and shopping options. You will, in other words, become immersed in your local communities and make a living doing it. This is by far the most popular of the real estate professions—80 percent of agents choose it as their field.

Residential sales agents are attracted to home buying and selling due to the highly personal and social nature of the field. Helping clients define the living environment that suits their needs naturally entails a personal analysis. It calls upon many different aspects of your persona, from decorator to therapist to lawyer and all things between. You will sometimes be called upon to handle emotional family issues, which can arise in a family home purchase. You will be in touch with the visual and decorative side of real estate, since personal creature comforts are at issue. In just a single day, you will wear many different hats and interact with many people.

These are some of the reasons that the vast majority of agents turn toward challenging and diversified residential sales. Because of the popularity of this field, this book looks most closely at the residential sales agent. Much of the next chapter is dedicated to examining a day in the life of the residential agent, along with her career experiences prior to becoming an agent.

FYI! _____

The average median income for all agents is $50,000 with the following breakdown:

$60,000 attributable to brokers

$47,000 to agents

$90,000 to commercial agents

$100,000 to property management

Extroverts prefer this field because the residential agent tends to have a commanding presence in transactions. You are a salesperson and require an assertive, outgoing nature with a good measure of confidence and persistence. You should have good people skills that come most naturally to people who are both Extroverts and Feelers. All these traits are discussed in more depth in Chapter 8.

FYI! _____

In *Do What You Are*, the sales agent personality profile of Extrovert, Sensor, Feeler, Judger (ESFJ) is described as follows:

"ESFJs are motivated to help other people in real and practical ways through direct action and cooperation. They are responsible, friendly, and sympathetic. Because ESFJs place such importance on their relationships with other people, they tend to be popular, gracious, eager to please, and talkative. Practical and realistic, ESFJs tend to be matter-of-fact and organized. They attend to and remember important facts and details. They are aware of and involved with their physical environment and like to be active and productive."

Although all people have the ability to use both their Sensing and Intuition, both aspects come in handy in residential sales since common sense and attention to detail, and imagination and creativity are all part of the successful agent's repertoire. Because of the personal and emotional aspects required of this career, Feeler types usually enjoy residential sales more than Thinkers. The residential agent needs to feel her client's considerations and understand them on an emotional level.

Real estate professionals who are Judgers and those who are Perceivers bring different gifts to the job. Judgers are usually well-organized, very productive, and closure-oriented. Perceivers are usually more spontaneous, flexible, and able to shift gears quickly—all characteristics that are required of agents on an almost daily basis. In the next chapter we will take an in-depth look at a typical day in the life of Julie, our residential sales agent.

Commercial Sales

Ideal personality profile: Extrovert, Sensing, Thinking, Judging (ESTJ); Introvert, Sensing, Thinking, Judging (ISTJ); Extrovert, Sensing, Thinking, Perceiving (ESTP); and Extrovert, Intuitive, Thinking, Judging (ENTJ).

Commercial, industrial, and farmland sales are included under the commercial category. Commercial agents specialize in income-producing properties, including office buildings, apartment buildings, stores and warehouses, and shopping centers. In order for clients to evaluate investment potentials, you need to understand growth factors, *capitalization rates* based on past income, and tax laws relating to real estate investments. Much of this career involves competency in objective analysis, number-crunching, and an emphasis on return-on-investment. It is not based nearly as much upon relationships as it is on hard, cold realities. This is why Thinkers clearly enjoy commercial real estate much more than Feelers do.

> **Real Estate Lingo**
>
> **Capitalization rates** represent the relationship between the value of the property and the income it produces.

> **Real Estate Lingo**
>
> **Zoning** is governmental regulation as to the use of a property. For instance, a property may be zoned for use by a single-family residence or it might be zoned for business.

Industrial and office real estate salespeople specialize in selling, developing, or leasing property used for industry or manufacturing. As this type of agent, you will understand the specific needs of different types of industries to determine variables such as transportation, proximity to raw materials, water and power, labor availability, and local building, *zoning*, and tax laws.

Land agents deal in land for farming and acquisition of rural land by cities for residential, commercial, and industrial expansion. Success as a land agent depends on accurately establishing the income potential of the property. As a successful land agent you will acquire a good working knowledge of agricultural and land-use factors in order to determine project feasibility.

Commercial real estate is far more analytical than residential sales. This field will appeal to you if you enjoy working with numbers and analyzing investment possibilities. Commercial agents often earn more than their residential counterparts, making income a consideration. They also enjoy schedules that conform more to regular working hours.

As a salesperson, the commercial agent has to be outgoing and assertive. Your advice should be based on hard facts and objective analysis (Sensing and Thinking characteristics), but the ability to see and present alternatives, creatively solve problems (Intuition), and be flexible when circumstances change (Perceiving) can also contribute to your success.

Mortgage Brokers

Ideal personality profile: Extrovert, Sensing, Thinking, Judging (ESTJ); Introvert, Sensing, Thinking, Judging (ISTJ); and Extrovert, Sensing, Thinking, Perceiving (ESTP).

A mortgage broker is a real estate financing professional who puts together a lender and a borrower. This is done after thoroughly reviewing the needs and capabilities of the borrower, the characteristics of the property, and the various lending programs available from a wide range of lenders. This occupation will appeal to you if you like working with numbers and monitoring the lending marketplace, which is constantly changing.

This occupation is deadline-intensive since loan approval is the last *contingency* in the transaction to be removed. You will have lenders, appraisers, real estate agents, and clients continually meeting deadlines through your services. You should therefore work well under pressure, possess good people skills, and have the ability to run an efficient, organized communication center. (Three key characteristics of Judgers are deadline-driven, organized, and efficient.)

You will also be discussing confidential information with clients and should be sensitive to

> **Real Estate Lingo**
>
> A **contingency** is a condition that is built into a purchase offer to make it conditional. The offer is conditional until such time that the conditions are removed. Then, the offer becomes unconditional and binding. The most common contingencies in the real estate transaction are the loan, the physical inspection, and the review of the title.

your clients' predicaments. As Jeff, the mortgage broker, describes in the next chapter, this job can be highly rewarding because clients are usually happy and appreciative after they get their loans. Jeff finds his job as a mortgage broker highly challenging and gratifying.

Property Managers

Ideal personality profile: Extrovert, Sensing, Thinking, Judging (ESTJ); Introvert, Sensing, Thinking, Judging (ISTJ); Extrovert, Sensing, Feeling, Judging (ESFJ); Extrovert, Sensing, Thinking, Perceiving (ESTP); and Extrovert, Sensing, Feeling, Perceiving (ESFP).

The property manager's principal role is to manage properties in order to produce the highest possible return on investment over the longest period of time. Managed commercial properties are likely to be office buildings and shopping centers; residential properties may be rental homes, apartments, and *condominium* developments. Property management generally brings higher financial reward to its agents than other fields of real estate. Property management also invariably involves more time commitment than its sister fields, as tenants must be found, qualified and maintained, while the property itself must also be kept in good repair.

Real Estate Lingo

A **condominium** is property developed for concurrent ownership where each owner has a separate interest in a unit combined with an undivided interest in the common areas of the property.

Since property management involves accounting and bookkeeping as well as dealing with owners and tenants, both the Introvert and Extrovert do well in this profession. Good people skills are mandatory since you will deal with owners and renters on a day-to-day basis. (While Introverts may be very good with people, Extroverts are naturally *drawn* to others and energized by being with them.) You will deal with raw data in the form of comparable rental values to establish lease rates for your owners (an excellent use of Sensing).

You will also deal directly with tradespersons in maintaining your clients' properties. Considering the number of people you deal with and the diversity of their capacities, patience is a requirement, not just a virtue, for a career in property management. Melissa, a property manager, describes in the next chapter the position she has been in for 21 years as anything but routine.

Appraisers

Ideal personality profile: Introvert, Sensing, Thinking, Judging (ISTJ); Introvert, Sensing, Feeling, Judging (ISFJ); Extrovert, Sensing, Thinking, Judging (ESTJ); Extrovert, Sensing, Feeling, Judging (ESFJ); Extrovert, Sensing, Feeling, Perceiving (ESFP).

Real estate *appraisers* do one thing and one thing only: they determine the value of properties. Real estate is appraised to determine many types of values: assessed value to establish property taxes, investment value for investor analysis, fair market value for market analysis, book value for accounting purposes, discount value for tax purposes, rental value for income projections, and insurable value for insurance purposes.

The science of appraisal presents varying methods to determine many different values. Most people think a property has one value and one value only—until they venture into a career in real estate appraisal where real estate is valued in different ways depending upon the purpose of the valuation. Appraisers must know acceptable principles of appraisal and have a good knowledge of mathematics, accounting, and economics. Appraisal is the most scientific of the many types of real estate careers. You might call these financial pros the CPAs of real estate.

Real Estate Lingo

An **appraiser** estimates the value of property as of a particular date.

This job requires tremendous focus and attention to details. Appraisers must be observant and accurate with facts. (Hence, all *ideal* types are Sensors.) While a lot of the job is done by oneself (the reason most appraisers are probably Introverts), appraisers often interact with different types of people including homeowners, town officials, and real estate agents, so the job can certainly encompass Extroverted activity and variety (which appeals to Sensing, Perceivers) as well. Appraisers must rely on established principles of appraisal and comparable sales.

FYI!

You can also use personality typing to increase your sales effectiveness. The book *The Art of Speed-Reading People* (Tieger & Barron-Tieger) teaches you how to quickly size up people and to speak their language. This book is available at www.personalitytype.com.

I think of the appraiser as the laboratory technician. Once he gathers supporting information, he establishes value according to a scientific system. The appraiser should be practical and oriented toward the use of methods and systems (which are also activities that appeal more to Sensors). In the next chapter, our appraiser, Paul, describes the required personality traits as practical and analytical, pointing out that you must be both, not just one, for this career to be a fit.

Take Your Time

As you can see, there are many careers under the umbrella of real estate agent. A career in real estate can be highly rewarding as long as you take the time to choose the right field and the right office. In other words, your initial decisions are imperative to finding the right fit. While this chapter and the next assist you in choosing the right field, Chapter 6 mentors you through your choice of office.

Take your time when deciding which field is right for you because where you start will probably be where you end. It's true. As creatures of habit, we generally enter a career and spend the next cycle of our lives trying to make it work for us. The time to be selective is now. Choose a field that matches your needs and your personality and allows you to work with energy, enthusiasm, and spirit.

FYI!

By spending more time typing your personality and assessing its suitability to your career choice, you should be able to head off impulsive choice-making. Taking the time for this important analysis before you jump into a career can mean the difference between a gratifying life-long career and a frustrating short-term one.

Maureen, a real estate appraiser, is a good example of someone who didn't take the time to scout the field before selecting her career. Maureen had worked as a tax preparer for six years when she realized that tax preparation was not what she wanted to do for the rest of her life. She decided that a career in real estate would give her more versatility, income, and the people contact she missed. She took the required courses and passed the real estate licensing exam. Her neighbor was an appraiser and offered her a spot in his firm.

Maureen began there, stayed there, and never realized her dream. Again she found herself working with numbers, which she likes, but she still does not have the interaction with people she desires. Maureen wishes she had taken her time to research the field better before choosing appraisal. She feels that commercial sales would have better suited her personality and her passion for working with numbers, but once she became established in appraisal, she did not feel like making yet another career transition. Maureen's story is an example of what can happen if you settle into a field before you carefully scrutinize the available career options.

Although the majority of real estate professionals I interviewed for this book shared positive stories about their real estate career choices, Bill had a story similar to

Maureen's. Bill obtained his real estate license after brokering securities for more than a decade. He fell into mortgage brokering when he answered an ad from a national bank. The interview went well and he accepted the position. Early on, he had inklings that mortgage brokering wasn't for him. The money was good, but he felt that office leasing would feed his creative juices far better. Each year he vowed to make his transition, but never did. He stayed where he began and feels frustrated and disappointed that he doesn't have the gumption to make the change.

Research the Field

Do yourself a favor and take your time when evaluating your options. You want to perform your analysis long before you begin your pre-licensing study for three important reasons. First, your investigation of the varied real estate career choices may tell you that the profession just is not right for you. Why take the required courses and the examination when real estate is not your answer? Second, some real estate prelicensing courses involve elections between varying courses. It would be wise for you to tailor your prelicensing education to the career you have determined is best for you. Third, when you study the required courses, you will naturally give greater attention to those involving the career you intend to make your own.

There is no rush when it comes to making a choice for the rest of your life, or at least for the foreseeable future. Talk to people, research, intern, join professional groups. Do anything it takes to introduce yourself to the inner workings of each facet of the real estate world. Ideally, you will undertake this level of examination while you are still involved in your current profession or schooling.

When you speak with others about your choices, take their advice with a grain of salt. Chapter 8 encourages you to be an independent thinker, which means not subjecting your ideas to public opinion, or if you do, not taking public opinion to heart. When you contemplate a change, conduct extensive research, but do not seek advice from others.

The independent thinker moves ahead despite public poll, oftentimes turning negative comments into reasons to be challenged. Each time I begin a new endeavor, while I often find a mentor to assist me with my transition, I do not seek validation from others. There is a distinction between sharing your ideas with others and the discerning process of receiving mentorship

---

The Inside Scoop

Peak earning years for people used to be in their 40s. Now it's mid-50s to 60s. The average age of agents is 52 years.

through your transition, both of which will be discussed later in this book. Get your mentorship but do not take public opinion to heart.

Remember also that you will most likely be guided away from the real estate agent profession by existing agents. They have found a good thing and they want to shelter their territory from interference by new wanna-bes. Through the processes described in this book, find your own passion and make your own decision.

What's Your Passion?

Since 93 percent of agents come to real estate in career transition, the odds are good that you are in the midst of your own professional evolution. Realize that you're in a natural life cycle. You have changed as you have progressed down the path of your life. Take time up front to investigate and try on these career options. If you don't, you may end up in a career choice that will invite yet another transition.

> **The Inside Scoop**
>
> What's your passion? Your passion may be bicycling. Specialize in a certain neighborhood and bike to client's homes. Your passion may be writing. Create the most laudatory, poetic brochures imaginable. You will have a lot of competition in this department. You can fit just about every passion you have into a career in real estate.

There is so much diversity available within the real estate field. It is very important to choose the field that is right for you. If you do, you will have the very best opportunity to stand out because you will enjoy what you do. The question then becomes one of exactly what it is that is right for you. What is your passion? In a later chapter, we explore this important question more fully. Now that you have reviewed the career choices and are about to step through a day in the life of each, pause to make this important inquiry of yourself.

Take a deep breath. Take another. Now close your eyes. Ask yourself, "What would I do as a career if I were guaranteed success no matter what?" Ask yourself a number of times. You have an answer. We have all thought about this. We may call our thoughts dreams, but dreams can be attained if they are acknowledged. What did you say? Say it again. Write it down. Remember, you cannot fail. You can have it.

Write your answer here:

_____

You have to know that you cannot fail in performing this exercise. You have to know you can be whatever you want to be. When I performed this exercise fifteen years ago, my passion was writing books. Within a year, I was writing my first book. It is powerful to acknowledge what you want within the safety of knowing you cannot fail.

You can then look at the fear of failure that stands in your way in a more objective manner, and perhaps even dismiss it as a factor that is no longer relevant in your life. For me, I realized that it was more important to go after my dreams than to fear some failure that may never happen.

Looking at our work on a more philosophical level, our work in life is so much more than just making a living. It is, in fact, one of the most vital places for us to grow and express our creativity. When you consider that many of us spend 50 percent of our waking time working, finding the right avenue for our work is certainly a pursuit worthy of some considered analysis.

I recently read a survey of a hundred people on their deathbeds who revealed that their greatest regret is for the risks they never took. They wished that they had followed their dreams. Now's the time to make your dreams come true through choosing the right real estate career and adopting a positive state of mind.

Carving a Niche

A niche is a specialty. It may be a special area of sales or a special location or a unique demographic target. As you review the standard careers described in this chapter, know that there are niches to be woven throughout the real estate field. Think of what you might specialize in. Once you have your license and begin accumulating experience, there is no limit to the niches you can carve out for yourself. If you understand from the beginning of your real estate career that the field is ripe for the building of niches, you will approach your career with a niche-building state of mind.

For instance, my real estate business is niche-oriented. Over my career, I have taken a little bit of this and a little bit of that and contoured my own special arena. Residential real estate appealed to me because I enjoy decorating and working with families. I was also interested in investment property because my expertise lies in equity sharing and tax-free exchanges. I melded these two aspects into a real estate brokerage practice, partnering investors and home buyers in *equity sharing* transactions.

More recently, as the stock market has grown into disfavor, my practice has taken a turn toward moving clients out of retirement accounts invested in the stock market and into

Real Estate Lingo

Equity sharing is a real estate co-ownership strategy whereby one party, the occupier, lives in the property and pays its expenses, while the other party, the investor, puts up the down payment funds. They share tax deductions and profit. Many other structures are also possible, but this is the most popular.

the more reliable real estate market. My real estate practice keeps shifting with the opportunities created by changes in the economy.

Carving out a niche is finding what you're good at and creating a professional position within the ever-changing real estate marketplace. It's about staying in tune with the market and learning and growing with it. The real estate market and its many faces is an enormously rich industry in terms of financial power and people power. It provides a changing stage on which to repackage yourself.

The Least You Need to Know

- ◆ There are many choices of careers within the real estate field.

- ◆ Knowing yourself and your personality will help you choose wisely among career choices.

- ◆ Each field has its advantages and tends to fit specific personality profiles.

- ◆ Take the time to research each of the real estate fields and determine your own passions before you leap into a specific field.

- ◆ Think about how you can develop a special niche for yourself that gives you opportunities to follow your passions.

Chapter 3

A Day in the Life

In This Chapter

- ◆ Julie, a residential sales agent—her story and her day
- ◆ Jim, a commercial sales agent—his story and his day
- ◆ Jeff, a mortgage broker—his story and his day
- ◆ Melissa, a property manager—her story and her day
- ◆ Paul, an appraiser—his story and his day

Did your personality profile spell property manager or sales agent? Are you more of an extrovert or an introvert? While the last chapter focused on personality profiling as a way of determining which career is right for you, this chapter looks at a typical day in the life of each real estate professional. This is the hands-on chapter, while the last chapter was a seat in the psychologist's chair. While this chapter focuses primarily on the residential sales agent, it also explores a day in the life for each career professional.

These agents also share their reasons for choosing the fields they chose and how their careers have evolved over time. By the time you complete this chapter, you should have a very good idea of whether or not the real estate profession appeals to you and which field fits best with your own professional interests.

For those of you already in the business, step through this chapter to familiarize yourself more fully with what your real estate peers do. If you don't already have solid referral relationships with these professionals, now is the time to develop them. In Chapter 9 we talk extensively about building your important Power Team with these other professionals.

Residential Sales

Since 80 percent of agents choose home sales as a career, we'll start with residential sales. I think that the hokey pokey was created to depict the life of a residential real estate agent. You put your feet in, your hands out, your elbows in, you shake it all about, and then you do the old soft shoe. It's the life of the residential sales agent, a never-ending flutter of people and activity. In just one day this agent can step through more roles than any other agent, ranging from mentor to decorator to therapist to financial analyst.

Julie's Background

Julie is our residential sales agent. She's on her way to Top Dog status. Julie's schooling and licensing was in social work. Working with people is her lifeline, but after ten years as a social worker she found it emotionally depleting and difficult to continue working within the confines of public agencies. The red tape was frustrating and unproductive. Seven years ago she left the profession to have her children. After that, she wanted to return to a career, but one without the structure or aggravation of social work. Following is Julie's story in her own words.

Why Julie Chose Her Career

After researching various professions, my career decision was a toss-up between real estate agent and financial planner. Since I have a knack for finances and a good business head, I felt financial planning would be a good choice, but I also felt that these talents would serve me in the real estate field. I had to complete a lot of classes to become licensed in financial planning, but I wasn't really interested in going back to school for a long time.

Since real estate investment has always been part of my plan for financial independence, I felt that a career in real estate made a lot of sense. I also felt drawn to real estate because it involves working with

> **The Inside Scoop**
>
> The average Realtor nationwide entered the profession at age 39 and has been in the profession for 13 years; the average age is 52 years of age.

people and an adjustable work schedule. I picked residential real estate sales because I like dealing with people and it is in line with my enjoyment of home decorating.

I knew some successful agents through my children's school activities and my yoga classes. After researching local residential brokerage firms, I interviewed at the international real estate firm that one of these agents worked for. I went with this firm because it had excellent support for its agents, an extensive program in real estate fundamentals, and continuing education courses presented at the office.

Julie's Career

I liked the office manager and felt comfortable with the other agents and staff. Then I arranged for the agent I knew to be my mentor. My initial assigned work area was small and unappealing, but I decorated it and made that little space work for me. Initially, most of my work was done at the office where I could get support from others and get as much floor time as possible. Now I do most of the paperwork from home before I go to the office and when I return home from my day. The office is primarily where I meet with clients and other professionals, get support, and attend office meetings.

I've been licensed for six years now. I'm very happy with my decision to work in real estate sales. I have been able to handle a full client load and take care of my young children and their schedules. I have taken a number of computer courses so that I can use technology fully in my business. I now have all the latest in computer equipment and I know that I use technology more than most of my peers. I've incorporated the computer into much of my activity and I find that correspondence, property searches, and general tasks go very smoothly because of this.

After I had been an agent for three years, I completed some additional real estate planning and investment courses, which were helpful to my clients and to me personally. I'm known as the office tax whiz. I've purchased a duplex as my own real estate investment and it already has a positive cash flow. I focus my continuing education courses on sharpening my real estate tax and investment skills.

Initially, I started with a 60-40 commission split where 40 percent of my commission went to the real estate company I work for, but now that I have a proven track record and my broker's license, I get a 70-30 split in my favor. I earn far more then I ever thought I would.

> ### The Inside Scoop
>
> Sixty percent of agents work under a commission split arrangement with their offices while 31 percent receive a 100 percent commission, compensating the office with set fees. The other 9 percent have other arrangements, such as a share of profits.

If I worked more, I would make even more. I put in about 35 hours a week and I cherish my time off. It took me about a year and a half to get going and build my own clientele. There were periods of uncertainty and scarcity, but I expected it to be rough as I started this new career.

After I had been a residential sales agent for four years, I started doing some business in the commercial residential market. That was a turning point for me. I began offering my clients multi-unit residential properties. I took my broker's examination and I am now licensed as a broker. I am still with the same firm, but if I decide I want to work harder I could go off on my own. I'm mentoring another agent who joined the firm a year ago.

I got a larger space in the office after I had been an agent for three years and I hired an assistant for 15 hours a week. My assistant now works 30 hours a week, mostly from her home. Last year I earned $140,000 from real estate sales and paid $22,000 to my assistant and paid about $20,000 in other expenses. The duplex I bought is bringing in another $550.00 a month above expenses. I love the diversity in my work and I enjoy helping people find the right home and the right investment property.

The Appeal of Julie's Career

This career will appeal to you if you like working with people and have good people skills. For independent people who like having their own business and control over their time, it is the perfect profession. You have to be organized, though. The money and personal satisfaction is good, as well.

A Day in the Life of Julie

Today is Saturday. It is June and business is very busy. Yesterday was a day off for me so today is also a catch-up day. My assistant is not working today so I send her e-mails to take care of when she works on Monday. Both my assistant and I receive our e-mail at home. I am set up to receive my e-mail at the office and at home. In the field, I can receive and send messages if I'm in a pinch.

FYI!

Many agents were formerly managers, salespersons, teachers, homemakers, or administrators. It's no surprise since agents are typically highly self-directed and independent.

Between my assistant and me, we write and produce beautiful sales brochures; staff open houses; write newspaper ads; prospect for new clients; follow up with old clients; work with property inspectors, appraisers, and mortgage brokers; and handle the many steps of the sales transaction. Yesterday my assistant took photographs of the home I will feature in an open house today and put the sales brochure together. Everything is ready for the open house scheduled for today.

Julie's Journal Entry for a Day

I receive a voice mail that another agent has an offer on one of my listings and wants to present the offer. I return his call and coordinate a presentation time of noon. One of my clients in contract to purchase a vacation home is set to remove her *inspection contingency* tomorrow. I call her and ask if she is satisfied with the condition of the property. I explain that this is the time to ask for a seller credit if she feels the price she has offered does not reflect the condition of the property. It is also the time to cancel the transaction if she is not satisfied with anything found in the inspection reports. My client feels she wants a credit of $7,000 for some work that will need to be done. I prepare a release of her inspection contingency subject to the seller crediting her with $7,000.

Real Estate Lingo

The **inspection contingency** is the period during which the buyer has the right to perform inspections he feels necessary to discover the condition of the property. This period may be as short as 15 days in a fast market.

10 A.M. Journal Entry: Hand Holding

I receive a call from clients who are feeling nervous. They are concerned because their home is listed for sale, but they haven't found a suitable new home. In the past ten days I have shown them every home listed in their price range and the location they want to live in. None of these homes have appealed to them.

Although the market is more of a seller's market than a buyer's market, it still is not typical for sellers to sell subject to finding a replacement home. They have reluctantly agreed not to make finding a replacement home a contingency of the sale. I just held the broker's open house on their home, and interest was high. I am expecting competitive offers in the next day or so.

My clients want to take their home off the market, concerned that they will be left without a place to live. I drive over and talk with them. We agree that the best way to proceed is to build in a customized clause that will give my clients a replacement home contingency, but one that will be more acceptable to a buyer than the typical open-ended contingency.

Noon Journal Entry: An Open House

I return to my office for the noon offer presentation with just enough time left to phone my clients and tell them the offer terms. At 2:00 P.M. I am holding an open house for another client. I like to do the open houses personally, because they are often excellent places to find new clients. My assistant has bought fresh flowers, some refreshments, the usual music to play, and printed marketing brochures. I drive by her house, pick up the supplies, arrive at the home early, and arrange the house with a few last items.

Last week I suggested to my client that professional *staging* of her home could make a big difference in marketability. A stager spent a day doing interior decorating, relocating furniture, and placing rental plants and artwork throughout the home. The changes were the perfect touch to make this client's property one of the most appealing homes on the market in its price range. The broker's open house was earlier in the week and this is the day to present the home to the public.

Real Estate Lingo

Basic **staging** involves giving the property an objective eye-over and rearranging the furnishings and accessories in the most appealing manner. Advanced staging involves basic staging and possibly minor remodeling and landscape improvement.

Real Estate Lingo

The **loan contingency** is the period during which the buyer obtains loan approval. The buyer makes the offer contingent upon obtaining the loan described in the offer. The loan contingency often expires 30 days prior to closing.

The open house brings about 25 people; some may be potential clients. The people who come to an open house sometimes have a house they are thinking about selling. Two couples sound very interested in buying a house. One has an agent already; the other wants to look at a few more houses but sounds interested in making an offer through me. Two couples found that the home did not meet their needs and we took a little time to review listings on my laptop. Next Wednesday I will show some other properties to one couple.

4:30 P.M. Journal Entry: The Day's End

At 4:30 P.M. I return to the office. I have frantic calls from a client whose *loan contingency* is due to be released in a few days. She reports problems obtaining loan approval. I have an e-mail from another agent inquiring about a property I have listed. But, before dealing with these issues, I call the clients whose home I received an offer on today to coordinate delivery of the offer to them and a meeting tomorrow to respond to the offer. I return a few more calls and leave messages that I will be available tomorrow between noon and 5 P.M.

Julie's Opinion of Residential Sales

Following are closing comments Julie made about a career in residential sales:

- **Personality type:** You need to be able to handle several deals at the same time, which requires a great deal of multitasking and multi-role-playing. Patience and persistence are part of every activity since a transaction can easily fall apart if you don't track it closely and stay in touch with everyone.

- **Character traits:** I think that honesty, a genuine liking of people, a calm demeanor and conversation, and an ability to track detail and understand options are all part of the successful agent. It may be that honesty is too high on my list, but the consequences of even a small white lie are not worth it. I like my clients to trust me, so my assistant and I do everything by the old golden rule.

- **Biggest rewards:** Satisfied customers; knowing that you got the buyer or seller what he wanted in the transaction and that you did it professionally; you are your only boss; being rewarded well for doing what you enjoy and; being able to see your children off to school in the morning.

- **Biggest pitfalls:** This is not the profession for a disorganized person. There is no room for forgetting a detail or confusing the needs of clients. Real estate draws its fair share of lawsuits, which is always a concern to me and most in my profession.

> **FYI!**
>
> Lawyers are known as deal breakers in real estate. They have reputations for analyzing all the should haves, would haves, and could haves, and often scaring their clients out of transactions. Real estate transactions end up in litigation more often than most other types of transactions. Generally, it is the buyer who sues the seller. The agent or real estate office is often also named in the lawsuit. A typical lawsuit is for failure to disclose a known condition to the buyer. Many buyers think the seller warrants the property's condition similar to a new product warranty. Actually, the seller's duty is to advise the buyer of *known* conditions. If the roof leaks and the seller did not know of the leak, he cannot be held liable.

Commercial Sales

While the majority of agents choose residential sales, commercial sales agents are sometimes thought of as the financial wizards of the real estate field. Commercial agents analyze investment potential and tax criteria of properties whereas their residential counterparts are primarily focused on property features.

Real Estate Lingo

The **CCIM** (certified commercial investment member) designation is granted by the National Association of Realtors upon successful completion of a prolonged course of study and experience. CCIMs are recognized experts in commercial real estate brokerage, leasing, asset management valuation, and investment analysis.

Jim's Background

Jim is our commercial sales agent. Seventeen years ago, after three careers, he got his real estate license. Jim had lived on both the East Coast and West Coast where he owned a boys camp, was a teacher, and then owned and operated a book publishing company. He has a *CCIM* designation (*certified commercial investment member*) and is in the top 10 percent of his profession. He has his broker's license, works for himself, and has a part-time assistant. He has a Bachelor's degree. (We will meet up with Jim again in Part 6 of this book, where Jim will share more details about his CCIM designation.)

Why Jim Chose His Career

I backed into commercial real estate as a result of selling my book publishing company. During the transaction, I was impressed by the broker who was a specialist in *business opportunities* as well as commercial investment properties. He was smart and professional and had a good sense of humor. We got to be friends and he suggested that I get a real estate license and join his small independent company of three brokers. I like people, action, and making a good living, and commercial sales seemed to fill the bill. I obtained my license and joined the firm. In my state, I was able to skip the agent's exam and sit for the broker's exam because I had a B.A. degree.

Real Estate Lingo

A **business opportunity** is a business for sale, generally with a proven track record.

The Inside Scoop

PDA stands for personal digital assistant. This is a generic name for a handheld device that keeps address and phone information and schedules.

I usually work about forty hours, Monday through Friday, a week. Sometimes I meet with a client on the weekend. I spend most of my work time in the office, although I have a home office set up. I use a laptop computer and a PDA. I now own and operate three commercial properties and about 30 percent of my time is spent on my own properties. I have made a very good living in part from commissions and in part from my own investments and taking an ownership interest in properties in lieu of commission.

The Appeal of Jim's Career

For a small investment of time and money, you can work for yourself and have control over your work time and playtime. You can also make a good living from commissions, and you can make a lot of money by investing in real estate. I wish I would have started in real estate when I was fresh out of college.

A Day in the Life of Jim

I arrive at the office at 9 A.M. and return two calls about my office complex listing. I assemble packages to mail to these inquiries. I call the *Wall Street Journal* to run an ad for a new listing of a medical office building. At 11 A.M., I meet with the owner of the office building to receive the rent roll and other tenant information so I can work up a package to present to the monthly commercial-investment marketing meeting next week. Commercial sales are tied to the income received by the property.

At 1 P.M. I have lunch with a prospective seller of a building. He wants to sell and lease back his office space. He is interviewing several brokers and wants a competitive commission arrangement. Since I work for myself I can work out any arrangement that suits me and my client. He also wants a broker who is a CCIM, a certified commercial investment member, and I qualify.

At 3 P.M. I meet the appraiser at an apartment building, now in escrow. At 4 P.M. I meet at the same apartment building for a contractor's inspection. We encounter a problem with two tenants who will not allow us into their apartments without 24-hour notice, which was given by phone yesterday but not acknowledged by the tenants. I reschedule the contractor to see these two apartments tomorrow at the same time. At 5 P.M. I return to my office to answer e-mails and phone calls. I begin to work up a medical office building package for a building a client will *exchange* out of, and then I submit the initial numbers to my client's accountant. As you can see, my days are often quite full.

Real Estate Lingo

An **exchange,** also known as 1031 Exchange or Starker Exchange, allows an owner to sell a property and reinvest in another property of equal or greater value without any tax consequence.

Jim's Opinion of Commercial Sales

Following are closing comments Jim made about a career in commercial sales:

◆ **Personality type:** Outgoing, friendly, patient, flexible, energetic, and detail-oriented. If you like and understand numbers well enough to do your own tax return, you may be good in this field.

◆ **Character traits:** I work with people and with their finances. I think a thorough understanding of investment returns is essential in order to represent income property. I also find that good listening helps in working with clients, especially the ones who are looking for space for their own businesses. It also helps to like being part of various community service groups, because networking is essential in the commercial sales business. I am active in two business networking groups.

◆ **Biggest rewards:** Knowing both parties of a transaction are happy about the outcome. I also thoroughly enjoy finding investment opportunities for myself. Each day is completely different from the one before.

◆ **Biggest pitfalls:** Liability for things you say or don't say. There are a lot of lawsuits in this business, so I keep careful records and am scrupulous about my paperwork.

The Inside Scoop

If you decide to become your own broker, make sure you get liability insurance, also known as errors and omissions insurance. Real estate transactions end up in litigation quite often. An agent should never practice without insurance with good limits of coverage. The agent who owns investment property would also be wise to own these properties in the name of a limited liability company to protect these assets from any personal judgment that may arise against him. Asset protection and good insurance coverage is a winning combination.

Mortgage Broker

Mortgage brokers are tied to the phone and the office more than any other agent. They have to be available during regular business hours and must continually stay in contact with changing interest rates and loan product criteria. These financial pros need to have nerves of steel to stay calm amidst ever-changing details and never-ending loan deadlines.

Jeff's Background

Jeff is our mortgage broker. He has been brokering for nine years. His wife is also a broker with the same company. Jeff graduated from college with a B.A. in economics and became a commodities broker. He transitioned to mortgage brokering because he was looking for more client satisfaction. In commodities, he felt his clients were never happy.

Why Jeff Chose His Career

I always liked finance and real estate and felt mortgage brokering provided the ideal blend of my two interests. My choice was also based on the fact that I liked determining my own income instead of someone else deciding for me.

The Appeal of Jeff's Career

This career will appeal to someone who enjoys working with numbers and likes challenges. It is the ideal profession for someone who enjoys independence and being his or her own boss.

A Day in the Life of Jeff

I arrive at the office at 9 A.M. and immediately gather lender rate sheets for loans to be *locked* in. I retrieve voice mail and e-mail messages, and pass some on to my assistant. I review pending loans with my assistant. We lock in rates for clients whose loans are in a ready-to-lock status. I work on tough-to-qualify loans, repackaging them for lender submission.

I answer the phone, which rings about 75 times a day, and read and respond to e-mail from clients, Realtors, and title companies. I usually spend about one hour a day prospecting for new clients, although 95 percent of my business is referral-based. I spend about an hour a day speaking with loan representatives discussing the loans I have to place. Nearly all of my time is spent in the office.

Real Estate Lingo

A loan is **locked** in when the lender guarantees the loan's rate and terms.

Jeff's Opinion of Being a Mortgage Broker

Following are closing comments Jeff made about a career as a mortgage broker:

- **Personality type:** In this business you have to be personable and outgoing.

- **Character traits:** You need to be detail-oriented, able to listen and process what a client is saying they are looking for. You need to be adaptable and creative in your thinking to package your loans, especially the difficult ones, for the best lender presentation. You need to be a good problem solver because most loans have problems one way or the other.

- **Biggest rewards:** Everyone loves you at the end of the transaction. Your income is dependent upon how hard you work. If you are organized, you can play a lot of golf and still have a good income.

- **Pitfalls:** Don't promise your clients anything until you lock them in. The market fluctuates continually and the rate you promise could be gone tomorrow when the loan is ready to be locked. A commission structure can be challenging when you first start out or when interest rates climb and no one wants a loan. I also wish I could have found someone to train me better at the beginning of my career.

Property Management

The property manager is a facilitator and a juggler all in one. This professional works with property owners, tenants, and trades people simultaneously. The job can require the patience of a saint, the people skills of a couple's therapist, and the ability to multitask to the extreme.

Real Estate Lingo

Master Property Manager (MPM) is a designation given by the National Association of Residential Property Managers (NARPM), a trade organization for the residential property management industry.

Melissa's Background

Twenty-one years ago, at 19, Melissa became a receptionist for the property management company she now owns. Prior to that she worked for a title company, which she found to be repetitive and uninteresting. Real estate has been her only real career. She now has seven employees, has her *Master Property Manager* (*MPM*) designation, and has served as President of the National Association of Residential Property Managers. (Melissa will also be featured later in Top Dogs.)

Why Melissa Chose This Career and the Appeal of It

I loved the "never-a-dull-moment" day of the property manager. Why might others choose this career? Property management is an exciting career. It is a salaried position for some people and provides a lot of people interaction.

A Day in the Life of Melissa

There is never a routine day. I start my day going through paperwork in the office. Many days in the late morning and early afternoon I meet with prospective clients. I am on the phone a lot returning calls and speaking to owners regarding repairs, prospective tenants, or the rental market. I usually work a long day that generally flies by, leaving plenty to do the next day. Many people call wanting to set up an appointment to see a specific rental that same day. Since I manage seven employees and own the company, there is a good amount of management work to perform.

Melissa's Opinion of Being a Property Manager

Following are closing comments Melissa made about a career in property management:

- **Personality type:** Property managers should be friendly, social people. They need to be able to handle several things at once and pay attention to the details and follow-up.

- **Character traits:** You are handling someone else's investment property and their money, so I recommend being honest and competent in bookkeeping. You are dealing with people from all walks of life from owners to tenants to trades persons, so liking people and being fair with them is also important. I remind everyone that we treat each rental as a business. This means never skipping credit checks on potential tenants because we might feel sorry for them. Decisions should never be based on how we feel about the owner or tenant.

> **FYI!**
>
> Property managers earn more than other agents. The norm nationwide is $100,000 per year. They also typically work longer hours than other agents and are subject to more complaints by virtue of the nature of managing property and dealing with both owners and their tenants.

- **Biggest rewards:** The variety and the excitement keep me hopping. I love the many different things I do in my day. I get a feeling of satisfaction in the upkeep and appearance of the properties I manage, and the high rate of occupancy I achieve for my clients. I enjoy working with the service people who do good work for me, like painting, carpet cleaning, groundskeeping, and more.

◆ **Pitfalls:** Sometimes an owner may be unwilling to keep his property in good repair. I hear many complaints every day from tenants and from owners. I also hear some sad personal stories from tenants who are not able to pay their rent on time, and I have to make some difficult calls in those situations. Complaints are the nature of this business since you are managing properties. You cannot take them to heart.

The Appraiser

When appraisers number crunch they can estimate value to a decimal point. These mathematicians of real estate assign numbers to features such as view, design, functionality, and outdoor space, to name a few. Through comparing these features to other similar properties recently sold, they arrive at an appraised value.

Paul's Background

Paul was a policeman and then a loan manager, when he gravitated to appraisal about 20 years ago.

Why Paul Chose This Career and the Appeal of It

I considered appraisal to be the area of real estate lending that allowed a good deal of independence. Since I was already in real estate lending, I thought that my employer and others in the lending field would probably be a good source of business. I liked construction and am good in math, both of which are helpful in the appraisal field.

I was also drawn to the freedom of being my own boss and working out in the field. Anyone who cherishes independence should consider a career as an appraiser. A person with good math and computer skills who enjoys analysis would enjoy this field. I'm out and about a great deal, and I enjoy the process of valuing properties.

A Day in the Life of Paul

I usually set my appointments for early in the morning, so at 8:30 A.M. I might be taking front, rear, and street pictures and measuring a large home. I pull *comparables* before I go out to the property so when I finish the inspection, I drive the comparables and take pictures of them. Back in the office I start populating the appraisal report software with floor plans, pictures, maps, and data. When the report is completely filled out, I convert it to a PDF file and e-mail it to my client.

Real Estate Lingo

Comparables are similar properties recently sold located in the same proximity. Recent is about six months. Proximity is within a mile or so. Other factors considered are amenities, condition, and location.

It takes about a day to complete a simple appraisal. Appraisals for attorneys and tax professionals involving income property require more in-depth analysis and can take as long as several days. I sometimes feel like a scientist at work since I pinpoint the value of a property through all sorts of logical steps.

I used to do everything by copier, mail, and photo processing through laboratories until technology allowed me to do everything out of my house. It has made a positive difference in the quality of my time and income. Clients are also more satisfied because they get their appraisals much sooner.

Paul's Opinion of Being an Appraiser

Following are closing comments Paul made about a career as an appraiser:

- **Personality Type:** Independent people who like working on their own and have a bent for math and technology are good appraisers.

- **Character Traits:** You must be practical and analytical. If you are just practical, you might be a contractor. If you are only analytical, you might be a loan officer. If you are both, you can be an appraiser. You need to be able to use a computer and to describe things simply.

FYI!

An average single-family home appraisal takes about an hour or so on-site, an hour to drive around the neighborhood and photograph comparable properties, and about four hours to gather some comparables and write the report.

- **Biggest rewards:** The biggest reward is freedom, lots of freedom. The money is also good. You also learn about good investment opportunities because you are often in on the first stages of someone wanting to sell a property. Another nice perk is that business is rather impersonal. An appraisal is ordered, it is worked up based on statistical information and methods, and it is produced. You have little dealing with clients and the problems that can crop up in representing them.

◆ **Pitfalls:** Most of the time the people that you deal with do not really want an appraisal. They call in an appraiser because they have to get one. They may be nervous if they want a low appraisal for tax purposes or a high appraisal for loan qualification purposes. You can't always plan your time in advance, because appraisals often must be done and submitted in a tight timeframe. Over the past few years licensing of appraisers has become far more complicated. There are all kinds of requirements and categories of designations that did not exist when I started in the profession.

FYI!

Real estate has become a mobile profession. Seventy percent of agents have a home office as well as their company office. They also employ cell phones, pagers, handheld devices, and laptops to do business wherever they are.

Which Is It for You?

If you are considering a profession in real estate, by now you should have a good idea of which career best suits your personality, your passions, and your objectives. Assuming you have decided to become a member of this very independent group of career professionals, the next two chapters will guide you through the prelicensing course requirements in your state and preparing for and taking the licensing examination.

Switching Careers Within Real Estate

If you are already a member of the real estate field, you may have found that a day in the life of one of these other careers appeals more to you than the field you're currently in. If so, do the career shuffle. It really is not difficult to transition between real estate fields. It's all in the same ballpark, it's just playing a different position in the game. And it is never too late. It won't be like starting over since you have your fellow agents in your current field to refer business to you in your new field.

Sometimes I hear agents complain that they chose the wrong field, but they don't want to switch because it will be like starting over. Sounds very much like the stories Maureen and Bill told in Chapter 2. Let's reframe this. Take the hundreds of agents who don't give you business because you do what they do, and convert them to referrals. Switching careers within the real estate field is actually an ideal way to create a never-ending market. It's really all about how you look at it, isn't it? You can miss a completely obvious market if you are not open to the idea of change.

The Least You Need to Know

◆ There are many career options under the umbrella of real estate.

◆ Each option has different characteristics and individual activities that make up a typical day.

◆ The residential agent has a flurry of activity and has the most personal involvement with clients.

◆ The commercial agent is similar to an investment analyst in some respects.

◆ The appraiser is like a scientific professional through his or her use of valuation methods and mathematical analysis.

Chapter 4

Your Prelicensing Education

In This Chapter

- ◆ A summary of prelicensing requirements
- ◆ An overview of the real estate principles course
- ◆ An introduction to property rights and the ways to hold title
- ◆ A look at the differences between condos and co-ops
- ◆ A survey of deeds used to transfer property

If you're reading this chapter, you have made the decision to become a real estate agent. Congratulations. You are about to enter an exciting and abundant profession. In all states, licensing is required to become a real estate agent. You have two steps in front of you to achieve your goal. One is to satisfy the prelicensing educational requirements. The second step is to take and pass the licensing exam.

This chapter covers step one, satisfying your state's prelicensing educational requirements for real estate agent licensing. Each state's requirements differ. A few states have no educational requirements. Most states require an average of 60 hours of education, while California and Quebec, Canada, tip the scales at 135 hours and 240 hours, respectively. Your state's requirements should be obtained from the Real Estate Commission in the state where you want to practice.

FYI!

The following states and Canadian provinces require 90 hours or more of courses before you may take the agent exam:

Arizona, California, Delaware, Idaho, Kentucky, Louisiana, Nevada, Ohio, Utah, West Virginia, Alberta, and Quebec. Some of these hours can be filled within a year or two after licensing.

FYI!

Appraisal is covered separately by a certification procedure, and is beyond the scope of this chapter. The entry-level certification is "residential appraiser," while the advanced designation, "general appraiser," requires additional education and experience. California has four levels of appraiser certification.

The Terminology

Here's how the real estate profession works. There are two categories of agents. The *entry category* is a salesperson. Some states refer to this entry licensing as broker associate, agent, or sales associate. The *advanced category* is the broker. Broker licensing is conferred on the agent after experience and additional education levels are met.

In this book I refer to each licensed real estate professional as an agent unless he has become licensed as a broker, at which time he is referred to as a broker. Part 6 of this book, which focuses on becoming a Top Dog, addresses advanced licensing and the examination of brokers. This chapter deals with licensing of agents only.

Requirement Exceptions

In most states licensed lawyers or graduates of law schools are exempt from some, but often not all, course requirements. For others, an exemption may apply if you took the required courses at a recognized college or university and achieved a passing grade. Most states's also accord reciprocity to licenses of other states, requiring that only their state's portion of the exam be taken.

Some states also provide exemptions from broker experience requirements, allowing qualified candidates to bypass the agent exam and go directly to the broker's exam, if you have …

♦ A 4-year college degree or a higher level of education.

♦ A certain amount of recent experience as a real estate professional in certain job categories not requiring licensing.

If you are exempt from the agent exam, then you may read the last section of this book on becoming a Top Dog, which discusses the broker exam and its prelicensing requirements.

Caution _____

Not all states and provinces have education or experience exemptions. Be sure to check on your particular state's requirements.

Prelicensing Course Procedures

The vast majority of states and Canadian provinces require license applicants to take prelicensing educational courses accredited by the state licensing agency before they qualify to sit for the exam. In other states, applicants can take these educational courses within a specified time after being licensed. Still other states require prelicensing courses to be completed before taking the exam as well as postlicensing courses targeted for one to two years after being licensed. There are significant differences between states. These additional courses are over and above annual continuing education courses that are required in all states to keep your license current.

FYI! _____

The following is a partial list of supplemental courses offered in California where other courses must be completed in addition to a course on real estate principles. If your state has supplemental course requirements, it is good to know which real estate career you intend to pursue so you can gear your courses toward that field.

♦ Real Estate Appraisal
♦ Property Management
♦ Real Estate Finance
♦ Real Estate Economics
♦ Legal Aspects of Real Estate
♦ Business Law
♦ Escrows
♦ Mortgage Loan Brokering and Lending
♦ Computer Applications in Real Estate

Prelicensing courses and the state exams cover the general real estate principles described later in this chapter as well as state-specific courses covering the laws specific to your state. Some states have additional course requirements. In those states, licensees are often given the option of selecting courses from a course list.

Determine Your State's Requirements

The best way to determine your state's licensing requirements is to search the Internet for "(name of your state) real estate commission." This search should bring you to the agency that regulates the licensing of real estate professionals. Mark the site as a favorite on your Web browser so you can easily return to it.

If you are not yet connected to the Internet, this is your ideal opportunity to do so. If you are seriously considering a career in real estate, you will require Internet access and computer experience, so now is the ideal time to begin. If you still haven't bridged the gap to technology, call your state Real Estate Commission or Department of Real Estate and ask them to send you an applicant package.

Take note of the following requirements and exemptions:

- License requirements, such as age, citizenship, and other factual information
- Prelicensing course requirements
- Postlicensing course requirements
- Course requirement exemptions
- Agent licensing exemptions

With this information you will know what courses you need to take, how many hours these courses involve, whether you can skip the agent exam and just take the broker exam, and whether there are courses you will have to take after licensing to complete the process.

Prelicensing Courses

Companies providing prelicensing instruction have programs tailored to meet state prelicensing course requirements. Some states allow all course work to be done online or in correspondence courses. Some states require all or some classroom study. To find these companies, do another Internet search for "(name of your state) real estate prelicensing courses" or look in the Yellow Pages under Real Estate Schools.

Some large real estate firms also offer prelicensing programs to qualify you for the exam and prepare you to take the licensing exam. If you are solo and have not yet affiliated with a firm, go to the Yellow Pages and look under *Real Estate Schools*.

FYI! _____

You want to locate a company that provides the training that suits you best. If online methods suit you and comply with your state's requirements, find an online company. If you feel you do better with human interaction for your instruction or if your state requires it, find a company that fits these requirements. These companies are set up to conform with your state's requirements. The vast majority of prelicensing instructors offer state-specific courses.

When you search for course instruction, make sure that the company you sign up with also has courses that prepare you for the real estate exam itself. You may wonder why you need an examination preparation course after you've just completed all these real estate courses. In Chapter 5, you will understand why. There is an art to taking the real estate exam, and there are courses to make you a master at the exam-taking process.

Timing and Surviving

On average, it takes about three months from the time you enroll in the pre-licensing courses to take your licensing exam. The average time for students to complete the prelicensing courses is six to eight weeks. You then receive your certificate of completion, apply for the exam, and take the exam, all of which takes four to five weeks. In other words, three months may elapse from the day you enroll in your pre-licensing courses to the day you sit down and actually take your state exam.

It's a good idea to take your coursework and the exam while you're still employed elsewhere. Start saving money on the side. Build up approximately six months of seed money so that you can start your new career without money concerns. Don't forget that you will be paid on an irregular basis by commissions earned, and in the beginning you may not earn a commission for some time. It takes a good amount of wherewithal both financially and emotionally to

Caution _____

Ideally, when you begin your practice you will want to have a nice car to tour clients in, a portable phone, a laptop computer, and a handheld organizer. All of these cost money. Make sure you are financially set to purchase your new needs and live your life comfortably for about half a year before you start your new career.

jump-start a new real estate business. But anything worthwhile takes some good advance planning and a strong dose of persistence.

Start telling everyone you know of your intentions to enter the real estate business and load up your database with names and contact information so you will have prospects to contact when you start your real estate business. Don't leave your employment until you have a good stash of cash and have passed the examination.

Real Estate Principles

The remainder of this chapter touches on the general real estate principles that are covered in your prelicensing courses and on your licensing exam. Of course, these principles do not include state-specific laws. For each course description, there is an average percentage of how much of the licensing exam you can expect each subject to cover.

Nature of Real Property and Ownership

The nature of real estate property and ownership should make up about 20 percent of the total exam.

Types of Real Property Rights

Real estate rights exist in many forms. The visible, or apparent, rights are the land and its improvements. Other rights also include the air, water, mineral and oil, and gas rights. There are also *real property* and *personal property* rights. Real property interests also come in varying types of estates, including *fee simple* (absolute and indefinite), life estates (measured by a lifespan), and leasehold estates (leases).

Real Estate Lingo

Fee simple is the most complete ownership one can have in a property. It establishes ownership of a property without limitation by time or any other factor. Most people own property in fee simple.

Real property is the land, its rights, and anything attached to it. The improvements (home, barn, or anything built on the property) is considered real property. Real property is transferred by deed.

Personal property is anything on the land that is not affixed and is moveable. For instance, furniture and farm equipment are personal property since they are not permanently affixed to the land. Personal property is transferred by bill of sale, not deed.

Here is an example of how property rights and ownership work: If I buy your property, you will most likely transfer fee simple title to me. With that title, I also receive the right to the air above the property, the resources below it (oil, for example), and the improvements on the property.

Holding Title

Title may be held by one or more persons and various different recognized entities. Methods of holding title, each of which has legal and tax significance, differ between the states. In some states, individuals can hold title in *joint tenancy*, meaning that the survivor of the owners becomes the sole owner without the necessity of probate. In other states, married couples desiring this type of *survivorship* hold title as *tenants by the entirety*. Community property states, representing a minority of states, permit holding title as *community property*. Your prelicensing course will instruct you on the ways for holding title in your state.

FYI!

If you live in a view area, your neighbors claim they have the right to a view over your property. They don't. Generally, you have the right to use the air above your property (the view) however you choose.

Real Estate Lingo

Joint tenancy is a way co-owners hold title in nearly all states if they want a surviving co-owner to receive the deceased co-owner's interest without probate. The co-owners do not have to be married.

Tenants by the entirety is the way a husband and wife hold title in 27 states if they want the surviving spouse to receive the deceased spouse's interest without probate. It is similar to joint tenancy used in other states.

Community property is a way of holding title without survivorship by married persons in states that have community property laws.

Community property with right of survivorship is a way of holding title by married persons in some states that have community property laws which allow the surviving spouse to receive a deceased spouse's interest without probate.

Survivorship. The co-owner automatically receives full title without the need for probate when a co-owner dies.

Tenants in common is a way for co-owners to own property together without survivorship rights. Their interests pass to their heirs, not to one another, when they die.

California and a few other community property states now permit married persons to hold title as *community property with right of survivorship*, a combination of joint tenancy and community property and similar to tenancy by the entirety. *Tenants in common* is usually the way co-owners hold title if they are not married. Each state's real estate laws provide detailed information on holding title.

> **FYI!**
>
> Community property states are Arizona, California, Idaho, Louisiana, Nevada, New Mexico, Texas, and Washington.
>
> Tenancy by the entirety states are Alaska, Arkansas, Delaware, District of Columbia, Florida, Hawaii, Indiana, Kentucky, Maryland, Michigan, Mississippi, Missouri, New Jersey, New York, North Carolina, Ohio, Oklahoma, Oregon, Pennsylvania, Rhode Island, Tennessee, Utah, Vermont, Virginia, Washington, West Virginia, and Wyoming.

Here is an example of how holding title works: If a married couple (Papa Bear and Mama Bear, for example) wants to hold title so the survivor receives the property without probate, they will hold title as "Papa Bear and Mama Bear, husband and wife, as tenants by the entirety."

If this married couple lives in a community property state they would hold title as "Papa Bear and Mama Bear, husband and wife, as community property with rights of survivorship."

If Papa Bear and Mama Bear are not married but want the survivor to have full title, title would be held as "Papa Bear and Mama Bear, as joint tenants."

If Papa Bear and Mama Bear do not want the survivor to receive title but instead want their heirs to inherit it, title would be held as "Papa Bear and Mama Bear, as tenants in common."

Common Interest Developments

Common interest developments consist of *condominiums* and *cooperatives*. In condominium ownership each unit has its own deed and is separately taxed and mortgaged. Governing functions are most often carried out by an elected association which assesses association dues to the condominium owners. Documents called *conditions, covenants, and restrictions* (CC&Rs) define what owners can and cannot do with their properties. Cooperatives are different since owners do not go on title, instead receiving shares in the cooperative and a lease of a unit.

Real Estate Lingo

Condominiums are properties developed for concurrent ownership where each owner has a separate interest in a unit combined with an undivided interest in the common areas of the property.

Cooperatives are ownership of property by a corporation in which each resident owns a percentage share of the corporation, but does not hold title to the property.

Covenants, conditions, and restrictions, often referred to as **CC&Rs,** are rules that govern how a property looks and is used. These limitations are most commonly recorded on title on properties in a subdivision by the developer of the property. They are common with condominiums and multi-use properties, but may also pertain to single-family homes.

Here is an example of how common interest development works: If I purchase an interest in a condominium, my name goes on the title and the legal description to the property shows exclusive occupancy of my particular unit and a non-exclusive right to use the common area of the property as a whole. For a cooperative, I would receive shares in the corporation and the lease of a unit, but my name would not go on the title.

Property Restrictions

Property restrictions include factors that restrict the use or ownership of a property. *Easements* and CC&Rs restrict the full and free use of property while judgments, liens, and mortgages affect the *equity* of the property. All of these restrictions are recorded on the title to the property.

Here is an example of how property restrictions work: An example of an easement is a right my property gives to a neighbor to run drainage pipes across my property at a certain location. In that location, I cannot build in a way that interferes with the easement right. There is an easement recorded on my property in favor of my neighbor.

In addition, CC&Rs recorded on my property may require that I must obtain the consent of the design review committee if I want to add onto my outdoor patio.

Real Estate Lingo

Easements are rights to use the property of another person for a specific purpose. Easements are recorded on the title on both the property enjoying the right and on the property burdened by the right.

Equity is the difference between the value of the property and the loans against it.

An example of a lien is when my lender records a lien (a deed of trust or mortgage depending on the state) on my property in the amount of $200,000 since they loaned me this amount. When I sell the property, this amount must be paid off. Another example is a money judgment someone obtains against me and ends up as a lien against my property.

Governmental Limitations

The use of our properties is subject to governmental restrictions in the form of zoning ordinances (regulation of the building of structures and use of the property for certain purposes) and building codes (standards of building and permit regulations). A process called *eminent domain* allows a governmental body to condemn a property for public use and pay the owner just compensation.

Here is an example of governmental limitations and how they affect property rights: My property is in an R-1 zone, which allows one, single-family home per one acre. (R stands for residential and 1 represents how many homes are permitted.) If the government decides it needs my property for the public good to extend the freeway, it exercises its eminent domain powers and must compensate me for the value of my property.

Real Estate Lingo

Eminent domain is the governmental right to take private property for necessary public use as long as it fairly compensates the owner. The process by which this occurs is called **condemnation**.

Land Description

The ways of legally describing a property consist of government survey systems (grids), *metes and bounds*, and subdivision lot and block number.

Here is an example of a land description: A metes and bounds description begins with a point of beginning and uses the four quadrants of the compass by use of degrees and feet, i.e., "beginning at the intersection of Main and Minor Streets thence along the south side of Little Street for 150 feet, thence south 45 degrees east … (360 degrees covered) … to the point of beginning."

Real Estate Lingo

Metes and bounds is a method of identifying a parcel by reference to its boundaries and its shape.

Valuation of Property

The valuation of property section of the exam makes up about 15 percent of the total exam length. The following sections discuss the various aspects of property valuation.

Appraisal

Appraisal is the process of creating an opinion about value by the use of accepted practices. It takes comparable recent sales, size, amenities, and condition of the property, *depreciation*, and several other accounting principles into consideration, depending on the type of property and the type of appraisal.

All lenders require an appraisal of a property to justify the real property loans they make. If I want to know the value of my property, the best method is to obtain an appraisal.

Real Estate Lingo

Depreciation is the allocation of the cost of an improvement over its life according to a set formula in the form of a tax deduction.

Taxes and Assessments

Income tax advantages relating to principal residences, vacation homes, and investment property are covered. The principal residence owner enjoys deductions for payment of loan interest and property taxes and exemptions from gain on sale. The investment property renders depreciation and other investment deductions and the ability to sell through a *tax-free exchange*.

The deductions an owner can take depend on whether the property is her principal residence, a vacation home, or investment property.

Real Estate Lingo

Tax free exchanges, also known as 1031 exchanges, allow taxes on profits to be deferred for real estate owners selling investment, rental, business, or vacation real estate and investing in other real estate.

Financing of Real Estate

Financing real estate accounts for about 20 percent of the exam. The following sections discuss the aspects of financing you can expect on the exam.

Types of Loans

There are many types of loans, including VA, FHA, and conventional loans. This is more of a memorization exercise than anything else. For example, if I am a veteran or qualify for an FHA-insured loan, I may be able to obtain a more favorable loan through these branches of the government.

FYI!

VA is the acronym for Veterans Administration. **FHA** stands for Federal Housing Administration. FHA loans allow qualified borrowers to obtain loans with as little as a 3 percent down payment.

Mortgages and Foreclosures

Nearly all properties are purchased with a loan that takes the form of a mortgage or deed of trust recorded on the title. These loans allow the lender to *foreclose* in the event of *default*. Lender requirements are discussed as well as consequences of default.

For example, if I buy a property worth $300,000 and the loan is for $250,000, the lender will record its security interest on the title as a deed of trust or mortgage, depending on the state the property is in, and will foreclose on that interest if I default on the loan.

Real Estate Lingo

To **foreclose** on a property means to liquidate the property for payment of a debt secured by it.

To **default** is to not meet a legal obligation.

Transfer of Ownership

Transfer of ownership accounts for about 15 percent of the exam.

Deeds

Types of deeds are *warranty deeds*, *grant deeds*, and *quitclaim deeds*. The type of deed used confers the type of guarantee given when a property is transferred. The wording of the deed is important to make the deed a valid contract. The process of *recording* deeds as well as the concept of *adverse possession* as a means to acquire title to a property are important to understand.

Real Estate Lingo

A **warranty deed** guarantees that the title is free and clear. A **grant deed** has fewer guarantees than a warranty deed. A **quitclaim** has no guarantees.

Recording is the act of entering deeds and other similar documents affecting title to a property in the public record.

Adverse possession is the acquisition of property through prolonged and unauthorized use of someone else's property.

Here is an example of a deed: If I sign a quitclaim deed, I make no title warranty to you. If I sign a warranty or grant deed, I do make title warranties to you. To claim your property by adverse possession, I file an action in the court system to quiet title (obtain title) to your property.

Closing Procedures

The acts of approving of clear title through a *title report*, ensuring a clear title through the purchase of *title insurance*, and completing the act of transferring title by recording the deed all serve to finalize the transfer of a property. *Settlement statements* allocate the amounts each party is charged for transferring title and itemizing its expenditures.

> **Real Estate Lingo**
>
> A **title report** is the report issued by a title company or closing attorney reporting the condition of the title to a property as disclosed by a search of the public record.
>
> **Title insurance** is a policy guaranteeing that the title is clear and the property is legally owned by the seller. Basic coverage does not involve a site inspection by the title company whereas extended coverage may. A site inspection allows the title insurance to provide coverage for more conditions.
>
> A **settlement statement** is a detailed accounting of buyer and seller debits and credits in the transaction.

The title report tells you whether there are easements, CC&Rs, or other restrictions affecting the property you intend to acquire. Title insurance ensures that you have clear title. Recordation of the deed in the public record makes the transaction part of the public record. The settlement statement describes how much you pay at closing for interest, insurance, purchase price, loan charges, agent commission, taxes, escrow fees, and so on.

Real Estate Brokerage

Real estate brokerage accounts for about 30 percent of the exam. The following sections describe the aspects of real estate brokerage.

Agency

Agency describes the relationships and obligations between the agents in the transaction and the buyers and sellers. For example, if I represent you as your agent in a transaction, I have an agency relationship with you. I become your legal agent and you become my principal.

There are many agency relationships, including seller's agent, buyer's agent, and *dual agent*.

Listings

A *listing* is the employment contract between a broker and a seller. These contracts provide for commission amount, term of the listing, agent's duties, and a description of the type of listing. Most listings are *exclusive right to sell listings*.

Here is an example of a listing agreement: When my client lists her property for sale with me, my exclusive right to sell listing agreement states that the listing is for four months, the listing price is $250,000 and the total commission to be paid is 6 percent of the sale price.

Real Estate Lingo

A real estate **agency relationship** is one where your client, or the principal, is represented by you, the agent, to act on their behalf. There are many legal obligations that arise because of this relationship.

A **dual agent** represents both a buyer and seller in a transaction.

A **listing** is a contract between the agent's broker and the owner that gives the broker the right to sell or lease the property.

An **exclusive right to sell** is a type of listing agreement between an owner and an agent's broker that pays the broker a commission even if the property is sold by someone else during the listing term.

Sales Contracts and Options

Purchase agreements include all the terms by which a buyer will buy and a seller will sell. It provides for the price, closing date, contingencies, and remedies on default. *Option agreements* are distinguished, as they establish a right to buy at a later time.

For example, the offer I make on a property becomes a purchase agreement after it is accepted by the seller. It regulates the entire transaction.

An example of an option agreement is if you agree to sell me your property in two years for a specified amount, I have an option agreement with you.

Real Estate Lingo

Option agreements give you the right to buy a property at a later specified time and price.

Federal Laws

You must be aware of fair housing laws relating to discrimination and disabilities, regulations that make loan procedures more understandable to consumers, and federally regulated environmental risks. Environmental issues include radon, asbestos, lead-based paint, and underground storage tanks.

In the practice of real estate, you need to be aware of protected rights afforded by discrimination and disability laws. These laws require specific steps to be taken by agents when dealing with certain classes of consumers. Fair housing laws must be memorized so you may be aware of when a particular law comes into play.

Consumer protection laws regulate the way loans are introduced to the public. These laws require finance charges and annual percentage rates to be expressed in simple, understandable ways. As agents, we must be aware of the requirements of these laws.

The government, too, protects buyers with respect to an ever-increasing list of environmental conditions. Sellers are required to disclose information relating to these conditions. As agents for buyers and sellers, we must be aware of the laws relating to environmental conditions and continually monitor this ever-changing body of law. For example, in the last few years, natural hazards such as earthquake propensity, the presence of mold, and the presence of lead-based paint have been added to the list of environmental conditions. The list seems to get longer with each passing year.

Property Management

The role and duties of the property manager, landlord-tenant relationships, leasing law, and laws relating to fair practices come under the heading of property management. There is a comprehensive body of law regulating leasing practice, which should be understood to some extent by all agents, even if they do not work as property managers. This body of law also involves fair housing practices, which protect renters from prohibited landlord acts.

Course Challenges

The previous discussion represents a highly summarized but rather complete overview of the real estate principles you will study in your prelicensing courses and what you will encounter on your licensing exam. Some of these subjects you will never encounter again in all of your real estate practice while others will be involved in your day-to-day activities. Your exam preparation course, described in the next chapter, will cover these subjects in detail.

The Least You Need to Know

- It can take three months to study and get your license, and longer to obtain your first commission.

- Each state has specific requirements for getting licensed, and there are entry level licenses and advanced licenses, with requirements for each level.

◆ The course work can be very interesting, with valuable information on property rights, ways to hold title, and differences in types of deeds.

◆ Property restrictions, such as easements and CC&Rs, can affect an owner's property rights.

◆ The steps you take in a real estate transaction are fully detailed in the prelicensing course.

Chapter 5

Preparing for and Taking the Exam

In This Chapter

- ◆ Applying for the exam and taking it
- ◆ Looking at a typical breakdown of the real estate exam
- ◆ Taking a real estate exam-preparation course
- ◆ Practicing for the exam
- ◆ Employing exam-taking strategies

You've completed your prelicensing courses. Now you want to apply for the exam, take an exam-preparation course, and take the exam. You're almost there. This chapter covers these steps and includes sample exam questions, so that you know what to expect when you take the exam.

A Checklist of Exam-Preparation Tasks

Follow a systematic checklist approach when preparing to take the exam. In this manner, you cover all bases allowing you to walk into the exam with confidence and assurance. These are the steps to take in the following order:

1. Apply to take the exam.

2. Determine exam procedures.

3. Gather information on exam content.

4. Take an exam-preparation course.

5. Simulate the exam conditions.

6. Master exam-taking strategies.

7. Adopt the right attitude.

8. Implement good exam-taking policies.

Apply to Take the Exam

Return to the website for your state's real estate commission and follow the instructions regarding applying for and taking the exam. Apply to take the exam before you undertake your exam preparatory work so that when you're done, you'll be ready to walk into your exam. You should find everything you need online, or in an applicant package you have requested from your state real estate commission.

After reviewing your state's requirements, you should be able to answer the following questions:

FYI!

A sample exam question:

Which of the following is the best evidence that the title has been conveyed?

A. The deed has been recorded.

B. The deed has been delivered to the grantee.

C. The buyer is in possession.

D. The deed has been acknowledged.

Answer: B.

◆ Do you need a broker to sponsor you, attest to your good character, or put up a bond for you?

◆ What is the cost to apply to take the exam, to take the exam, and to have your license issued?

◆ What documents must you submit, such as proof of age, financial responsibility, high school or college completion, and residency?

◆ Are you required to submit photographs and/or fingerprints?

◆ Do you have proof of completion of your state's course requirements?

◆ Do you have proof of veteran or disabled veteran status, if it is applicable?

When you have your complete package assembled, send it by priority mail, or drop it off yourself if the office is close by. Keep a copy of everything in case your package is somehow misplaced.

Determine Exam Procedures

Obtain the dates and locations of examinations. Some states offer exams only twice a year and only in one location, typically the state's capital. Others offer the exam frequently and in many different locations. Depending on your state's policy, you should be able to schedule your exam date for when you are done with your examination-preparation course. This is the information you want to ascertain when determining exam procedures for your state:

◆ Examination dates and locations.

◆ What is the deadline to apply for your exam date of choice?

◆ Exam format, whether pencil and paper or examination machine.

◆ What you must bring to the exam: registration confirmation, pencils, scratch paper, application documents, calculator?

◆ Exam-grading procedure: Is each section separately graded or are the sections added up basing your score on an overall score?

◆ Exam grading: How long will it be before you are notified of your results?

◆ Exam performance notification: Are you directly notified or is someone else notified, such as your sponsoring broker, about how you did on the exam?

◆ Exam result advisory: Are you advised about your score or just informed of whether you passed? Will you be able to review your exam to see where you excelled or where you made mistakes?

◆ License issuance: Is your license automatically issued or does it just make you eligible to apply for licensing? How long do you have after passing to obtain your license?

◆ Retaking the exam: How soon after failing the exam may you retake it and how many times can you retake it?

FYI!

A sample exam question:
We call the instrument used to remove the lien of a trust deed or mortgage from record a ...

A. Satisfaction.
B. Release.
C. Deed of reconveyance.
D. Certificate of redemption.
Answer: C.

- Pass score: What is your state's passing score? (In most states you have to get 70–75 percent of the questions correct to pass.)

- Time allowed to take the exam: Most states allow between three and four hours to take the exam. A few states allow two to three hours.

- Pass statistics: What is the pass rate in your state? Most states average a 65 percent pass rate.

Gather Information on Exam Content

All exams are multiple choice consisting of 100 to 150 questions. Most state exams consist of two parts: a longer portion and a shorter portion. The longer portion with typically 80 to 100 questions is the general real estate exam covering the real estate principles you studied in your prelicensing course described in the last chapter. The shorter portion, typically 20 to 50 questions, covers licensing law in your particular state.

Your state's Real Estate Commission or the company it hires to administer the exam will provide you with a wealth of information about the exam, including sample questions and exam content. Some states give you a breakdown of the percentage of questions relating to certain subjects.

As an example of the information you'll gather, I've noted here a summary of what is on California's website:

> **What the exam tests for:** Appropriate knowledge of the English language, including reading, writing, and spelling; arithmetic computations common to real estate and business opportunity practices.

> An understanding of the principles of real estate and business opportunity conveyancing; the general purposes and general legal effect of agency contracts, deposit receipts, deeds, deeds of trust, chattel mortgages, bills of sale, mortgages, land contracts of sale, and leases; principles of business, land economics, and appraisals.

> A general and fair understanding of the obligations between principal and agent; the principles of real estate and business opportunity transactions, and the code of business ethics pertaining thereto; provisions of the law relating to real estate as administered by the Real Estate Commissioner.

Examination topics and percentage of exam coverage:

◆ Real property and laws relating to ownership (approximately 11 percent of exam), which includes ownership of property, encumbrances, and public power over property

◆ Tax implications of real estate ownership (approximately 8 percent of exam), which includes knowledge of current tax laws affecting real estate ownership

◆ Valuation/appraisal of real property (approximately 15 percent of exam), which includes methods of appraising and valuing property and factors which may influence value

◆ Financing real estate (approximately 17 percent of exam), which includes sources of financing, common clauses in mortgage instruments, types of loans and terms and conditions

FYI!

California's website lists 50 sample questions. You can get there directly by searching on the Internet for "California department of real estate salesperson exam sample questions." The first listing takes you directly to the sample questions under "the real estate license examinations." These exam allocations are similar to those described in Chapter 4.

◆ Transfer of property (approximately 10 percent of exam), which includes title, escrow, and reports

◆ Real estate practice (approximately 22 percent of exam), which includes listing of real property, sales contracts, and marketing

◆ Broker's responsibility for agency management (approximately 17 percent of exam), which includes state real estate laws and regulations, laws relating to fair practices, knowledge of trends and developments and knowledge of commonly used real estate forms and math calculations

Take an Exam-Preparation Course

After you apply to take the exam and gather information on it, take an examination-preparation course. You need it. The real estate exam is unique. You want to take a preparation course that will tutor you in the art of multiple-choice testing and in repetition of the concepts studied in your prelicensing courses. Your intent is to take the exam once and move on into your new career from there. The best way to do that is by taking a preparatory course. The pass rate for the exam is about 65 percent. The pass rate for preparatory-course attendees is 85 percent. Convinced?

The company you took your prelicensing course from also has exam-preparation courses geared toward your state's exam. Most courses cover about 2000 questions which are very similar to what you will encounter on the exam. These companies have reconstructed the exams so that their sample questions nearly simulate the licensing exam. They are also aware of the topics that cause the biggest problems for examinees and emphasize these problem areas throughout their practice exams.

Generally, real estate math and contracts are considered the most challenging areas. Math is what you took in the seventh grade. You're just a little out of practice. About 25 percent of the general examination covers math. Most states allow the use of a pocket calculator. Math principles that are covered include commission, interest calculations, depreciation, *prorations*, and *amortization*.

Real Estate Lingo

Prorations are the division of a property's expenses between the buyer and seller as of the property's transfer date.

Amortization is the gradual paying off of a debt by periodic payments.

Contracts intimidate people because they think that only lawyers can understand them. Don't buy into this. The principles are easy and pertain to agreements we make every day of our lives. What did you agree to do and what did they agree to give you in return?

Find the course that is best for you. Courses are offered in person, by correspondence, and online. Find what best suits your needs and your level of discipline. If you feel you will need support from instructors or students, find a course that you can attend in person. Some people consider exam simulation to be highly valuable. The in-person courses put you in a room while an exam is administered under circumstances very similar to those used by your state examiners. If you do not require interaction and want to work at your own speed, go with an online or correspondence course.

Simulate the Exam Conditions

Some states require good old-fashioned pencil and paper while some states require computer usage for taking the exam. Know in advance what your state uses and simulate it many times before taking the exam.

Pencil and Paper or Computer Terminal

Some states use computer answer forms that you fill in with a pencil. The instructions ask you not to write in the exam booklet or on the answer sheet other than filling in your answer choice. You should then indicate to yourself which questions you want to come back to and which questions are math-related problems that require your math analysis hat. Note on a separate piece of paper "To come back to" (for questions you get stuck on) and "math questions" (for all math questions so you can tackle them at one time). Then come back to those groupings of questions after you complete the rest.

Most states are converting to computer entry instead of pencil and paper entry. You are placed in front of a keyboard and monitor similar to what you might have at home or at work. Questions with their answer choices are displayed and you enter your answer on your keypad in the blank provided. You can erase an answer and scroll back and forth to advance and return to questions.

If this is the method used by your state, make sure you are familiar with computer use. The last thing you need is to spend valuable time fumbling with the computer. The exam administrators will provide detailed instructions on use of the equipment and give you a brief practice session. But this is not really enough time to become comfortable with computer test taking if you don't know the basics of using a computer.

FYI! _____

A sample exam question:
When an obligation is paid on an installment basis, it is known as …

A. Acceleration

B. Conversion

C. Amortization

D. Depreciation

Answer: C

The Simulation Process

If upon completion of your examination preparation course you do not feel comfortable with exam taking, buy one of the many books or online courses and practice more. In this case, practice does make perfect. Sit yourself down with a simulated examination according to the rules that will be followed in your exam. You have probably already done this in your preparation course. Use all the exam-taking strategies discussed in this chapter in your simulation sessions.

Master Exam-Taking Strategies

The national part of the exam is always multiple choice. Most states also use this format while very few states have a true/false or fill-in-the-blank format. If you gather information and take an exam-preparation course, you will know your state's format in advance. Here are some practical tips on answering questions:

1. For multiple-choice questions, realize that you are looking at the right answer. You do not have to pull it out of your head. It lies before you.

2. Identify keywords. Often these questions have keywords that guide you to the answer. The first step is to locate the keyword and relate it to the answers. Often, keywords come in the following forms: *always, never, not, but, if, incorrect, must, best, normally,* and *except.* Make sure you choose the answer that incorporates the keyword distinction. When you see these words, train your mental alarm clock to automatically go off.

3. Go with your first impression. It's usually correct.

4. Don't make it complicated. These exams test for minimal levels of competence. Don't look for the hidden meaning. There is no hidden meaning.

FYI!

A sample exam question: A, B, and C are joint tenants. A conveys his interest to D. This changes the ownership as follows:

A. B, C, and D are joint tenants.

B. B, C, and D are each one-third tenants in common.

C. D owns one third as a tenant in common with B and C, who now own two thirds as joint tenants.

D. None of the above.

Answer: B

Adopt the Right Attitude

Adopting the right attitude is an important step to achieving success on the exam. It consists of the following:

◆ Shore up your confidence

◆ Feel good and sleep well

◆ Look at the worst-case scenario

◆ Look at the best-case scenario

◆ Walk into the exam with a positive attitude

Shore Up Your Confidence

If you have been out of school and out of practice taking exams, you can be equipped to handle any jitters. After completing your prelicensing courses and an examination-preparation course, you will have all the knowledge you need. In your preparation course, you will take several practice examinations. You will probably obtain sample questions from your state licensing body. You know exactly what the exam will consist of, and you will have mastered multiple-choice testing. The only unknown is the exact wording of the questions. In other words, you have taken all the right steps. There is no reason to lack confidence.

Sleep Well and Feel Good

Rest and relax the day before the exam. The day before that, do a little studying, especially on subjects you feel weakest in. If you do opt to study the day before, don't spend more than a few hours studying and make sure you are finished at least two hours before your regular bedtime. Get some exercise the day before and do something to take your mind off the exam. A movie or something that takes your mind off the task of taking the exam is ideal.

Don't eat a heavy meal the night before or the day of the exam. Get good directions to the test location, including where to park and how to get into the building. Make sure you arrive at your testing location early. If you arrive late, you will not be allowed to take the exam.

Caution

The lowest pass rates are in Alaska, Arkansas, California, Colorado, Kentucky, Pennsylvania, South Carolina, Tennessee, and Utah.

The following states have the highest pass rates: Arizona, Georgia, and South Dakota.

Look at the Worst-Case Scenario

The pass rate in most states is 65 percent. The worst that can happen to you is you will be one of the 35 percent who do not pass. If you took the suggested preparation course, your odds of passing have increased to 85 percent. Do you really think you'll be one of the unsuccessful 15 percent? What is it that makes you feel that you will be among those fail? The facts before you do not support this conclusion.

Look at the Best-Case Scenario

Chances are almost nine out of ten that you will pass. You've taken all the right steps to put yourself into the 85 percentile. Why wouldn't you pass? Why look at the glass as half-empty when it's nearly full?

Have a Positive Attitude

What's not to feel good about? You've looked at your career options and made a decision to have a career in the real estate field. You've taken and passed the courses you need to qualify for the licensing exam. You have most likely taken an exam-preparation course to prepare for the big exam. If you have taken your examination-preparation course in person, you have a group of other attendees to support you and positively influence you.

Your life is about to take a turn in a new direction entirely of your own making. Your decision has come out of a desire to make your life better. Keep these thoughts in mind as you take the exam. This is an exciting time for you and everything is looking up. Bring your positive attitude with you when you walk through the examination door.

Implement Good Exam-Taking Policies

The following is a checklist you may want to adopt when you take the licensing exam:

◆ Don't pay attention to anyone else. If you do, you will think everyone else is calm and you are nervous. Everyone is nervous, but some people don't show it as much as others do. Do not look around during the exam when you are stuck. Just move on to the next question. Most states use several different test versions in each sitting. The person in your view will most likely not even have the same test you have.

◆ Read the instructions. Do this to make sure you understand the rules.

◆ First answer the easy questions. Some people get stuck on a question, run out of time, and are unable to answer the easy questions. Don't let your focus and attention become distracted by one question. Remember, you can get up to 30 percent wrong. If you answer the easy questions first, you will have a number of correct answers already in your bank account. Your primary objective in the exam is to answer as many questions as you can correctly. You will not get more credit for the ones that are more difficult. So, why belabor one when you can move on and potentially get five more correct?

♦ Answer the math questions at the same time. In this manner, you can put your "calculating hat" on instead of taking it off and on. You will have your calculator, if your state allows one, and your scratch paper and you'll save time by working one problem after another.

♦ Come back to the hard questions after you have answered the easy ones. On your second pass, do the same thing you did initially. Spend a little time with each question. If you're stuck, move on to the next one. Give yourself a little more time than you did with the first pass. However, don't struggle or stay on one question too long. You can come back to it, or just leave it as one of the 30 percent you are allowed to get wrong.

♦ Answer every question. Most exam proctors will provide warnings at certain time intervals before the exam ends. When you receive that warning, make an assessment of where you are in the exam. For instance, if you have ten questions you are stuck on, give yourself enough time to choose an answer. First, eliminate the answers you know are incorrect. Then choose one of the remaining answers.

The Inside Scoop

Some of the professionals you met in Chapter 2 had the following comments about the licensing exam:

"The salesperson exam is definitely not easy. The subject matter is very technical. What helped me the most was the practice exams that were included in my preparation course. They were very similar to the real exam. The exam seemed very familiar to me when I tested, due to the many practice exams I had taken."

"The exam is difficult. The secret is to take lots of practice tests."

"The test items are often ambiguous. The best way to pass the test is to take a preparatory course and memorize answers to hundreds of test questions you get in the preparatory course."

"I rate the exam eight on a scale of one to ten, with ten being the hardest."

"I made sure that I was averaging 90 percent or better on the practice exams, which made the real thing seem easier. Practice; it makes a difference."

What's the lesson to learn here? Although the test might be difficult, the preparatory class and practice questions really do prepare you to pass.

- You should know in advance whether there will be a time warning. If there isn't one, keep track of time yourself, and make sure you know when there are only 15 minutes left before the exam ends to give yourself the time to make final decisions.

- Don't leave the exam early unless you feel sure of all of your answers. Spend the extra time to review any questions you have concerns about.

- Every once in a while take a few deep breaths and stretch your arms.

The Least You Need to Know

- The Real Estate Commission for your state can provide information about licensing requirements and the exam.

- The Real Estate Commission for each state often provides a complete breakdown of the exam, so you know what to study for.

- The real estate agents exam is usually half a day long, while the brokers exam is usually one day long.

- The main secret to passing the exam is practice.

- A real estate exam preparation course is helpful and highly recommended before you take the exam.

Part 2

Getting Started

Although many career choices are available to the real estate agent, this book focuses on the residential sales agent. This part takes you through the business formation stage so you can successfully launch your business with a solid working foundation. The building blocks consist of …

- ◆ Choosing the right office.
- ◆ Formulating and instituting a good small business plan.
- ◆ Incorporating personal and professional power into your business.
- ◆ Creating a power team of professionals to support you.

Chapter 6

Choosing Your Office

In This Chapter

- ◆ The importance of real estate associations
- ◆ A checklist for interviewing the office you join
- ◆ Training and support from your office
- ◆ Fees and commissions you pay the company you choose
- ◆ A list of regrets from seasoned agents

Although many career options are available to the real estate agent, this book focuses on the residential sales agent. This chapter is about choosing the real estate office where you will begin your real estate sales career. This choice is one of the most important you will make since the office you select will mentor you into the practices and principles that will mark your career.

At the end of this chapter you will benefit from the hindsight of agents who wish they had started out their careers differently. A majority of them said they would have chosen their first office more carefully and begun their careers with more office involvement and better initial training.

Before you begin looking at which office might be right for you, you should develop an understanding of the real estate industry. I refer to it as the real estate country club because it consists of a closely-knit community of very social people. You don't have to be a social butterfly to be a member of the real estate community, but if you are, you have found your niche.

Socializing with the Real Estate Country Club

The real estate club is made up of agents and affiliates of agents. Its members consist of lenders, property inspectors, title and closing professionals, and the many categories of real estate agents. The agents are members of the local real estate association and its multiple listing service, while the rest are affiliates. The affiliates provide services to the agents and their clients and are always courting the agents.

The real estate professional is part of a large, active community. It's as if real estate has a flashing sign that says "Join me and you will never be lonely or broke again." It's true. Real estate takes care of its people. While you don't want to test your local real estate agent by asking to be personally invited into their well-protected domain, the real estate community itself is a large, highly cordial, supportive group of professionals.

Some people would contest this viewpoint, finding the real estate industry to be a cutthroat, fiercely protective community. However, this book is written from the perspective of *The New Ideal*, where old competitive attitudes give way to more compassionate, integrity-based ideals.

The Inside Scoop
More than any other group of professionals, real estate agents will steer you away from their terrain. They will not admit to the merits of their profession, nor will they make you feel there is room for you. "It's a dog-eat-dog industry. You really do not want a part of it. We work 24 hours a day, seven days a week. There is no rest for the agent. We really don't make a lot of money; it's a myth."

Don't Believe All Agents

Real estate is bountiful. It provides unlimited financial opportunity to those who know how to tap into it. While the average income for agents is $50,000 a year nationwide, those who become Top Dogs earn extraordinary sums. Real estate is social. Real estate is flexible. It assures independence. Your typical agent works 43 hours a week, including driving time, with a schedule entirely of his or her own making.

The local real estate association you may join is a constant flurry of activity. They're always sponsoring educational programs and social events. The events can make you feel that life is one big party. The educational programs draw top motivational speakers, trainers, and educators providing the latest in information and methods. Between the firm you choose to affiliate with, the professional board you may join, and your mentors, you should be able to get all the support, both socially and professionally, you will need.

> **FYI!**
>
> To get an idea of what your local real estate association offers, search on the Internet for your locality and "Association of Realtors," for example, "Boston Massachusetts Association of Realtors." Some of these sites require membership and passwords to access some information, but you still may be able to get a good idea of the programs and services they provide. When you interview an office manager, ask him or her to step you through an online tour of what their office and the local association provide in terms of education, training, and community. Chapter 7 provides more information about the many benefits association membership offers.

Understanding the Relationship

If you are still researching the real estate sales field, undergo what I call job security training. The would-be agent needs to understand that there is no job security whatsoever in real estate. Understand this before you even decide to study for the licensing exam.

This step consists of contacting a firm that you are considering joining and interviewing the office manager to gain preliminary information about the office and its services. Note that I said you will be interviewing them. I mean this. You will be paying them up to half of your earnings and additional fees. You will begin your real estate professional career under their tutelage. There is a lot you need to know about this office to determine whether you should associate with them.

They are happy to discuss your potential career choice with you; they would prefer to dispel any doubts now instead of after you've joined their office. The purpose of this meeting is to get an idea of how the office operates, what they offer for training and support, and the financial arrangement you can expect. There's no need for a resumé or any other type of formality.

In fact, with some larger firms that provide license exam-preparation training, you can begin your association before you get your license. In this way you join the team before you're licensed and go through the pre-licensing process with others of similar interest.

The job of the office manager is to recruit new agents as well as manage existing agents. They are always looking for new talent. The real estate sales office thrives on agents making money for them. Their policy is the more the merrier, although they do want you to produce if you are going to take up space in their office. When you contact an office asking to meet with the manager, recognize that this is a standard part of the manager's job.

Caution

Your skill as a real estate agent ultimately determines your income and success. There usually isn't a benefit package or retirement package to rely on. Always know that being a real estate agent means working for yourself but giving a part of your income to someone else. After working for another firm, you can become a broker and work for yourself if you choose.

Caution

As an independent contractor, you work for yourself, pay your own taxes, and track your own deductions. One of those deductions will probably be a car lease. You need a good-sized, four-door, high-quality car for driving your clients to view property.

Potential real estate licensees often have a misconception about the career they are considering. The number-one confusion in real estate sales is that you will be employed by one of these offices. This is not true. Although you will work under the name of the company, you are not employed by the company. You are an independent contractor.

The analogy is more of a franchise than one of self-employment. You purchase the right to come under the logo of the company you join and to use its tools. Let me repeat: You *purchase* the right. There are no benefits or pay provided by the company. In fact, it's the other way around. You pay for everything you get.

You will pay for errors and omissions insurance, board dues, multiple listing dues, desk fees, and administrative fees. You may pay for any training you receive. You will pay for the equipment you may need: typically a laptop, a fax machine at home, a cellular phone, and a handheld organizer for use in the field. You will pay for your car, auto insurance, and gas. You will pay for your health insurance and retirement benefits. And on top of that you may share a significant portion of the commissions you earn with the office you join.

You pay the company you hang your license with a high price for the privilege of using its name and placing your license with that company. When you have your broker's license, you will still pay these fees, but your commission split will probably be more in your favor. Over time, as you bring in more commissions, you will keep a bigger percentage of it.

Supporting the Fable

It is quite common for an office manager to watch the potential licensee's face turn white as she describes the financial aspect of the office-agent relationship. Both the agents and the real estate offices encourage the misconception that the agent works for the firm. According to a recent survey of real estate owners, their choice of agent is often due to the reputation of the firm they are associated with.

FYI!

Most people believe that the real estate firm has invested significant time and energy in their employee-agent relationships and continues to do so throughout the agent's career. This could not be farther from the truth. Once the agent concludes any required office training, which can be as brief as a few hours or as long as ten days, the agent is on his or her own. While the office broker is legally required to oversee your transactions, her presence is often more of a supervisor touching base than anything else.

So you see that your future is all of your own making. Take the steps described in this book and you will achieve a success that will make you proud to have chosen real estate as a career. It's not an easy career to begin, but once you define your market and implement good work habits and a productive business plan, it can be a very fulfilling one.

Choosing the Right Office

How do you know which office is right for you? You want to choose a company that will mentor you in customs and practices that will serve you throughout your real estate career. Many factors will go into your decision: your own personal needs, the firm's reputation, the office manager's style, and the agent package the firm offers. Selecting the right office is second only to choosing the right business partner.

The Inside Scoop

Choosing your first office is like hiring a mentor. It is essential that you get the right training and support when you start out your real estate career. This training will set the tone for your business practices and ideals throughout the rest of your career.

The following categories will guide you in making this very important career decision:

◆ Company ideals

◆ Training and support

◆ Company reputation

◆ Financial considerations

◆ Office manager

◆ Company-generated business for you

◆ Office spirit

◆ Your working area

◆ Awards and clubs

You should analyze the benefits each office has to offer for each of these categories and then decide which best meets your needs.

Company Ideals

As with all industries, the real estate brokerage industry is experiencing massive change. Some companies encourage high integrity and clients' needs as top priority, while others continue to rely on old-fashioned selling techniques and outdated business practices. The office you choose will mentor you into your new professional life, so choose carefully.

FYI!

Some companies align themselves with self-empowerment and motivational platforms. They partner with their agents and provide personal development programs to support the agent's personal and professional development. It's a new concept that encourages a heightened sense of teamwork and support.

As with all times of change, innovative new companies are springing into existence. Some of these new companies have grown quickly and have gained both a national and international presence. They have a more democratic way of doing business with their agents, supporting teamwork. They also encourage and advocate higher integrity in interacting with and representing clients. Naturally, this type of company fits in with *The New Ideal* stressed in this book.

Make sure your research of the firm you are considering includes their philosophy on the following issues:

◆ Does the firm promote high-pressure selling techniques?

◆ Does the firm endorse the client's interest first and foremost, even if it means losing the deal?

◆ Is the firm technologically innovative? Does it support the agents' use of computer-based, contact-management programs and agent web pages?

◆ How much does the firm charge agents, whether by commission split or other fees? Does the firm have any type of profit sharing or retirement programs for their agents?

When you sit down with the office manager, explore every one of these subjects.

Training and Support

One of the most important benefits you will receive from the company you choose is training and support. You want to establish good habits early on and set up tools to support you throughout your career. Some offices have full-blown training programs; others give you a cubicle, desk, and phone and say, "Go get 'em." Some Internet-based brokers don't even have offices, nor do they provide one for you. Typically, the larger the firm's national presence, the more training they offer. Remember, though, you pay for the training the same as you pay for everything else you receive from your office. Why? Because you are not an employee of the firm.

The training you may receive from the office will vary. Some offices offer highly sophisticated, in-depth new agent training by experienced trainers with a full curriculum covering agency relationships, *fiduciary duty*, the listing agreement, the purchase agreement, dealing with contingencies, seller disclosures, buyer due diligence, prospecting, and marketing. Each of these subjects is discussed in Chapter 19, as they warrant a chapter of their own.

Real Estate Lingo

In a real estate transaction, the agent has a **fiduciary duty** to his client. A fiduciary duty is acting on behalf of your client with the utmost of care, integrity, honesty, confidentiality, and loyalty. Your mission is to take all steps with your client's best interest in mind. You are your client's trusted advocate.

Although you pay for everything you receive, at least it's there for the asking. It can be scary and lonely to be the new kid in the office and not have any support. With the tools and education provided by the larger firms, you have an abundant supply of resources for any type of situation. A highly detailed training manual can be an invaluable resource for the beginning agent. It's the built-in mentor that never leaves your side.

At the end of this chapter, you will find a list of steps agents would have done differently if they had to do it all over again. One of the most common regrets agents have is that they did not receive good training and support from their first office.

FYI!

Some cutting-edge firms provide ongoing empowerment programs for their agents. These are designed to increase personal productivity and provide career development. These online *universities* provide education, training, and tools. Some forward-looking companies provide peer partnering, matching agents with similar goals and production levels. These partners mentor each other and hold one another accountable for their goals. Some of these partners choose to share their work and profits and become true business partners, a subject that will be discussed later in this book. Others limit the relationship to acting as coaches for one another, which can be an extremely useful tool to the new agent.

One type of training offered by one national firm is called *mastermind training*, which stimulates its participants to expand their thinking in a setting that motivates and mentors them. *Shadowing* is another variety of training where the agent spends the day with a top producer, focusing on personal productivity, time management, and goal-setting techniques. This type of hands-on mentoring can jump-start the career of a new agent.

Some companies have online systems for their agents to download forms, promotional materials, and prospecting kits. Some firms offer ongoing online and in-person courses to increase the agent's technology base, marketing, time management, and legal and life skills. Some have online and conference-call coaching programs by top trainers to motivate you to higher production. Some have tools you can download to assist you in setting up your own website. Others ask you to download your listings directly to their website. Some provide in-house and online continuing education programs.

Caution

As a new agent you can become insecure and alienated if you don't immerse yourself in your office and the real estate community. You need to get experience and these contacts are very helpful sources.

On the agent-support websites for many companies, you get a shopping cart, fill it with the support you need, and pay as you go. You could get this type of training and support just about anywhere in the classroom or on the Internet, but these firms offer everything in one handy spot. When you begin your real estate career, it's a good idea to avoid the urge to reinvent the wheel. Multitudes have come before you. The process is all set up in a cookie-cutter fashion; you just need to decide which process you want to call your own.

Sizing Up the Company Reputation

Throughout your affiliation with the first company you sign on with, you will be thought of as an extension of that company. You therefore want to very carefully select the company that will hold your license, train you, and share its image with you. Research the company well to ensure that it has a solid history, credibility in the community, and a good share of the market.

Real estate relies on looks. What does the office look like? What do its agents look like? If you were a property owner about to sell a home, would you receive a good impression of this firm by walking through its doors? Does it have an image that shows responsibility and credibility?

The *multiple listing services (MLS)* provide statistics on how much of the market share each firm has. Have someone run those statistics for you before you join an office, or better yet, ask the office manager you're interviewing. Consider those numbers when you choose your firm. Drive around the community and observe the presence of this company on for-sale signs. Look at its presence in the local real estate section of the newspaper. Talk to other agents and property owners. Get the hard facts about this company; it will appear on all your cards, contracts, and flyers for years to come and will earn up to 50 percent of every cent you make.

> **Real Estate Lingo**
>
> A multiple listing service (**MLS**) is the database of properties listed for sale and rent within a certain locale. Only real estate agent members may use it. It also includes tax information, member information, and market statistics.

Sizing Up Financial Considerations

Since the real estate sales industry is undergoing enormous change, the industry standard for financial arrangements with agents is also undergoing changes. Not long ago, it was fairly standard for a new agent to share his commission 50-50 with the company, and most often the agent paid no expenses after that. Now, the split is all over the board.

With some companies, you earn the full commission and pay a per-transaction fee or a monthly fee. Some charge you fees in advance, which can be intimidating when you're paying for a new car, a new image, and your traveling high-tech office and you are not yet bringing in an income. Some take some commission and charge some fees. Those that split commission have sliding scales depending on your sales volume. Get a copy of their scale. Some flat fee–based companies allow you to pay for only what you use.

FYI!

Some firms have instituted profit-sharing for their agents in an effort to address agent long-term financial planning objectives. These more-innovative companies encourage their agents to incorporate income-producing strategies into their business plans. Previously, this type of support of independent contractor agents was unheard of. Now it is just starting but will spread through the industry in the future.

Find out how much you pay the company and what they give you in return. Only you can evaluate whether what you pay justifies what you receive. Make a detailed list and scrutinize the options, the way you might compare loan options when buying a house. When analyzing your choice of office, there are important distinctions unrelated to company charges that can tip the scales in favor of one office over the other, such as company reputation or team spirit.

Sizing Up the Office Manager

The office manager will be your mentor on some level for years to come. This will be a very important person in your early career development. Spend some time with him or her discussing office philosophies and procedures. Describe situations that might develop and ask how they should be handled. For instance, you're handling the floor at the office and something comes up that you don't know the answer to. The manager is not in. What should you do? Is there a backup person in charge, or can you contact your manager when you're in a pinch for the first few months?

> **The Inside Scoop**
>
> A recent survey of 1,500 agents showed that the top three reasons agents joined their current firm were company image (54 percent), broker's ethics (41 percent), and the company's business philosophy (34 percent).

Get permission from the manager to interview the agents and receive their candid input. If you do this, the agents will be far more willing to talk about their experiences. You need to be able to know that this manager will be there to support and guide you through your first year of practice. Make sure you know you can work well with this person and will receive support when you need it.

Getting Leads from the Company

Your focus here is to determine what this office does to develop business for you. Does it regularly promote the services of the company? How frequently? What is the quality of its advertising? Does it have a Web presence? If it has a Web presence, will you be able to upload all of your listings to its site? Does it have a program to mentor you through setting up your own website?

How much floor time will you have? In the beginning of your career, you may depend on folks who walk in the office or phone the office as vital lead sources. You want to make sure this office does not have too many agents who would limit your floor time. With the increasing use of agent direct phone lines, floor time is quickly becoming something of the past. If the company you interview has a floor time policy, examine it carefully. For the new agent, floor time is invaluable in terms of acquiring leads and clients.

Office Spirit and Agent Support

Does this office operate from a base of teamwork, or are the agents working strictly on their own? Many offices give lip service to teamwork, but operate as a collection of competitive individuals. Other offices are built on teamwork, providing in-house mentorship to new agents. As a new agent, you want to operate within a team environment as much as you can. Talk to top agents in the office and find out whether you can work as an assistant for them for a while until you can break away on your own. In this manner, you will receive the best hands-on training available and receive pay while you learn.

Find out whether agents in the office are open to your sitting at open houses for them and even shadowing them for a day. See whether agents in the office are open to letting you "house sit" their listings while they take short vacations. Talk to agents about whether they will refer business to you that they don't want or can't get to in exchange for a referral fee from you. The best way to approach these issues is to have a generous attitude, not one of selfishness. In other words, your intention is to contribute to their well-being while they contribute to your learning and well-being.

Do some agents within the office partner with one another for mentoring purposes? Are some also partnering as full business partners? If you can find an office that has a long practice of team spirit, weigh this strongly. The office that provides very little in the way of formal training and high-tech strategies, but has good old-fashioned manager-agent relationships and team

The Inside Scoop

Teamwork and support are very important to agents starting out. If you can find a mentor and are comfortable with most of the other agents in an office, you can gain immeasurably from their experience. At the end of this chapter, you will see that teamwork and support were priorities for a majority of agents when choosing their first office.

spirit, will guide you smoothly through your apprenticeship. At the end of this chapter you will see that agents regretted that they had not created more teamwork at the office they joined.

Sizing Up Your Work Space

This issue is based on personal preference. One person can be put in the bullpen cramped in a small cubicle in the loudest area of the office and be delighted. Another may find this a reason to have her head examined. Make sure you have a good idea of exactly what your work area will look like and whether you will be sharing it with others.

What will it feel like when the office is full of agents and their clients conducting business? In your first year, you will probably want to spend most of your time in the office where you can get support, rather than in your home office. How conducive is your space to your own personal productivity? Only you can answer that.

Getting Recognition

Many offices have special awards, clubs, and distinctions to honor achievements of their agents. Real estate is a social club and the offices are part of this. The larger offices have all kinds of awards and designations to celebrate staff. There are the million-dollar clubs, the best of the office, the best new agent. It's like being back in school again.

The agents receive their awards, and then publicize them to their sales communities. Yesterday they were just an agent. Today, they are a member of a multimillion-dollar club, tomorrow it may be the President's Club, and in the not-so-distant future it could be the Chairman's Circle of Excellence.

Some companies have their very own designations they give to experts in a given area of specialization, such as luxury home specialist, vacation home specialist, new home specialist, and farm and ranch specialist. It's another gold star on your business card that makes clients feel you are the top of your field.

Awards and designations are very important to agents. On their business cards, after you get past the gorgeous smiling mug, note the many designations and awards the agent has. These days it doesn't take much to join the million-dollar club. In areas of the country where the average-priced home is $700,000, you're in the door with one or two sales. Official designations are another story to be covered in later chapters.

Interviewing Firms

For this interview, you should bring a resumé that details your education, prior work experience, and affiliations. Make it one page, choose an impressive font, and use sturdy paper. There is a way of taking factual information and presenting it in an impressive way. It's not misrepresenting; it's making the most out of what you have. You need to learn this art for real estate sales, so you might as well begin with yourself.

The Inside Scoop
If you don't have prior resumé preparation experience, search the Internet on resumé preparation or pick up a book on the subject. You will soon prepare a bio for clients based on your resumé. Spend a little time cultivating your resumé-writing talents. You may want to pick up a copy of *The Resume Handbook: How to Write Outstanding Resumes and Cover Letters for Every Situation* (3rd Ed.) by Arthur D. Rosenberg, David V. Hizer.

The interview is the time to cover all the bases you discussed in this chapter. Bring this book and refer to it, or photocopy the pages you need. You'll be quite impressive when you present these topics for discussion. It will show that you are serious about your vision and intend to make the most of your career.

You will probably already have many of your answers from the preliminary research you have done. There will be areas to be discussed and negotiated. Most importantly, you need to evaluate the level of rapport you have with the office manager. The interview should take an hour to an hour and a half.

You should interview at least three companies. If you were interviewing someone you wanted to hire, you would be sure to interview at least three people. Make sure you do the same with the company you will hire. Then, take time to compare your notes and deliberate over your important decision. You should know which office is right for you. If you don't, interview more companies until you have a strong feeling that you have found the office for you.

New agents are often unaware that *they* are in high demand, feeling intimidated by the interviewing process. When an office manager invites them on board, the agent gladly accepts, so pleased to have been accepted. If this is your inclination, put the shoe on your other foot. Nearly every office you interview with wants you in their money-making pool. Always remember, you are interviewing them; they are not interviewing you. Make your choice prudently.

Regrets of New Agents

You don't have to say, "I wish I had known then what I know now." Hindsight is always 20-20, and with this list of agent regrets you can learn from others who came before you. Here is a list of some of the major obstacles new agents face. Take each of these ideas to heart and consider them seriously when you begin your new career.

One agent points out that you have to be the one to seek out help from others:

> I wish I had involved myself more fully in my office. There is nothing that makes you feel more insecure than watching these gung ho producers handle five deals at a time and you don't even know the first step to take. Don't sit there. Find mentors, go to open houses, scout out a subdivision and find out everything about it, ask agents in your office to let you tag along.

From this agent's advice, you learn that discipline is important when starting and sustaining your real estate career:

> I should have disciplined myself more from the first moment, but most especially when I felt I wouldn't make it in the business. The last thing to do when feeling insecure is to cut back on good work habits. Always remember, the road to success is under construction. You can only pound one nail in at a time, but you've got to be disciplined to finish the job.

FYI!

Other regrets not as high on the list include:

- I wish I had learned more about technology.
- I wish I had understood the agent smiling at you will stab you in the back.
- I wish I had understood that my choices have nothing to do with my client's choices.
- I wish I had understood the low regard agents are held in so I could build a model without those traits.
- I wish I had understood the official designations and received some early on.

This agent comments on the importance of building niches:

> Real estate sales is about creating markets everywhere you go. The best way to do that is to continually build niches. You live in a community. Be the agent who specializes in the 10-block radius around your home. Do this from day one. Also, make sure you use technology as much as you can, and have your own website.

Concerned about money when starting out? So was this agent. Here's some advice:

> Building a new career and a new business can be overwhelming if you don't have a stash to get you through the first year. Yes, I mean a year. You'll more than make up for it after that many times over again. In the beginning, though, you need to focus on the many challenges of your new business instead of worrying about making ends meet.

This agent comments on choice of office:

> I wish I had chosen my first office more carefully and found more mentors to guide me through my first year. I would have chosen my office based on its training program and its new agent support. I needed a training manual that was far more detailed than the skimpy notebook they handed me. I would have preferred an office that set me up with a mentor-agent to help me through my first few transactions.

This agent comments on creativity in the business:

> I wish I had opened my mind to the many creative ways an agent can make real estate work for them as a source of creative income, excellent investment potential, and for creating a specialized career niche.

> **Caution**
>
> The National Association of Realtors reports that the typical agent has been in the business for 13 years, having been with the same firm for five years and only one firm prior to that.

These "If-only-I-had" regrets are discussed throughout this book.

The Least You Need to Know

- Your local real estate association sponsors educational programs and social events for agents and affiliates.

- When you join an office, you become a franchisee of sorts, paying the office while, in turn, you receive support.

- Selecting the right office involves many factors: your own personal needs, the firm's reputation, the office manager's style, the agent package the firm offers, and more.

- Throughout your affiliation with the company you sign on with, you will be thought of as an extension of that company.

- Evaluate the philosophy and ideals of the company you intend to join to ensure that they are in line with your own philosophies.

Chapter 7

Building Your Business

In This Chapter

+ Real estate associations and the multiple listing service

+ Your small business as a productive, organized enterprise

+ An intensive tutorial in understanding market indicators

+ Computer technology as the foundation of your business

+ Continuing education is important to Top Dogs

This chapter is a recipe for beginning your career with a solid foundation. After all, you've just become the CEO of your own company. It's time to implement a plan so you can capably steer your new company to success. When you start out in real estate sales, a good business plan is a must because you are beginning not only a new business, but an entirely new career. To ensure your success, you need many levels of business-building training.

This chapter only touches on the basic steps you will need to take to set up your new business. These are just the starter steps, whereas later chapters on marketing, computer technology, database management, and representation of your clients will round out the training you need. They didn't build Rome in a day and you won't build your new business in one day either. If you begin it according to the steps in this chapter, it will be assured of a good foundation. The first step to take is to get some reality training.

FYI!

Many excellent books have been written about setting up your new business. Don't reinvent the business model. Follow the steps in this chapter, but also read some books on small business procedures. The Small Business Administration has all kinds of resources and information on its website at www.sba.gov.

A Dose of Reality Training

Realize that you are not prepared for the job ahead. Many people earn four- to eight-year degrees in institutions of higher learning to engage in professions that feel like kindergarten class compared to the transactions you will handle. Yet the real estate industry turns out agents to handle complex, multifaceted real estate sales transactions with just a few months of preparation. You therefore have a tremendous reality gap to bridge between what you know and how to make a living in real estate.

Unless you spend two years assisting a top producer before you handle your own deals, you must come to terms with the fact that you will not have enough time to gain the experience you need. You may make some serious and frustrating mistakes. For the first year or two anything that can go wrong will go wrong in varying stages of your transactions.

FYI!

Ask each of the experienced agents in your office whether they will let you track one transaction with them. This will be invaluable for you. If you limit your request to just a single transaction, you are more likely to receive a gracious response to your request. Although busy agents are hesitant to commit to mentoring you for any period of time, offering to help them on one transaction has an altogether different ring.

It often works like this: You master multiple listing entry, but then handling contingencies plagues you. You get contingencies down, and then dealing with price reductions becomes the new monster. You feel like you're back on track, and then a title issue comes in the side door. In real estate, where there are so many different roles and issues to deal with, the only way to ward off problems is to be a seasoned agent.

New agents are often taken advantage of by the public; often clients expect new agents to drive them all over the universe. You are likely to be abused by other agents who forget they were once in your position. You may also be led down a rosy path by those who see new agent naiveté written all over you. You may even make legal mistakes and you might get involved in unethical situations without even knowing it.

When these things happen, as they shall, don't be surprised. If you're not surprised, your clients and peers won't be surprised. Stay calm, and sit down with your mentor or your manager and discuss situations as they arise. Don't take these issues to heart, but learn from each situation. With that said, let's plan your business so you can get through your experiences with as much ease and support possible.

Obtain Office Training and Support

Remember the number-one regret agents had about the beginning of their careers? Let me remind you in the words of one agent who mirrored what a large group of her peers had to say:

> I wish I had involved myself more fully in my office. There is nothing that makes you feel more insecure than watching these gung ho producers handle five deals at a time, and you don't even know the first step to take. Don't sit there. Find mentors, go to open houses, scout out a subdivision and find out everything about it, and ask agents in your office to let you tag along.

 FYI!

A little farther down the list of agent regrets is this:

> I wish I had chosen my first office more carefully and found more mentors to guide me through my first year. I would have chosen my office based on its training program and its new agent support. I needed a training manual that was far more detailed than the skimpy notebook they handed me. I would have preferred an office that set me up with a mentor-agent relationship to help me through my first few transactions.

The very first step is to immerse yourself in your office. Hopefully, your office will have a well-developed training program and a good office manual. If the mentoring you need isn't available, find it. Your local association, discussed later in this chapter, will have a variety of programs and support aids available. If your office manager or the rest of the agents are not very forthcoming, you may have to reel them in. Everybody is busy doing what they were doing before you joined the office, so it is probable that you will have to build your own office support.

If your office manual isn't detailed enough, supplement it. It is helpful to everyone in an office, and others are often willing to participate in sharing information with you because they will benefit from your product. A detailed office procedures manual is worth its weight in gold. It will get you through those inevitable difficult times during your first year when you have no idea what to do. Statistics show that you will stay at your office for at least seven years. It is worth spending the time to set up a system that works for you.

You should also establish relationships with key players in your office. Don't come with a "what you can do for me" attitude. See what you can do to assist others and become a member of their support team. Determine who the top producers are and offer to assist with their transactions without pay, or offer to act as their administrative assistant. Seek to learn and contribute to the office. Top agents are the very best training tools you could ever pay for. Give thought now to choosing a person in your office to act as your mentor and possibly another person to partner with you.

Participate with Your Realtor Associations

After you seek training in your office and after you make the best of your office situation, obtain training and support from your local real estate association. Each locale has its own real estate association that provides social and educational support to its members and affiliates. Along with your office, your local association will become the heartbeat of your real estate community. Get to know your local association and its staff. This association is like family to Realtors, and you can reap the benefits of its education, social events, and unbeatable community.

When you join an office, you become a member of your local association. You may also choose to join the statewide association and the National Association of Realtors. None of these memberships is mandatory. The only mandatory membership is with the real estate commission that issued your license and monitors your continuing education requirements. Your local Realtor association will have a continually growing list of educational programs and social events. The educational programs are usually very good as top educators and motivational speakers tour the real estate associations providing quality programs for continuing education credit.

> **The Inside Scoop**
>
> Did you know that the term *Realtor* is trademarked by the National Association of Realtors and can only be used by members? Go to www.realtor.org to find out more.

The social events are usually loads of fun. There are bowling events, ski trips, golf trips, gambling excursions, and cruises. The local Realtor groups celebrate everything.

And if there is nothing in particular to celebrate, there is a dance or an auction just for a reason to get together. They also sponsor events supporting local charities. Real estate has a unique sense of vitality and community that is not as common to other professions.

Your local real estate board, your state's board, and the national board also have websites with databases of statistics and other valuable information you should review regularly. These excellent websites are sources of legal, economic, and educational information as well as standard transaction forms.

Your local association also has a store where you can purchase signs, forms, and just about anything you'll need to practice real estate. You can also lease your *lock boxes* and keys through the association. Your association also has boards and committees you can serve on. This type of service doesn't network you with clients, but it does present valuable opportunities to learn and to bond with your fellow agents. In the bigger picture, this type of service will gain you recognition from both clients and other agents as you will be thought of as one of the movers and shakers of the real estate community.

FYI!

When you become a real estate licensee, bring out the teacher in yourself and develop a program accredited by your state real estate licensing organization. Through this, you will be more closely connected to the community and become recognized as an expert in the subject you teach. Why not teach a course on helping new agents set up their new business after you get yours running smoothly?

Real Estate Lingo

A **lockbox** is an attachment to a door that holds the key to that door. Agents have access to the lockbox so that they can obtain the key to a property on-site. Many areas have adopted electronic lockboxes that track which agents visited the location, so that the listing agent has another tool for follow-up.

Know the Market

It's time for boot camp. Put on your boots, or at least your comfortable walking shoes, and walk the market, talk the market, and see the market. It will take time for you to talk market, but you will begin to if you saturate yourself in it. So, how do you get prepared?

Check Out the Multiple Listing Service

Each locality has a multiple listing service (MLS) for its sales and rental listings. Most multiple listing services operate independently from real estate associations. Just about every licensed agent or broker belongs to the MLS, which provides a database of current and past listings of properties for sale and for rent. Through the MLS, the agent lists a client's property for sale or rent, and all agents belonging to that service can view the listings. Some services provide listings for an entire region; others handle one specific geographic area.

FYI!

The listing on the MLS will tell you specific information about the land, its building(s), and its listed price. It will also tell you commission amount and the property's showing information. There is a photo (or multiple photos), an embellished description, and contact information for the listing agent. There may be additional information, such as a date that all offers will be received, or any special terms, such as whether the owner will carry back financing or a special closing period.

Most services also provide a great deal of information beyond listings. For example, they provide tax assessor information and data regarding other agent and office information so you can track market share. We now have the capability for e-mails of new or changed listings to automatically be sent to designated clients and prospects. Marketing is at its best when it happens entirely without you. The more computer-savvy you become, the more benefits you will obtain from the MLS.

The MLS is your best course in real estate economics and statistics. Using the MLS is the course you did not receive in preparation for your license, but it *is* the one that really makes you a real estate agent. Once you understand the local real estate market and its statistics, you will begin to think like a real estate professional.

Here is a list of the primary statistics to study and compare to the same timeframe from the year before:

♦ Active listings in the area of your practice

♦ Average list price

♦ Average sales price

♦ Average time on market before sale

♦ List price versus sales price ratio

♦ Number of sales year-to-date

♦ Current interest rate for 30-year, fixed mortgage

Each MLS tracks these statistics. They are easy to retrieve, but you need to *understand* them. Sit down with your mentor or office manager and talk about these numbers. Only by comparing current statistics with one another and with statistics from the year before can you establish and track the economics of your market. You will see how prices compare to the year before, whether the market is slowing or quickening, and whether it is a seller's market or a buyer's market.

Now see how your area's statistics compare with surrounding areas and with the state and country as a whole. The website for your state association will provide data on where your area ranks within your state. How does its median home price compare to the immediate surrounding areas? Compare your local and statewide median home price to the national median by going to Realtor.org, the site of the National Association of Realtors. It gets very interesting when you start to put these statistics into perspective.

The Inside Scoop

The National Association of Realtors has two websites, Realtor.com for the consumer and Realtor.org for agents. You should familiarize yourself with the consumer site so that you can direct your clients there. The agent site includes business management tips, breaking news, and the latest industry statistics and trends, sales and marketing tools, legal tips, and educational opportunities. In Canada, the national website is www.crea.ca.

Tour Houses

Study homes on the MLS, the inventory that makes the statistics. It would take you three hours to physically tour three properties. On the MLS website, you can tour at least a hundred in that time. It's not like opening the kitchen cabinets or walking through the garden, but you can see all of the properties' statistics along with a variety of pictures for each.

Through a careful study of the current active and recently sold listings, you will begin to understand value in a specific area. You will also start to understand per-square-foot figures when you divide the square footage of homes into their sale prices. You will see which areas appreciate more than other areas, and you will gain a sense of how long homes take to sell.

To complete your boot-camp training, move offline and into the field with some of the active listings you studied, physically touring these properties. This is where it gets fun. The numbers you've studied become homes and gardens. Hold the listing in your hand as you tour a property so the property's statistics are at your fingertips.

Make sure you know the number of bedrooms and baths before you tour. Know what the siding is and how many fireplaces there are, and so on. Your primary reason for touring is to match up the physical product with its listing price and listing features.

The market statistics you studied and the physical features of these properties will begin to relate to one another. An updated bathroom spells value, whereas a fully landscaped garden may spell work. Watch these listings as they travel through sale, and you will understand what makes one property more marketable than another. You may get a feel for why one property gets an offer in just a few days while another one goes through multiple price reductions and becomes stale.

> **Caution**
>
> Go to properties on your own or with your mentor, hold the listing in hand and make believe your clients are with you. Now's the time to perfect your touring style, not later when potential buyers are bombarding you with questions.

Let seasoned agents in your office know you want to be included in listings they have obtained. Offer to sit for them when they hold open houses. Keep up your study of the market and tours of properties until you have a true understanding of value, property features and your own local real estate market. Make sure you track the status of properties you tour. This type of monitoring will give you the very best sense of your local market.

Get to Know Your Local Neighborhoods

Tour a different neighborhood every few weeks. Pull the active and sold listings for that neighborhood. Get a feel for neighborhood value in relation to your entire area. Drive around and become acquainted with the amenities that make a certain sector a unique community. Know its proximity to transportation, major city centers, and other neighborhoods. Find out about the local schools and their reputations. Develop a neighborhood analysis based on your observations and the values you have established.

It will take about three months of constant study and touring about ten homes a week to get a real feel for the market. If you religiously perform neighborhood analysis for the same period of time, you will develop a good understanding of your area as a whole and the difference in value among neighborhoods. You will tour a home and know which improvements increase value and which features make it more marketable. You will develop the ability to look at homes and come close to estimating the value without even reviewing computer statistics. One day you will drive by a house for sale, a price will come to mind, you will stop and pull the flyer—and you will be on the money. You will become a real estate pro without even realizing it.

Manage Your Own Business

When you decided on a career in real estate, you made a decision to become a small business owner. If that scares you, a career in residential real estate sales is not for you. Although you come under the umbrella of a real estate office, you are actually the owner and operator of your own real estate sales practice. There are some important administrative steps you must take as a small business owner. The following sections explore these.

Incorporate Technology Fully

Because the MLS is Internet-driven and the business model in this book is computer-driven, it is imperative that technology become the foundation of your business.

Thus, Chapter 12 is devoted entirely to it, covering the computer programs you will require to manage contacts, e-mail and calendaring functions, word processing, Internet access, and accounting. Most agents have two offices and field locations from which they need the ability to access information and to communicate by voice, fax, and e-mail. The challenge of the highly portable nature of your business is solved with a laptop, a cell phone, and a handheld organizer, all of which must work together.

Caution

Don't take your energy away from the real estate business by becoming a computer nerd. Get some basic training in how to connect your equipment and how to share information. Find a person who knows computers to help you. Otherwise, you'll add a level of frustration to your business that will decrease, not increase, your productivity.

Include Web Technology

Web-based technology is also a subject you need to seriously consider. The way we communicate with others and receive our information has changed, as has the way we market ourselves. Just as every business has a physical address, most now have an Internet address. The office you work for probably has a Web presence.

Statistics show that agents who have their own websites earn twice as much as agents who don't. You therefore want to give serious consideration to having your own website separate from your

FYI!

The percentage of Realtors who believe having a website and using the Internet has changed the way they do business has increased to 64 percent in 2003 from 50 percent in 2002. Over 60 percent of Realtors have a personal website, either their own or through their brokerage.

office's site. Do yourself a favor and do more than just hire someone to put your site up for you. If you don't know how to interact with your site, you won't get the most out of it. It can be an incredible marketing tool for your existing clientele and a source for ongoing, new Internet-driven clients. Website creation and administration are discussed later in this book.

Open Your Bank Accounts

You will need a business operating account for the commissions you earn and a client trust account for costs your client may deposit with you for payment of expenses. Your business operating account will be the main account for your small business where you will keep track of the income you receive and the deductions you take.

> ### The Inside Scoop
>
> Your trust account may have money from your clients for various expenses. Perhaps these are fees to a stager, a painter, or a carpet-cleaning service. Sometimes the client is not local to the property and asks you to coordinate with many people to prepare a property for sale.

You'll pay all your expenses out of this account, so you must therefore track them to count as deductions on your tax return.

The trust account is required by law if you hold funds for others. It will hold any funds your client has entrusted to you which are to be used on their behalf. Until these funds are spent according to their instructions, they belong to the client and must be kept in a separate trust account. You are not required to have a separate trust account for each client, but you must separately account for their funds within your trust account.

Prepare for Tax Time

Now that you work for yourself, you are responsible for calculating and paying your own taxes. The days of receiving paychecks with taxes already deducted are gone. You have state and federal income, Social Security, and Medicare taxes to pay. You will pay a rather steep *self-employment tax* for the privilege of being self-employed. I realize it should be the other way around, but it is not. These taxes can easily eat up 40 percent of your net income.

The time to make your tax payments is as you go along by payment of quarterly estimates. You don't want to get to tax filing day without budgeting for taxes. There are penalties to pay if you do not make tax deposits as you go along. With most accounting software programs, your tax payments can be calculated as you deposit commissions.

If you have employees who are not *independent contractors*, you will also have to calculate and pay their taxes. An assistant will most likely meet the criteria of independent contractor, which means the assistant pays his own taxes. Workers are considered independent contractors if they have the right to direct and control the way they work, including the details of when, where, and how they do their jobs. If your assistant works out of her home at her own pace and works for others in addition to you, the independent contractor test has most likely been met.

When and if you hire an assistant, make sure you have him or her sign an independent contractor agreement that says what is described above. There is a fine line between employee and independent contractor status, so always watch that you do not cross it. If you do, the taxing authorities can assess you for any taxes that have not been paid both by you and by your employee. The very best way to stay on the right side of the independent contractor fence is to define only the work you want done, leaving your assistant to control how, when, and where the tasks are accomplished.

Real Estate Lingo

Self-employment tax: Social security and Medicare tax paid by self-employed taxpayers on the net income from their trade or business.

Independent contractor: A worker with the right to direct and control the way he works, including the details of when, where, and how he does his job. The independent contractor receives a 1099-Misc form by the end of January if he has earned over $600.00 from you.

Deduct Most of Your Expenses

Now that you are self-employed, all business-related expenses are deductible. You pay self-employment taxes, so you want to meticulously claim all the deductions that you can as a small business owner. Pay all tax-deductible expenses out of your business operating account and itemize these expenses under the appropriate deduction category.

Know what deductions you can and cannot take. Your car is now a business expense, as is the business use of your home. All expenses you pay for education, including books you read, are deductible. Dues for clubs you join are also eligible as a deduction. Office equipment you use for your business is deductible. If the expense is related to business, take it as a deduction. This also applies to gas, auto repair, and auto insurance expense.

Save all your receipts for business travel, entertainment, and restaurants. You are required to itemize the specific people you met with, the dates you met, and the business purpose. This is the reason those big, ugly manila envelopes exist—to hold all your receipts in case you are audited. The reason is not to pull the receipts out at tax time and tally them up. You should implement a far better accounting program that tracks these expenses on computer as you go along.

FYI!

Here is a list of common deductions available to the real estate agent who works as an independent contractor:

- Advertising
- Assistant wages
- Automobile expenses and lease
- Books and publications
- Business travel
- Dues to business-related organizations
- Education
- Entertainment necessary for business
- Equipment (including computers, phones, handhelds)
- Gifts to clients (all those gifts described in the Referral Stream System)
- Home office use
- Insurance
- Licensing once licensed
- Supplies (including software)
- Postage
- Professional services
- Rent for office space
- Stationery and printing
- Telephone

There is a whole world of deductions available to you now that you are self-employed. From now on, whenever you pay an expense, go through the mental process of determining whether it is an expense related to your business. If it is, be sure you deduct it. The best way to track expenses is to pay them all through your business operating account or a business credit card. Make sure you have separate business and personal bank accounts and credit card accounts. The accounting becomes simple when everything associated with your business accounts is segregated.

When you pay your business credit card each month, allocate each item to its deduction category with your accounting software. You "split" the total bill into your deduction categories. For instance, your bill is $1,500, $230 of which was for advertising. Itemize this expense as "advertising." The categories you use should be the same categories you will use on your tax return.

It is especially important to scrupulously document your deductions because they determine the net income your taxes will be based upon. You therefore want to have as many deductions as possible. If you earn $75,000 and deduct $15,000 for expenses, your taxes are based on $60,000 net. Your expenses are your way to receive tax-free income as long as you choose them carefully and document them well.

Set Up Your Retirement Accounts

Many agents miss out on retirement planning because it dawns on them late in the game that nobody else is going to do it for them. We CEOs of our small businesses don't get the huge stock option packages others do, nor do we automatically have retirement accounts building for years as we toil away. We get nothing, a big zip, unless we begin saving for retirement early. When you set up your office, set up your retirement accounts. Build retirement into your overall business plan. If you set up these accounts with automatic payments from your operating account each month, you won't even feel the bite.

When you start out knowing you are the only one who will take care of your retirement, you will build in the steps required to fund your retirement. Don't just open a simple IRA, review the options, talk to your accountant, and determine whether a Roth IRA or SEP, or other retirement option, is the best plan for you. Why pay taxes on income when you can legally divert income into tax-deferred or even tax-free retirement accounts? Setting up the maximum leveraged retirement accounts and creating future income streams (addressed later in this book in Part 6) will assure you financial abundance throughout your later years.

FYI!

Take the time to consider available retirement options and build them into your business and accounting plan. Go to www.irs.gov/ retirement/article/0,,id=10897 5,00.html and review the simple information the government provides on Traditional IRAs, Roth IRAs, Simple IRAs, and SEPs.

Package Your Business

Set yourself up as an entrepreneur with an entrepreneur state of mind. Every successful entrepreneur sets up his business according to business opportunity resale standards to be sold later when it's a profitable venture. Any business that has a long-standing client list and a good history of income can be sold as a business opportunity. The longer the business has operated and the more net income it receives, the higher its value.

This is the frame of mind you want to have when setting up your business. The last section of this book describes business opportunity resale packaging of your business in more detail. It is important to set up your potentially sellable business now in its beginning stages for resale later. Here are a few tips to consider:

- Keep good, clear, verifiable records.

- Have a good accounting program that tracks all income and expenses.

- Have your tax return mirror your accounting income and expense categories.

- Set up systems for doing business that will allow your buyer to operate your business as successfully as you did.

The Inside Scoop

Surf the Net for business opportunities to get an idea of resale standards. Just having the intention to build an enterprise that will have resale value gives you an entrepreneurial state of mind. See if there are any real estate practices for sale in your area. Why start from scratch when you can step into someone else's successful shoes?

Each step you take with your business plan takes into account the marketability of your business. Will this feature make this business more marketable when later sold as a business opportunity? If you revise your business procedures, do it in a simple, straightforward way. If you have a choice between technology and archaic methods, choose technology. Make sure your records, both on the computer and hard copy, are clear. Keep your client base well organized in your contact management program. Your intention is to sell your flourishing enterprise when the time is right, even if it remains a one-person business.

Check Your Insurance Coverage

You will also need to contact your vehicle insurer to report that you are using your vehicle for business and chauffeuring clients. Otherwise, your insurance may not cover you for a business-related loss. Your office will also likely require you to list it as an additional insured on your policy. Your vehicle insurance will increase, so be prepared for that.

You also want to check on your new professional liability insurance. Lawsuits are a part of real estate. They go with any territory that involves high stakes. Real estate is about as high as you can get. Your liability insurance is called *errors and omissions insurance*, and covers you for any claim made against you for your real estate services. Typically, you pay your insurance through the office you hang your license with. Make sure the coverage is high and your deductible is low.

Real Estate Lingo

Errors and Omissions Insurance is known as E & O Insurance. This insurance provides legal defense and coverage for claims made against you in your capacity as an agent. Most real estate offices provide this insurance for their agents as part of the fees they charge.

Take Construction and Architecture Courses

Real estate lingo is a vocabulary of its own. You need to know the industry-accepted terminology for all parts of a building, its components, its décor, and its land. The appraisal industry has its way of speaking. The construction industry has another. Architecture has its own. Decorating has its share. Landscaping has yet another. You need to know them all so you can intelligently communicate the names of features of a property. Some you met up with on your real estate exam. Much of this terminology may be new to you.

FYI!

Here are a few sample terms you will come across:

♦ **Construction terms:** dormer, wainscoting, rafters, trusses, load-bearing wall, joists

♦ **Decorating terms:** foyer instead of hallway, swags, cornices, valances

♦ **Furniture styles:** Chesterfield sofa versus the camelback sofa, Chippendale leg versus French provincial leg

♦ **Architectural terms:** crown molding and cove molding; peninsulas and islands; granite, marble, slate

♦ **Landscaping:** hardscape and softscape

♦ **Engineering:** septic systems, wells

When you get your license and become involved in the real estate industry, you are immediately catapulted into a whole different language. Read books on these subjects. Watch Home & Garden television and acquire an education in a week that will serve you well in your new career. Surf the Net. A dictionary of real estate terms will do once you know the words, but until then you need to learn what each feature is by touch, feel, and sight.

Take Continuing Education and Specialty Training

As with most other professional licenses, you must fulfill continuing education requirements to retain your license. These courses advance your expertise in your chosen field of real estate or help you to transition into another real estate field. If you plan ahead and choose your continuing education courses wisely, you will continually enhance your practice by broadening your marketplace and establishing your com-petence in chosen fields of expertise.

The Inside Scoop

Continually monitor the continuing education courses offered by your local real estate association, your state association, and the national association. Why not take the best courses to help you specialize and become a Top Dog? You may want to begin working toward a special designation like Certified Residential Specialist (CRS) or Graduate of the Realtor Institute (GRI) offered by the National Association of Realtors.

Although your job is not to give tax advice or legal advice, by honing your understanding of tax laws and contractual issues you will become indispensable to your clients and yourself. You will stand out as a career specialist who understands and takes advantage of the full benefits and ramifications of real estate ownership.

Build in continuing education, not just because it is required by your license, but because you want to be a Top Dog in your business. Don't wait until your continuing education hours are due to be turned in to take the week-long Real Estate Agent's Grand Riviera Gambling Cruise. You may get a good tan and have a lot of fun, but it won't boost your career in the least. Instead, continually monitor courses and pick and choose the ones that will enhance your marketability, your personal knowledge, and your own entrepreneurial skills.

The Least You Need to Know

- Your local, state, and national associations provide educational tools, statistics, and other valuable resources.

- The information and statistics on your local multiple listing service will become your education for the rest of your career.

- Now that you are a small business owner, payment of taxes, claiming deductions, retirement allocations, and resale value should all be built into your business plan.

- Training in computer technology allows you to market and organize your business and bring it everywhere you go.

- Use your continuing education courses to specialize and define a market as your own.

Chapter 8

Building Personal and Professional Power

In This Chapter

- ◆ Understanding the seven principles of personal and professional power
- ◆ Viewing work as an extension of your passion
- ◆ Having an independent way of thinking
- ◆ Being powerful means having self-discipline
- ◆ Practicing good people skills is essential

This chapter describes the character traits and ideals that lead to personal and professional power. Cultivate these principles as the core of your real estate practice. While a good business plan and computer technology can make the difference between financial success and mediocre achievement, personal and professional power assure you of wealth of a different kind. It brings your heart and soul into your work and makes something more than profit your bottom line.

I refer to your real estate business as a real estate *practice* because personal and professional power is based upon the premise that you render a quality professional *service* to your clientele. Your business is far more than a high-pressure real estate sales office. It is a real estate practice based upon customs and practices that dispense client-first loyalty and high-ethics service.

The Seven Principles of Power

Powerful people believe in themselves and their ability to make things happen. They have confidence that their ideas will manifest. They subscribe to the centuries-old concept of "you are what you think." They have mastered the skill of empowered thinking, a talent essential to achieving success.

> **FYI!**
>
> The philosophy of "you are what you think" began centuries ago when Buddha expressed it as, "All we are is the result of what we have thought."
>
> In articulating a religion called Christian Science, Mary Baker Eddy affirmed that if you hold a thought of perfection, you will be perfect.
>
> "Think who you want to become and you will become it" is the foundation of Napoleon Hill's formula to personal achievement and enrichment in his empowering book, *Think and Grow Rich*.

Dale Carnegie, Thomas Edison, Henry Ford, and Franklin D. Roosevelt all based their success on the ability to hold a vision and work toward it. The "you are what you think" concept is expressed in more modern times in many ways. Affirm what you want and it will be yours. Be positive even if you don't feel it, and you will begin to feel positive. Do not fear failure; it is just a stepping stone to success. Believe you will achieve, and you will. Give, and you shall receive. Seek your passion, and you will find abundance. An open mind leads to true abundance.

The following seven principles represent the ideals found to be most essential to achieving personal and professional power within the real estate sales field:

- ◆ **Principle 1:** See your work as your passion.
- ◆ **Principle 2:** Develop a burning desire to succeed.
- ◆ **Principle 3:** Be an independent thinker.
- ◆ **Principle 4:** Have a positive attitude.

- ◆ **Principle 5:** Be self-disciplined.
- ◆ **Principle 6:** Be ethical.
- ◆ **Principle 7:** Have good people skills.

Personal power is premised on the belief that you can affect an outcome through the power of your thinking. Self-defeating attitudes are replaced with empowering ones. You think it, affirm it, and expect the result. Whether you prescribe to personal empowerment philosophies doesn't matter. These principles have worked for centuries to create personal and professional success. What does matter is whether you are willing to use these tools to have the best chance to achieve personal and professional prosperity in your real estate career. If you are, the steps follow.

The Inside Scoop
If these concepts appeal to you read Napoleon Hill's book, *Think and Grow Rich*, by Fawcett Columbine, New York. It was one of the important books that assisted me with my path to personal achievement. Many other books and tapes on personal empowerment will coach you with this concept. Tony Robbins, Joe Girard, Dr. Norman Vincent Peale, Zig Zigler, and Og Mandino, to mention a few, are available as your mentors.

Principle 1: See Your Work as Your Passion

Proverb: A little of what you fancy does you good.

The first step to personal and professional power is to see your work as the source of good things, as the outlet for your passion. This takes a transformation of the way we as a society feel about work. For as long as history tells the story, we have suffered in our work, equating pain with work and pleasure with home. We must shake loose of these archaic attitudes that announce that the source of our livelihood has to be hard in order to be worthwhile.

In many other professions, it is difficult to adopt a change of heart regarding work. Finding passion and meaning in a career is in conflict with the typical corporate hierarchy and its rigid chain of command. Most of us have taken that path. When we couldn't reframe our views about work from within that culture, we went in search of fulfillment outside of it. In real estate we recognize that our work can be an outlet for our personal passion.

Caution

You cannot find your passion unless you believe that you can make a difference to more than yourself. This is presented in Chapter 15. It is about treating our clients in a more integrity-driven manner, and bringing our deeper morals and creative spirits into our work as a whole.

In Marsha Sinetar's book *Do What you Love, the Money Will Follow*, she pronounces that when we do what we are passionate about, abundance follows—not just financial abundance but personal abundance as well. The soul-searching question then is, "What do you love doing? What feeds your spirit?" In real estate it's not hard to find the answer because the job encompasses such a diverse range of qualities. Architect, analyst, attorney, therapist, decorator, negotiator, marketer, and advocate are just a few. My passions are property staging, negotiating, and problem solving. The real estate practice I have developed feeds each of these passions and gives me a wealth of personal and professional power and satisfaction.

Go on your own personal hunt to determine what it is that speaks to your soul. What gets your juices flowing? Just looking at your day and pinpointing specific roles you play that make you feel good will result in a new appreciation for what you do. Instead of experiencing a day that just passes like any other, doing too many things with not enough time, your day involves several roles—a little bit of decorator, a lot of an advocate. Sometimes you'll play of the role of marketer, or of a therapist.

If your passion does not exist in your day, bring it into your day. If you love to drive and should have been a race car driver, take the long route, get off the beaten track, and drive. If gardening is one of your passions, spend more time in clients' gardens. Help them spruce up their gardens when they buy or sell. If marketing brings out the best in you, as you'll find out in a later chapter, Marketing is your middle name. You'll have no trouble putting this talent to use and frolicking in the results as well.

The answer to enjoying our work is really in knowing that work can be a source of pleasure and in taking the time to incorporate the activities you feel passionate about into your daily work life. The proverb goes, "A little of what you fancy does you good." Let's change it to "A lot of what you fancy does you really good."

Principle 2: Develop a Burning Desire to Succeed

Proverb: Where there's a will, there's a way.

In his work, *Think and Grow Rich*, Napoleon Hill coined the term "burning desire." His philosophy is that in order to acquire deep-seeded abundance, you must have a burning desire. You must desire your objective so fiercely that you are willing to persist time and time again in the face of defeat. You must taste it, feel it, see it.

You must use your five senses to visualize it. Then you must dream it until it bursts inside of you. Once you have reached this stage, you will find that the dream has manifested into reality. Hill even went so far as to call the fully developed burning desire an obsession.

This is how I became the national expert on *equity sharing*. It began with a good concept in its embryonic stages. I obsessed on it for about five years, and before I knew it I was writing a book, doing radio shows, touring the country, giving seminars, serving as an expert witness, and facilitating equity-sharing transactions across the country. My obsession with equity sharing has brought me satisfaction, enjoyment, a well-known reputation, and a good income stream.

> **FYI!**
>
> For some of us strongly motivated by a desire to serve, you may want to change the name of this principle to "a burning desire to serve." Since service is at the core of the real estate profession, it's really just a philosophical difference between a desire to succeed and a desire to serve. For you to succeed in real estate, service has to be a goal. The reason equity sharing appealed to me so strongly is I was born with a deep desire to bring equality to others. Is it any wonder that something called equity sharing became my obsession?

This willingness to be fully engaged in our work is one of the essential elements of powerful people. When you begin to pinpoint your passion and cultivate it in your work, you will automatically want to commit yourself more fully to your work. You will feel more interested in and satisfied by it. Each day that you practice these principles, you will engage yourself more fully in your work and you will naturally reap the rewards of your commitment. It takes a strong commitment to be the very best. The result will be that you will operate with confidence, diligence, ethics, and passion.

The real estate field is like no other. It is enormously wealthy with unlimited possibility. It is easy to find something that interests you, like equity sharing did for me, and tap into it. If it has not already been created, Principle 2 coaches you in how to build it. Let "Where there's a will, there's a way" be your motto. Combine it with Principle 3, independent thinking, and these principles will carry you a long, long way.

Principle 3: Be an Independent Thinker

Proverb: Life is what you make it.

Another essential ingredient to personal and professional power is independent thinking. You have to believe that "Life is what you make it," and have the vision to make your dreams happen. Most people tap their creative visions but are soon derailed by the opinions of others. They fail to commemorate their dreams, instead subjecting them to the negative thoughts of others.

FYI!

As Nathaniel Hill so aptly put it, "Opinions are the cheapest commodities on earth. Everyone has a flock of opinions ready to be wished upon anyone who will accept them." Successful independent thinkers don't share their visions. We think out of the box, create out of the box, and do not subject our ideas to the scrutiny of others.

Real estate abounds with independent thinkers. Many people are drawn to real estate because of its unstructured environment and flexibility. Far too often, the attraction stops there. Most agents say, "I'm so glad to be out of the rat race of the workaday structured world. I have independence and financial reward in my work," and independent thought ends.

In the real estate field, you are in the middle of a goldmine as long as you retain your independent thinking. We are exposed to deals every day of our lives. Just think of how many times in a day or week you are asked if you know a source of ready cash or a good real estate deal. The independent thinker jumps on these opportunities, continually expanding her vision, and is always on the lookout for deals.

The independent thinker sees a need and fills it. She thinks of real estate as an investment first and the source of a commission second. She keeps track of good real estate deals and puts people together, herself included, to provide funding for these deals. She acquires an investor state of mind and builds future income streams that sustain her throughout her career.

Real estate's possibilities are infinite. As you increase your professional expertise, you serve your clients and manage your own investments better. In real estate, if you follow your passions and let your dreams evolve, you can build a business that will sustain you for years to come. I know this from personal experience. I started out in real estate law, then ran the gamut to real estate litigation, mediation, sales, equity-sharing facilitation, exchange facilitation, real estate seminars, consulting on real estate issues, and writing real estate books. The entrepreneurial-minded independent thinker can find a place in real estate's expansive universe and create a niche that will attract clients, wealth, and opportunities. "If you build it, they will come."

Principle 4: Have a Positive Attitude

Proverb: Count your blessings.

A positive attitude is essential to the achievement of personal power. When you enter the real estate profession, you see cheery people everywhere. Not only is the agent's smile plastered across business cards, it is who the agent is—at least who the successful agent is. Real estate draws people who are able to look on the positive side of things. After all, they've chosen a profession that is marked by freedom and flexibility. What's not to smile about? Let it be a touchstone for you. It can be contagious if you let it. Remember, "you are what you think."

Take real estate legend, Danielle Kennedy, for example. When she became an agent she was six months pregnant with her fifth child, yet through persistence and a positive attitude she achieved success few have seen. Within four years she closed on over one hundred homes and has since become a well-respected motivational speaker and author of several sales books. This lady was empowered and determined to make the grade. Read her fine work, *How To List & Sell Real Estate*.

FYI!

If you have a positive attitude, you see the glass as half-full. Back in the early twentieth century, when men of unparalleled fortune and power like Franklin D. Roosevelt and Thomas Edison needed to create a state of mind that was essential to getting what they wanted, they used the power of affirmation. They affirmed what they wanted on a continual basis and watched it materialize. Just start acting like a positive person, associate with positive people, and pretty soon you will find that you have a positive state of mind.

Once you cultivate a positive attitude, it's time to create a positive work environment. The first step is to identify and limit your susceptibility to negative influences. Watch your everyday life, both work-related situations and the rest of your life. What causes you to feel negativity? Write these conditions down.

Next, spend time noting the things that make you feel good. Create a "count-my-blessings" list. These may include beautiful scenery, pleasant company, your family, and satisfaction with your achievements. Stop, watch, and identify exactly what makes you feel good. Then set boundaries to protect against the negative influences and to bring in the positive ones.

Caution

Negative influences come in various shapes and sizes. They may be conditions with family members and friends, the media constantly sensationalizing negative events, the agent in the next cubicle relentlessly complaining about her husband, and so on.

The final step of the Positive Life Plan is to deliberately seek out people and circumstances that influence you positively. Positive people are magnetic. Everyone wants to be near them.

People are drawn by their genuine smile and their contagious feeling of good will. Take steps to attract and surround yourself with these people. When you choose real estate as a career, select an upbeat group of people to surround yourself with. Let it work for you. Pick Power Team members (discussed in the next chapter) who have a positive spirit.

FYI!

I often take my dog to the office with me. I drive over the Golden Gate Bridge just for the joy of it. It does help that my office is only ten miles from San Francisco. I take my morning walk each day before I work. I have my afternoon tea. I sit with clients and help them resolve their real estate woes day in and day out. If I find a client is impossible, I gently pass them on to some other less discerning professional.

Creating positive spirit can be a real challenge for the new agent who often sets up shop in the least desirable spot in what is probably already a crowded office. In addition, everything he's doing is brand new. Setting up your workspace after you have conducted the previous analysis makes the difference between a haphazard work environment and one that supports a positive state of mind. Bring in a picture of the dog if you can't fit your dog under your desk. Wear headphones if you can't concentrate because your cubicle is in the middle of a busy walkway. Build in those creature comforts that make you feel like a worthwhile creature.

Principle 5: Be Self-Disciplined

Proverb: If at first you don't succeed, try, try, and try again.

Henry Ford and Dale Carnegie knew it. You can have a burning desire to the extent of it becoming an obsession, but if you don't have the self-discipline to go after the object of your desire, you will never get it. Self-discipline, therefore, is a necessary quality for true personal power. In real estate you've got to have self-discipline for about a hundred reasons.

The number-one reason you need self-discipline is that you work for yourself and you are the source of your income. Number two is that you work for yourself, but the show goes on without you. Most self-employed people have to show up to get the show rolling. That in itself is an incentive for self-discipline. In real estate, the office opens, the phones are answered, and life marches on without you. There is no office rule that says you have to be there. Number three is that when the show goes on without you, you earn no income. Your business makes no money without you.

And, in offices where you pay fees on top of commission, you lose money when you don't show up.

> **FYI!**
>
> Remember, one of the major regrets of seasoned agents is the lack of self-discipline, as this agent states:
>
> "I should have disciplined myself more from the first moment, but most especially when I felt I wouldn't make it in the business. The last thing to do when feeling insecure is to cut back on good work habits. Always remember, the road to success is under construction. You can only pound one nail at a time, but you've got to be disciplined to finish the job."

The best way to start out on the right foot is to act as if you have a regular job. Of course you don't, and that's why you're smiling. But if you adopt the work ethic an employer would require of you, you will develop a discipline that will serve you for the rest of your career. Keep regular work hours. Get there early. Be part of the team. Allow the office environment to work for you. Let your office and your Power Team be a central part of your business. Without self-discipline on the part of all Power Team members, the Power Team will not have power.

The number-one obstacle of self-discipline is that nasty human foible called procrastination. When you join the real estate club and its share of amenities, determination and persistence are the name of the game. There is no room for procrastination. If you stop doing it in real estate, very simply, real estate stops doing it for you. The business moves too fast to allow procrastinators aboard its fast track for more than a short ride.

I would like to share a story about the life of one man we all know and respect. His story may be a bit historical but it so perfectly depicts the self-discipline a person develops when he manifests a burning desire and perseveres until he achieves his goal. Here is this famous gentleman's resumé:

- ◆ 1831   Failed in business
- ◆ 1832   Lost election for the legislature
- ◆ 1834   Failed in business again

The Inside Scoop

M. Scott Peck's *The Road Less Traveled*, published by Simon & Schuster, discusses self-discipline when he begins his international bestseller with "Life is difficult." He describes self-discipline as one of the tools required to solve life's problems. I highly recommend this book.

- ◆ 1835   Sweetheart died
- ◆ 1836   Nervous breakdown
- ◆ 1838   Defeated in second political race
- ◆ 1843   Defeated for Congress
- ◆ 1846   Defeated for Congress
- ◆ 1848   Defeated for Congress
- ◆ 1855   Defeated for the U.S. Senate
- ◆ 1856   Defeated for the vice presidency
- ◆ 1858   Defeated for the U.S. Senate
- ◆ 1860   Elected president of the United States

This man is Abraham Lincoln. He is a deeply inspiring model of what happens when you burn with your desire to the point of obsession and persist until you achieve your goal. For the thirty years before he was elected President of the United States, he was continually defeated in all his major undertakings. He was defeated so often it's surprising that he had enough energy to come in for yet another round. He was just simply obsessed and had the self-discipline to persevere.

> **The Inside Scoop**
>
> Here are some inspiring quotes from Abraham Lincoln:
>
> "Leave nothing for tomorrow which can be done today."
>
> "I have been driven many times upon my knees by the overwhelming conviction that I had nowhere else to go. My own wisdom and that of all about me seemed insufficient for that day."

Although Abraham Lincoln was not in real estate sales, he was in sales of the highest order. Hopefully, we don't have to lose a loved one or have a nervous breakdown to achieve our goals in the real estate field. But it has been my experience that the most successful of us come through a fair share of life challenges before we discover our own personal and professional power.

Principle 6: Be Ethical

Proverb: As you sow, so shall you reap.

Good ethics are at the heart of personal power. *The New Ideal* mandates that you represent your client first and foremost. Don't focus on the close and don't rush clients through the process. Focus instead on assisting your client by applying your highest integrity to each and every step of the transaction. Your mission is to make your client's welfare your top priority. After all, you are his or her legal agent.

Take each step slowly and carefully, explaining *the* many options available to your buyers and sellers. Allow yourself to be guided by your integrity as you skillfully discharge your legal duty. To the personally powerful agent, client advocacy and quality personal service is far more important than the close. The commission we make at closing is just a by-product of serving our clients according to this ethical code and our legal obligation. It's no longer a job of salesmanship. It is now a job of ethics.

Chapter 15 carries this principle farther. Let it now be a seed that begins to germinate within you. Erase the artificial line between business and personal ethics that was drawn so long ago. Because our work becomes the source of our passion, personal ethics come into play. They go hand in hand with true passion. Allow yourself to cross the bridge into a more conscious livelihood of ethics-based action. If you do, you will exude a professional power that draws others to you because "as you sow, so shall you reap."

Principle 7: Have Good People Skills

Proverb: Do unto others as you would have them do unto you.

Real estate is a people place. For the real estate professional, good people skills are mandatory. Everything you do involves relationships with clients, other agents, and various other professionals. Your work on behalf of your client is that of a counselor, a friend, a strong negotiator, a shrewd analyst, and a facilitator. In order to have personal power in real estate you have to develop strong people skills. You must develop the principle of "Do unto others as you would have them do unto you."

In the real estate field, good people skills mean the application of skillful listening. We need to hear what our clients have to say from both their words and emotions. As a society, our ears have failed as instruments of understanding others. We must learn to listen in new ways. Begin to give your clients 100 percent of your attention as they describe what they want. This is the only way to truly understand their needs. Remember, you are their fiduciary agent. Your job is to be loyal to them and take care of their interests above all else. How can you do this when you haven't heard what their interests are?

Problem solving is another people skill the powerful agent should possess. The residential real estate transaction is particularly susceptible to high levels of stress because of its fast track, high stakes, and personal nature. Clients can become unglued in any phase of the deal. Your role as the caretaker of these transactions makes you an essential member of your client's problem-solving team. Legally you become their fiduciary, but emotionally you become part of their problem-solving team. By continually cultivating sensitivity and compassion, you will have the patience and understanding to problem solve in a professional manner on these occasions.

The Inside Scoop
For the next week, pay attention to the way others listen to you. You know the difference when someone is doing ten things at one time, and you are one of those ten things. In these days of quick action, particularly within real estate's fast pace, everyone seems to be continually multitasking. Be fully present when you are listening to your clients. Don't multitask. They know the difference, and so do you.

Client representation is not the only role in which good people skills are required. You will also be called upon to display your negotiating skills. At the drop of a hat, an emotional buyer or seller can come up with the most confounded demands. Your job is to take this transaction and carefully maneuver it through another phase that no one really planned upon. Armed with good people skills and effective negotiating expertise, you will work through this obstacle and turn it into a mere bump in the road.

Always draw upon the proverb of "Do unto others as you would have them do unto you" when dealing with all parties in your transactions and your people skills will be a quality others will admire in you. Most of all, you will have inner peace and will have earned the respect of your clients.

The Sum of the Parts

I have my seven principles on a card in my wallet and on my wall at the office and at home. They are with me wherever I go. They have become a part of me and I can truly say I have personal and professional power. It's been a long, soul-searching road, but one that I would not trade for all the money in the world. The richness you will receive if you incorporate these seven principles into your real estate career will be equally rewarding to you as you step into your personal and professional power.

The next chapter is on choosing your all-important Power Team. Take the qualities you have reviewed in this chapter and apply them to the criteria you use to choose Power Team members. If you do, you will have an unbeatable Power Team that will serve you and your clients in a truly powerful way.

The Least You Need to Know

- Personal and professional power can come through a belief that you can affect your outcome through positive thinking.

- One way to become a powerful person is to enjoy what you do and express your passion through your work.

- Persistence and the application of independent thinking can lead to personal and professional power.

- Because real estate is a field that deals with people, having good people skills and being a good listener are important traits to acquire.

- Personal and professional power come to those who operate with high integrity.

Chapter 9

Building Your Power Team

In This Chapter

- ◆ Your Power Team members
- ◆ Partnering with another agent
- ◆ Where to find Power Team candidates
- ◆ Qualifying your Power Team members
- ◆ Team meetings and motivation

The foundation of every agent's business is his Power Team. Thus, one of the first steps you will take is to build your own essential team. Your Power Team members are real estate professionals who will make your transactions seamlessly travel through the many stages to closing. It is these professionals who become a pipeline for client referrals for a lifetime. You will refer to them; they will refer to you. And they will help provide professional service to your clients at its very best.

Be picky about who you choose for your team. Make sure your candidates provide quality service and have good professional ethics. Each member is vital to your reputation and your success. Talk to your mentor or office manager about candidates for your team. If you feel you don't have enough experience in the field to make these important choices, don't make them. It is better to defer building of your team until you are able to build a team that is personally and professionally powerful.

When you interview members, have a mental checklist in place for the important qualities you seek in each. While reading this chapter, compose your own list of traits that are important to you. The checklist approach works best since you will apply the same criteria to a number of different candidates, some of whom will not meet your standards and some of whom will become qualified Power Team members.

Choosing Your Power Team Members

The Power Team members will consist of the following:

- ◆ Your mentor(s)
- ◆ Your agent partner if you have one
- ◆ Mortgage broker
- ◆ Closing professional
- ◆ Professional stager
- ◆ Pest control inspector
- ◆ General property inspector

FYI!

You can easily put together a Power Team at just one Chamber of Commerce mixer or civic organization meeting. When you are new to the business and don't really have many contacts yet, this may be an ideal way to assemble your first Power Team. In the beginning, the job is more about creating an energetic and supportive team. Over time the team will refine itself into an efficient, productive, powerful group.

During the first year of your career, your mentor is your most important tool for motivation and guidance. If you cannot find mentor qualities in one person, select several mentors each with a different expertise. It would be ideal to get everything you need in one person, but if you can't, don't stop looking.

The person you choose should be a fellow agent and must be able to give you the time and expertise you need. Although your mentor will not officially be a member of your Power Team (at least the team that works together servicing clients and meets regularly), this guide should have many of the traits described in the prior chapter on personal and professional power. You want to learn from a pro—not just any old pro, but a personally powerful one.

Now on to your official Power Team members. If you have partnered with another agent, this agent will naturally become your most important Power Team member. If not, the mortgage broker is the most important member. There are two reasons why. First, a good mortgage broker can make the difference between a deal plagued with stress and a smooth, calm transaction. Second, this is the team member you are likely to get the most referrals from. Make sure your qualification of these team members is thorough. Act like you're getting married when you qualify both your agent partner and your mortgage broker members. These people can make the difference between a good life as an agent and an average one.

Other optional members are a real estate attorney, a certified public accountant, and an exchange intermediary. You should have affiliations with each of these professionals since their services are often required in transactions. Including them in your Power Team family depends on whether their presence has a benefit. If they enhance the team spirit, pass the team qualification test, and are willing to reciprocate with referrals, sign them up.

Partnering with Another Agent

It can be a real challenge to beat the time crunch of the swiftly moving real estate transaction. Given the importance of each step in a transaction and the brief period assigned to each, emergencies threaten even the most well-planned time off. Agent partnering is a welcome relief for the agent who feels pulled in many directions.

Through job sharing, one partner is on call while the other is off, confident that her clients are being taken care of. The well-chosen partnership can be the ideal answer for weary agents who have felt captive by work and responsibility.

If you decide to partner with another agent, your agent partner will naturally be one of the most valuable members of your Power Team. Believe it or not, sharing your listings with the right agent-partner can be the way to increase

> ## The Inside Scoop
>
> When you are a new agent, consider partnering. When you're a pro, consider teaming up with a novice. As in anything else, selective partnering can make the difference between a solitary career experience and one filled with sharing of rewards and woes.

your market appreciably. It may sound strange to describe sharing listings as a way to increase a market. You might think that this would break a market or at least cut it in half. Actually, it can double your market and create a synergy that occurs when two people work well together.

New agents teaming up in partnership with one another can be the perfect solution to even the odds when pickings are slim initially. One commission between the two is better than no commission at all. In the beginning, it's also helpful to have a colleague in your corner when you're fumbling through new experiences, even when your partner fumbles with you. It can get lonely at the new agent's desk without a phone that rings while you're trying to master a highly detail-oriented profession.

If you are a new agent and you find a seasoned professional to team up with, you are two steps ahead. The commission split between you and partner will not be equal in this relationship, but the advantages are easy to understand. You have found a built-in mentor, someone who has learned the ropes and can guide you through the obstacle course. The skilled agent, on the other hand, will reap the rewards of sharing time and responsibilities and have fresh enthusiasm from you as his partner.

Arranging the Partnership

You and your partner can have any arrangement that suits your fancy. It can be a 50-50 split, a 10-90 split, or anything in between. You can have an on-call arrangement that does not involve commission splitting, but is purely a time trade. For example, Tom and Anne have an on-call arrangement. Tom is on call for Anne's clients when she is off and vice versa. They do not share commissions.

> **Caution**
>
> Prepare a *written* partnership agreement signed by you and your agent partner that reflects what you have agreed to, especially how you have agreed to share your commissions. In this manner, you can eliminate areas for potential misunderstandings and future problems. Include a clause on how you will dissolve the partnership should either of you seek a change.

Or you may choose a time trade coupled with a fee for time spent. In that situation, Tom and Ann would time-trade but keep track of the time they spend on the other's matters. At the end of the month, whoever has spent more time gets paid an agreed-on hourly rate for the excess time.

There are as many variables as you can dream up for agent partnerships. As long as everyone works in the same office, there should be no problem since everyone is on the same insurance policy, has a commission split with the same company, and has the same manager. Agents have found that job sharing and on call partnering enhance their use of time.

Using a Professional Stager

Most agents who deal with high-end properties have a stager on their Power Team. The stager accompanies you to listing presentations. He provides design and decorating recommendations, hopefully in a very sensitive manner, on how to best stage the home for sale. Sellers usually find staging quite helpful and often engage the stager's services. I think every agent, not just high-end agents, seriously interested in listing a home for sale should recommend the services of a professional stager. This is why the stager is included on your Power Team.

Your stager is a designer or decorator versed in staging properties for sale. For high-end properties, a stager is hired with expertise in interior decorating, contracting, and landscape architecture. The value and condition of the property indicate which type of stager is used and the budget for this professional. Chapter 22 describes the role of the stager in more detail.

FYI!

You can find stagers in the yellow pages of your phone book. Look under Interior Designers, and note which ones have added home staging to their specialties. Pay attention to their suggestions, so that you can make similar suggestions for clients who do not want to pay for this professional service. I found my stager in the very next town through an Internet search that brought me to bhammil.com.

Stagers may use the furnishings already present or might rent furnishings, artwork, and plants for a home. They usually reduce the clutter so that the space shows to its fullest advantage. They also recommend painting and other spruce-up steps. These talented people can work wonders with very little expense. A staged home may greatly hasten the sale of that home.

Finding Power Team Members

Where do you find these professionals that will become your essential Power Team members? You will find them in local real estate circles. They will also be looking for you since they, too, need a powerful Power Team.

Each real estate community has a number of professional marketing groups. If you can't find one, check out your local real estate board or the local chamber of commerce. These groups generally meet once or twice a month. Your local board consists of agent members and affiliates. Affiliates are your potential team members. You may want to monitor new affiliates as they join since they are probably new to real estate or to your territory and obviously want a larger market. They will be motivated. Of course, motivation isn't everything, but it is a start.

If you are partnering with an agent who has been practicing for any time, he will have his own Power Team in place. If you use his team, you won't have to build your own. Sometimes that is an advantage; sometimes it is not. Talk to your agent partner about his team with the thought of ensuring that this team is the very best for both of you.

FYI!

Here is a list that may guide you in your search for Power Team members:

◆ Your local real estate board

◆ Your mentor

◆ Your office manager

◆ Yellow pages and Internet searches

◆ Community groups

◆ Your agent partner

The Inside Scoop

Make sure you don't settle for an existing Power Team. There is nothing worse than a stale team. If the team members do not represent your ideals or quality of service, then they should be replaced. You want to have a powerful team to support you in being successful. Remember that this is a business decision, not a friendship decision.

Your partner may have wanted to replace some members, but has not had the time or has been embarrassed to do so. His partnership with you is just the excuse to reassess and revise the team as needed. If you perform your own interview of an existing team, do it with a good deal of deference. You're the new kid on the block and they are veterans. Don't rock the boat, just watch and inquire with manners and humility.

If you're not partnering, ask your mentor or office manager for referrals. The people they refer you to may not be available to the extent your Power Team members need to be, but they can refer you to other potential candidates in their field. Go to the yellow pages under the category of professional you are looking for. Tell them you are interested in building a Power Team and would like to speak with them about their participation or a referral to someone in their field who may be a benefit to your group. If you have a group affiliation, look for your team members there. In this way, you'll be starting out with someone who has a similar outside interest. Sharing something in common, aside from career objectives, makes for a solid Power Team partnership.

Qualifying Power Team Members

As you qualify candidates, ask them for their lists of existing Power Team members. You may want to tap resources they have already found success with. You want to pick your Power Team members according to your list of important criteria discussed in the following list:

- Commitment to a Power Team plan
- Availability
- Quality of services
- Personal and professional power
- Good people skills
- High integrity

Commitment to a Power Team Plan

One of the most important criteria of your team members is their ability to commit to you. Your candidate may already have one or more teams in place and may not be able to give you the service and referrals your Power Team needs. You want this relationship to be as important to them as it is to you. With that comes a commitment to continually upgrade services as the market changes and spend time with team members motivating and assisting one another.

As a real estate sales agent, your transactions always need the services of your team members, whereas their transactions rarely need you because they do not have agent choice in the majority of their transactions. This makes their ability to commit to you and give you quality service all the more important.

It may take some searching efforts to find team members who can give you this commitment because often the quality candidates already have teams in place. You will probably end up with someone relatively new to their field, as you are new to yours. A new person may be able to give your clients more attention. If they have good practices in place, they may be as capable as someone who has been in the profession for a long time.

Availability

You want to make sure your Power Team members are available. Because of the flexibility afforded by the industry, many real estate professionals suffer from poor self-discipline when it comes to keeping a regular schedule. You want to be able to contact your team members during regular working hours to be able to keep your transactions on course and full speed

> **The Inside Scoop**
>
> If e-mail will be your primary source of communication with Power Team members, make sure they have built e-mail services fully into their business model. Some people only use e-mail as a secondary source of communication. If you are e-mail–based, your Power Team members need to be as well.

ahead. Find out what their regular hours are and make sure their hours conform to your schedule and the schedule of the rest of your Power Team.

My team members primarily keep in touch through e-mail. When we are working on the same transaction, we include the rest of the team on communications with one another so everyone stays on top of the transaction's status. E-mail provides a highly efficient way of keeping everyone in the loop in the most time-efficient manner possible, as long as your Power Team members are technologically versatile.

Quality of Services

Your members should provide diligent, competent services. They should be professionals who will go the extra mile for you and your clients. When you put together a new team, you will not yet know how team members measure up to this standard. As you encounter someone who falls short, talk to him or her immediately. Make sure the situation is corrected. If, after thorough communication and a good opportunity to correct, your team member continues to fall short, replace him or her. Do it with permission of your team members, and do it compassionately, but do it.

You are building an important enterprise with your Power Team. Do not underestimate the value of each member, especially your agent partner, mortgage broker, and closing professional. You want to do business with and have your clients served by the finest in the field. Do not feel that you cannot have the best because you're new. Remember, you are operating under *The New Ideal*, and you will bring this distinction to any Power Team you build. Be proud of who you are and expect others to treat you with respect just as you treat them with respect.

Personal and Professional Power

Repeating the last chapter on personal and professional power here would be worthwhile. You want your Power Team members to share the qualities of personally powerful people. Develop a mental checklist of the qualities described in the last chapter. Your team members may not possess all criteria required of the person with personal and professional power, but if each team member possesses a few of these skills, you will be well on the path to creating a top-notch Power Team.

If your entire Power Team has developed its own version of personal power, your team will be exceptional. Each team member will attract his own market because he will be motivated to provide outstanding service, and clients will naturally gravitate his way. With this special synergy, your Power Team will be a magnet that will draw clients and their referrals.

Good People Skills

Your Power Team members should be likeable, since you will be working closely with them. You will pull them into every transaction you have. If you enjoy working with them, your clients will, too. In the beginning, check in with the clients you refer to team members at each stage and make sure they are well taken care of. If they aren't feeling taken care of, look at the reason why. Transactions can become stressful, and how we deal with one another during times of stress is extremely important. It is the difference between good people skills and bad people skills. You want each member on your team to demonstrate good people skills.

High Integrity

You want your team members to share your values relating to integrity and ethics. Your team should not only be capable and enjoyable to work with, they should be a team deserving of your respect and that of your clients. You want to stand out in what you do because of your sense of service and integrity, and you want your Power Team to do the same.

Your Power Team can produce phenomenal teaming power if each member is aligned with a similar mission statement about excellent service and caring for people. An ideal way to make sure your team shares the same vision is to develop a mission statement together. At your first Power Team meeting, put the creation of a mission statement on the agenda.

Team Motivation

If you aspire to have a truly empowered Power Team, a motivation plan is important. Your team might start out upbeat and positive, but it is susceptible to negative professional influences. Weekly or bimonthly meetings can provide just the right amount of motivation and support to keep your team upbeat and on track.

The Inside Scoop

My first Power Team gave monthly seminars to the community, sharing valuable information about the real estate purchase and sale process. By holding these seminars and becoming a quality team, we built a referral stream that lasted for many years. We also provided invaluable support to one another on both a personal and business level.

Title and closing companies often have conference rooms they will let you use to put on community service seminars. Use a flyer to announce your seminars to the community. You can also post notices in the Community Calendar of your local newspaper.

You may want to appoint one team member on a rotation basis to serve as the motivational coach each month. This person can perform the roles of the troubleshooter, problem solver, and facilitator for a period of service. Scheduled meetings provide an extra, all-important bond among members and a forum for open discussion of challenging situations.

Transaction and Quality Control

Set up a method of communicating on each transaction so that all involved members can track the progress of a transaction. I set up individual transaction pages on my website so Power Team members and our clients can track the progress of our transactions. These pages are confidential and can only be accessed with the URL of that page.

You also want to conduct your own diligent quality control to ensure that each member provides the level of service and integrity that your clients deserve. On your Power Team, quality control occurs as each member holds the rest accountable for timely, quality services promised.

The Least You Need to Know

- ◆ Your Power Team provides stability to your transactions and credibility to your business.

- ◆ Partnering with another agent provides you the ability to share benefits and burdens with someone else.

- ◆ Qualifying your Power Team members is essential to building a team that has a solid foundation and shares your values.

- ◆ Keeping your team motivated and in line with high ideals is as important as finding the right team members.

- ◆ Have regular meetings and monitor the performance of Power Team members.

Part 3

Building an Unbeatable System

Get out your tool belt. It's time to build your unbeatable system. It's a three-level structure constructed of the following:

> Top level: Marketing strategies
>
> Middle level: Time management techniques
>
> Bottom level: Computer technology

Always think of your business as a three-level enterprise since these three components are essential to optimum performance of your business. When you decided to become a real estate sales agent, you adopted two middle names: Marketing and Computer. Your name is now Real Estate Marketing Computer Agent.

Chapter 10

Making Your Market

In This Chapter

- ◆ Your sphere of influence as your first market
- ◆ Consider specializing as a way to make a market
- ◆ Broaden your community involvement
- ◆ Put up your own website
- ◆ Give free seminars
- ◆ Prospecting expired listings and "for sale by owner" properties

Make Market your middle name. Since nearly everyone you bump into will buy or sell real estate, you are continually surrounded by potential markets. Why not let everyone you meet know what you do? What you do is a large part of who you are, especially if you have come to your profession after having been down many other roads. This chapter will assist you in identifying and creating markets. It will start you out with your personal sphere of influence and take you through many different markets from which to pinpoint your expertise.

Real Estate Lingo

A **contacts database** is the computer-based program you use, such as Microsoft Outlook, for your address book and calendar. These programs allow you to easily manage a high volume of information in an organized, efficient manner.

Spend time taking note of your life. Notice the many groups in which you become involved. You'll be surprised to see how many lives you touch and communities you interact with. This is an important process for many reasons. It defines your first list of prospects, allowing you to begin your all-important *contacts database*. You become more community-minded and begin to define the many markets you will interact with over the course of your new career. Most important, it gives you some valuable ideas about markets you may want to specialize in.

Tap Your Sphere of Influence

Let the bells toll and the story be told that you are now an agent. Tell all your friends, relatives, acquaintances, shopkeepers, and everyone you meet about this new career you have begun. Don't forget schoolmates, past co-workers, neighbors, parents of your kid's friends, and anyone affiliated with activities you regularly engage in. Tell folks in your wider communities, such as religious organizations, parent-teacher associations, volunteer groups, exercise groups, country clubs, or golf clubs. Did I forget to include everyone you have ever come in contact with from your first memory on? These important people make up your initial sphere of influence, which will become your very first market to tap.

FYI!

The third most common thing seasoned agents wished they had realized in their early years:

Real estate sales is about creating markets everywhere you go. The best way to do that is to continually build niches. You live in a community. Be the agent who specializes in the 10-block radius around your home. Do this from day one. Also, make sure you use technology as much as you can and have your own website.

Start assembling your contact list even before you are licensed. Begin the computerized database you will use for all your future mailings. Don't let your mental critic send messages such as, "This is stupid. I haven't even passed the exam. What if I don't?" You will pass the exam. Everyone does. So if you have the time before you are licensed and the flurry of activity begins, take steps right away to create your first contacts database.

Once you define the spheres in which your life has traveled, you will have a good basis for identifying markets. For instance, if you previously worked with retirees, or you are a member of a country club with many retirees, you may want to specialize in marketing to people retiring or downsizing after the kids have left home. This group often trades in a large home for a smaller one or a multilevel home for a single-story home. They also have a high degree of interest in purchasing in a retirement community.

When you have determined the spheres of your life, gather names and contact information for people falling within that category. For example, you meet with a book club once a month. List book club as a sphere and obtain names and contact information for that sphere. You don't even have to mention your purpose to these people. Input them directly into your contacts database according to the instructions in Chapter 14.

If you have decided to partner with another agent, tap their sphere of influence. Many agents from the old school focusing on salesmanship instead of what this book advocates as *The New Ideal* (a new, more-ethical way of representing clients described in Chapter 15) may never have marketed to their own sphere. Even if they have, this is the opportunity to notify them again. Why? You have something to announce. The two of you have teamed up to provide unparalleled service to clients.

Let your contacts all know you are ready to assist them with their real estate needs. Don't limit it to the sector of real estate sales you have entered. Tell them to come to you with any real estate matter, and you will handle it if it is your specialty or refer them to someone who will do a first-rate job for them.

Real Estate Lingo

Your **sphere of influence** is everyone you have known or associated with throughout your life. Pull out those dusty yearbooks, tap into your memory banks, and remember all those folks whom you have had contact with. Track down your childhood friends and the parents of your children's friends. It is time to remember them all.

The Inside Scoop

Your contacts database usually comes packaged with computer word processing (such as Microsoft Word) and Internet access programs. Microsoft's contact program is called Outlook. Your sphere of influence contacts are input into this program or any other program you choose for preparation of the mailing list for career announcements and more.

The first reason you want them to come to you for everything is that you will be the best person to research the field and find the best person for them if you are not

Real Estate Lingo
A **referral fee** is a fee paid for referral of a client.

suited for their situation. The second reason, and I do mean second, is that you will receive a *referral fee* from the lucky agent you refer them to.

I have always invited people to come to me for any real estate or legal matter. They think of me as law and real estate. Most of the time, I refer them to someone else since I am quite specialized in what I do. But they enter my marketplace first. And, when they come, they are served well. They are either served by my office, referred to my *Power Team* members, or referred to others who will provide good service. The true marketer knows that what goes around comes around. My *Power Team* members refer people to me. Those who come to me and are referred out, refer to me. Other professionals who receive referrals from me reciprocate.

Specialize

One of the best ways to create a self-fueling market is to specialize. There are as many categories to specialize in as you can dream up. If you have a special interest in or knowledge of bowling alleys, you can specialize in the purchase and sale of bowling alleys. It doesn't matter where you are located; you act as facilitator of these transactions. Through specializing, you create your very own market through which clients will find you.

The Inside Scoop

Here is a list of general categories you can specialize in that might interest you:

- Relocation
- Buyers agent only
- First-time home buyers
- Military housing
- Retirement housing
- Luxury homes only
- Specific town residential only
- A specific neighborhood

The list of specialties is never-ending. If you live in an area with many golf courses, specialize in golf course homes. If you're in a beach area, focus on beach-front properties. In Sedona, Arizona, you might specialize in spiritual centers. Marketing is all about being creative.

Market to Your Neighborhood

A specific market for each residential agent consists of neighbors. For the commercial agent, your market is your office neighbors. Let them know you are down the street and well aware of the market for their properties. Often an agent specializing in a neighborhood will list recent comparables on their mailers. The recipients are interested in the comparables because they own property in the area. The *comparables* listed are not even properties the agent has sold, but they are a good attention getter and provide valuable information.

You don't even need an affiliation with a neighborhood to make it your market. All it takes is carving a niche by letting people know you specialize in a particular area. The job then is to find out everything you can about that area and let your name be known in that area in as many ways as you can. A blimp would be ideal, a banner across city hall would be better, and then there are more traditional ways, like newspaper advertising.

When I get mailers, I throw everything away except the ones that give me the comparables for the real estate I own. Every agent should mail to his or her neighbors, not just at home but at the office. The people who live close to your office are also your market and you will be surprised to find that even the 15 other agents in your office haven't tapped this valuable group of prospects. When it comes to defining the extent of your group, go beyond what you feel is reasonable. If 50 feels right, double it. We're only speaking about $15.00 more for postage, and when you bring in a new client your return can be a thousand times that much.

> **Real Estate Lingo**
>
> **Comparables** are similar properties recently sold located in the same proximity. Recent is defined as within about the last six months. Proximity is defined as within a mile or so of each other. Other factors considered are amenities, condition, and location.

Do More of What You Like

In line with the principle of "do what you love and the money will follow," build your business around your passion. If you enjoy golf, play more and let everyone know what you do. Make golf and real estate go hand in hand. In fact, they do. The golf course is one place where business is done and is done well. If you're an avid hiker, hike more and do it with hiking groups whose real estate needs you will fill. If cooking is your thing, create delicacies to serve at open houses. Sailing is what you enjoy? Join the local sailing club and jibe less and talk real estate more.

Bring your passions to your work and you will be a magnet for others. You will dazzle. Even if it doesn't bring business, and I cannot imagine that it wouldn't, at least you will be enjoying yourself. Instead of forcing yourself to make cold calls, do something you love where you gather with others. Entertain the many ways in which you can join your passion with your work. Got a dog? Walk the dog and talk to other dog lovers. I meet more people and do more business when I walk my dog than when I engage in some planned marketing activities. When you orient your business around your likes rather than your dislikes, it's surprising how much fun you can have and how much business will show up in your path.

Join Organizations

Real estate is a social club. Joining organizations is something agents do because agents are always busy creating new markets. You will find an abundance of agents buzzing around at any social or fraternal organization. Why? Because agents are community-minded. Their job is to service the real estate needs of the community. Community service is therefore essential to a flourishing real estate career.

There are so many types of organizations to choose from. Your town will have a chamber of commerce. There are benevolent societies. Find one or two that align with your philosophies and make that group a part of your community. These groups are all about engaging with and serving one another; in other words, carrying out the job of your middle name.

Remind Past Clients

Never lose track of your past clients, or better said, never let your past clients lose track of you. Include them on your list to receive your marketing mailer. If your list is still a reasonable size, follow up the mailing with a quick call to check in. You'll probably get an answering machine, but your voice will remind them of you and your services. Your past clients are your very best market as they will return to you and refer their people to you as long as you stay in touch and provide excellent service. Never lose contact, even if it is just by way of your smiling face on a postcard or flyer.

Give Free Seminars

People love getting something free. It's just a part of human nature. Why not begin your own free seminar series alone or with your *Power Team* members? It is where I can be found every Tuesday evening. Weekly may be too often for you, but it works for me. Talk about some part of what you know that will be of interest to your market.

I have become an institution in my area through providing weekly public service seminars for nearly a decade. My seminars are information-packed and on cutting-edge real estate and legal subjects. They provide a community base for people to come and bring with them their real estate and legal issues. They are also a magnet for people who need my legal and real estate services.

Don't feel that you are not experienced enough to give a seminar. People like to come together just for a place to share their ideas. Sometimes it's not you they come to hear; it's the subject that interests them and they have their own thoughts to impart. Successful seminars can consist of a room full of people sharing their ideas with others. Real estate is always a subject of interest to people because it is a part of everyone's life.

Remember that the purpose of the seminar is to provide community service, not to market your services. You will nevertheless want to add the names, addresses, phone numbers, and e-mail addresses of the attendees to your ever-growing contact list, include them on your mailers and keep in touch as warranted.

FYI!

An interesting seminar will bring you a market year round as long as your primary motivation is to give information, not to sell your services.

Seminar title: How to Make Maximum Profit on the Sale of Your Home

Place: XYZ Title Company

Price: Free

Caution

A lot of people won't attend seminars because they know they will be marketed to, or they will have to sit through a marketing presentation to get to the real reason they came. Don't get gimmicky with your seminars. Just provide useful information, give your audience a chance to provide input and ask questions, and stay away from the services you provide.

List on Others' Websites

The multiple listing services are private. Despite this privacy factor, your listings will appear in many places on the Internet after you list them on the MLS. The MLS allows the agent to indicate whether the listing may become part of these public domains. If you choose to make them public, they are broadcast over the Internet periodically.

For instance, the National Association of Realtors automatically picks up listings from the many listing services around the country, as do other services. In this manner, an interested buyer anywhere can search listings through the National Association of Realtors site (NAR) at www.realtor.com.

Consumer access to listings is valuable for you and your buyers. Because your listings on the MLS are private, you either print out or e-mail properties you feel a client may be interested in; or sit your client at your computer and perform searches. On NAR's site, clients can search on their own at their own pace. This is an advantage to you and your client. It takes a while for data to be picked up by NAR, so its information is not as fresh as that on the local MLS, but it is still advantageous for your clients to have listing information at their fingertips.

Many websites sell listing space. Some cater to people selling "for sale by owner" (FSBOs) properties, while others cater to specific types of listings. There are sites for luxury homes, vacation homes, lots for development, investment property, and so on. Newspapers also have Internet listing sites. Only you can determine whether listing on these sites justifies the expense.

Use Your Own Website

There many reasons to have your own website. One is to attract Internet-savvy clients interested in your services or your listings. A website allows you to market more competitively since the Internet gives small business the same exposure as big business. All websites are treated equally. Some Internet search engines do assure higher placement if you pay a fee, but the fees are not high when compared with the benefit a priority listing can bring.

The key to insuring that your site will receive top presence in a keyword search is to make sure *each* page contains the proper tags for search engine reporting purposes. To keep priority placement, you should update your website often, have proper keywords on each page, and provide links from your site to other sites. So many people go to the time and expense of putting up a site, but fail to implement the important steps relating to search criteria. They have a website but no one finds them without knowing their specific address. They are not picked up in any searches.

The Inside Scoop

According to the National Association of Realtors, agents with a personal website earn twice as much as those who don't, and four out of ten Realtors have a business website.

My website brings me a fairly large market because I perform a few highly specialized services. Because of my specialization and how my website is set up, the search engines locate my site under certain key search words. It isn't difficult to have a commanding presence as long as your market is well-defined, unique, and meets search-engine criteria.

More and more people are looking to the Internet when researching products and professional services. Soon more people will find agents by searching the web than by browsing the yellow pages; any agent who does not have web presence will be unable to compete. So join the ranks of those agents with Internet addresses as soon as possible.

The Inside Scoop

Go to the Internet and search under keywords that describe the services you provide. Now, narrow that search by more specifically describing your service and the location in which you provide it. Through this process you should be able to identify a service you perform or will perform that is unique enough to come up in the top 30, as long as your site is indexed correctly. The truly creative agent searches for a specialty few others share and begins to specialize in it! Your next step after you come up with the right keywords is to make sure your website is properly coded so the search engines index your pages under these keywords. Go to www.websitetrafficbuilders.com for more.

Promote Your Listings on Your Website

For the active agent, a website that displays your listed properties gives you and your listings additional exposure. Some agents do a grand exposé on unique properties complete with historical and legal data, comparables, and a picture gallery that vies with most virtual reality tours. Clients love it. It also makes buyer and agent calls very easy. Just refer them to your website.

Web listing has become so popular now that you will sometimes see a website address dedicated to just one listing. For instance, your new listing is at 287 Hometown Drive. Your sign includes a tag that says see www.287hometown.com. The website process has become so easy that vendors now give you a listing-specific website address and design and host that listing for less than $100. The site also points to the rest of your listings and includes your bio and tools to help buyers.

FYI!

I use hidden pages on my website as a tool to communicate status and activities on my transactions. I create a confidential web page for each transaction and give clients and team members the address for that page, which I update as the transaction progresses. It's actually easier than e-mailing everyone to report the status of a transaction. The page has no keywords and is not linked to the web pages accessed by the public. It provides a handy confidential way for people to track the progress of my transactions.

Once you become accustomed to administrating your website, you may want to use it to its full extent in marketing your business. You can include resource pages of steps for buyers and steps for sellers. You can dedicate a page for FSBOs (for sale by owners) to assist them in handling their transactions. Include links to your *Power Team's* sites. Include a page for referrals to other professionals.

Because I have web presence and use my site extensively as a forum for existing transactions, as a place to post listings, as a resource for valuable legal and real estate information, and as a calendar to my free seminars, my market stays in touch with my site. I also receive traffic from Internet searchers for the specialized services I provide. The information, on my site changes frequently as my business moves to its next level. Clients appreciate the free resources made available to them.

Planning Your Website

Websites begin with your ideas, which then can be implemented by you or by vendors that you hire. Many real estate associations have vendors they recommend for website production, or you can do a search on the Internet for these professionals. These developers have the website production process down to a science. When I put my site up, the process was complicated and unsophisticated. Now, it is simple and streamlined.

> **Caution**
>
> Do another search on the Internet, this time searching for "real estate website developers." This search will give you companies that develop agents' sites for a living. Just be careful with the extra fees they charge. Make sure you ask all the questions and get all the answers when it comes to ongoing extra charges and making changes to your site.

If you want to make changes to your site to add new listings and other information on your own, make sure the company that creates the site for you is able to give you that capability. Confirm that you can also add new pages on your own. Some will not give you this flexibility, wanting to obtain payment for each change you want to make and requiring you to take extra steps that make the updating process frustrating. Chapter 12 suggests some software you may use to administer your site. It's quite simple if you buy the right program.

Send Mailers

The *Referral Stream System* business model presented in Chapter 14 is about the circle of prosperity that results from continual marketing to your clients and prospects. Your business model is based on keeping track of people, acknowledging them, and staying in touch. This begins with sending announcements to your sphere of influence described earlier in this chapter. Send out these mailers the first day you join an office. Coordinate with the office you've joined and find out if they will take any part in this venture.

They may not be willing to financially contribute, but using their name on your announcement can give you just the right credibility to make your proclamation sound like one of monumental importance. Many offices have these announcements all set to go; all you need to do is pay for them.

Once you have current and sold listings to rave about, you will want a mailer to describe them. Until then, just let everyone know you've joined an office and are ready to assist them in a first-rate manner. The mailer options are endless. Keep track of those you receive in the mail. There are postcards, one-page letters, flyers, four-page mailers, four-color mailers, double-glossy newsletters, and everything in between. It all depends on how much you want to spend and your belief in the productivity of mailers.

> **The Inside Scoop**
>
> "The _____ Company is proud to welcome Sam Agent (specializing in _____) to its residential real estate division." (If you have not identified a specialty, leave that out.)
>
> This is much better than this:
>
> "I have joined the office of The _____ Company."

The frequency of mailings will also depend on your budget. Monthly is the most often you should mail; quarterly is the minimum. The purpose of this outreach is to remind people that you are there to assist them and their peers with their real estate transactions. The numbers game says that the more frequently people see your name, the more often they think of you.

When it comes to mailers, develop a mass marketing state of mind. Unless you're doing a newsletter, your cost is nominal when compared with your return on this investment if you bring in a new client. Compare the cost of postage to a $15,000 commission. This reminder causes you to always push the envelope when it comes to making your market. When you plan your budget, target as many mailings as you can afford.

Advertise Effectively

There are many ways to advertise, and savvy agents know that this is the key to successful marketing. Agents advertise more than any other profession because the game is market, market, market. You see these agents' faces peeking out at you everywhere: in the newspaper, on supermarket carts, in magazines. They believe in getting their name out even if they have to pay dearly for it. Since many of these forms of advertising are expensive, the cost must be measured against the results obtained.

There is a lot to be said for repetition. An agent can become well known through seeing her name continually in the same media. The Top Dogs have so many "for sale" signs broadcasting their names that they do not have to worry about using paid-for advertising. Some do, though, and that's one of the reasons their signs are everywhere.

The Inside Scoop

Here's an example of an advertisement slogan a local agent runs in the real estate section under the town where she specializes: "Audrey Agent, specializing in Middleburg luxury homes." Audrey identifies herself with the Middleburg luxury home market because of her constant advertising. If she provides excellent services as well, she may have a corner on that market.

A face photo is one of the trademarks of agents. Not any old mug shot, but one that's personal, friendly, and close up. Agents are famous for plastering their smiling faces everywhere they can. We are now beginning to see agents smiling from their "for sale" signs. Forget the name of the company. Give us an agent smiling and that's all that matters. It's a reminder about the social nature of real estate.

Your decision as to which type of advertising is best for your business will depend upon the market you want to capture and the amount of your advertising budget. If you cater to the residential market, the local newspaper's real estate section might be just the right place for an ad if it is affordable.

Broadcast Your Career

If we all walked around with our professions taped across our foreheads, especially personal service providers, we'd probably have a better world. After all, who we choose to give our business to is often an emotional decision. It usually comes down to, "Do I like this person and feel comfortable in his or her presence?" Putting your name on your forehead isn't really practical, nor is painting your career on the side of your car. You need the personal contact. So let people know what you do at your first possible opportunity.

If you mention your profession right at the start, your contact can begin his mental and emotional assessment of you early on in the conversation. As you converse, place your card in his hand, reinforcing what you said both by touch and by a card he can carry with him. This is one very good reason why your photo on your card is important. Your contact will remember his conversation with you and when he comes across your card, he may remember his contact with you by looking at your picture.

Prospect for Gold

The word *prospecting* always reminds me of mining. I see the miner's light on a sooty forehead searching for gold. Although the new agent is looking for clients, not gold, his clients are his gold. Prospecting in the real estate world means contacting potential clients with one purpose in mind: to see if you can be of help. Two of the most valuable ways of prospecting in the real estate world include working the expired listings and FSBOs. People with expired listings or FSBO properties need help since they obviously have a property to sell and no one to help them.

 FYI!

Prospecting in the real estate business is a way of targeting potential clients and appealing to their real estate needs. The choice of term is good since in real estate our clients bring us financial reward similar to the miner's reward when he strikes gold.

The Philosophy That Works

Ask these prospects why their listing expired or why they are selling on their own. Ask them to share their war stories. Be generous. Share useful information with them. Then, don't push them. Leave them your name and number and tell them to call if they want more help. Then, continue to check in with them on a weekly basis.

Many FSBOs have had bad experiences with agents in the past. They do not want to repeat their mistakes. Those with expired listings probably feel let down by the agents who were unable to sell their properties. They will be reluctant to deal with you because of this, and nothing will change that except for genuine sincerity.

The sales trainers give you scripts with which to prospect. You just need to pick the right one out of your bag of tricks to fit the right situation. Prospecting within *The New Ideal* has nothing to do with trying to pull a fast one on someone. It is not about instilling fear in others as a way to get their listing. Always remember that you are not from the old school of agents. You are from *The New Ideal*. Your purpose is to genuinely offer your help, and if they don't want it, that is their prerogative.

Former President Clinton demonstrated the importance of making one's desire known to others. His slogan in his presidential campaign was "I desperately want to be your president." I'm not saying that this is the exact terminology to use with this less-than-friendly group of prospects, but do let them know you have the answer for them and make no bones about the fact that you want their listing. Authenticity and good service make an unbeatable combination.

The Inside Scoop

The National Association of Realtors reports that agent sales of comparable properties resulted in sales prices 27 percent higher than those sold by FSBOs. This means that if the FSBO is selling without an agent to save money, they are not accomplishing their objective. (This statistic is derived from the 2002 NAR Profile of Home Buyers and Sellers.)

Dealing with FSBOs

The FSBOs are found through buying FSBO lists for your area and reviewing the classifieds. They are the advertisements that say FSBO, or do not say agent. Many FSBOs can be downright hostile to agents. They have issued a directive to the world that says, "I am selling on my own and I do not want to use a real estate agent."

If they are in the initial stages of marketing, they are gung ho and ready to take on the world. All the new agents and some of the old ones approach FSBOs, each trying out their best script from their sales technique bag of tricks. This type of prospecting is not what *The New Ideal* encourages its professional real estate agents do.

Instead, be real. The biggest mistake agents make with FSBOs is to come on strong when the FSBO has just begun his job. FSBOs resent agent intrusion more than you could ever know. They have made a decision to do it their way without your help, and they do not want you taking their job away from them. Go ahead and contact them early on in their marketing, but be gentle.

Tell them you understand their reasons for wanting to sell on their own, and that you're an agent who has signed onto *The New Ideal*; then invite them to tap you for help as they go along. If you have a web page for FSBOs on your site, direct them there. In other words, you're agreeing to no listing and offering free help.

If you are still at the stage of your career where handling an open house would be advantageous, offer to handle your FSBO's open house free of charge. Explain that it's an opportunity for you to meet prospects and help him all in one sitting. You will earn your FSBO's appreciation, possibly his listing, and probably a few more prospects, too.

> **FYI!**
>
> Offer FSBOs the following proposition: "Fred, I'll prepare you an in-depth comparable market analysis supported by current market data. My package also includes a market analysis sheet that is useful in understanding current market statistics. I'll prepare a property profile that shows where your property lies in conjunction with your neighbors. If you still don't want my help, take these documents and use them to sell on your own. They will help. If you want my help, it's there for the taking." It is hard to say no to this kind of proposition, especially when the agent really means it.

Dealing with Expired Listings

You find the expired listings through a simple database search on the MLS. Then you match up the property with the owner name through tax records. Most multiple listing services also include tax records. Title companies will also provide you with a *property profile* containing the information you need. If a phone number doesn't come up in the data you receive, try one of the cross-indexing services available through an Internet search for mailing list vendors. In the real estate world, information is plentiful. In this industry, where there is a will, there is a way.

Many listings expire because they are priced unrealistically. The owner undoubtedly insisted that her price be used rather than the market price. This is a conversation you will want to have and perhaps you will be able to explain this in a manner that will be more palatable to your prospect. Price is always a touchy subject with the seller who knows it all. All you can do is be honest and sincere, watch the listing, and check in from time to time.

> **Real Estate Lingo**
>
> A **property profile** is a report a title company provides as a customer service that includes a property's title vesting, loan, tax information, its legal description, and information on surrounding properties.

The Least You Need to Know

◆ Anyone you meet is a potential client and should be added to your contact list and categorized according to the following chapter.

◆ Scrutinize existing markets that surround you and consider specializing in one or two of those markets.

◆ There is no reason to be without your own website in the real estate business where marketing is essential.

◆ Keep your name in front of your potential clients with mailers and other forms of advertising.

◆ Respect and understand FSBOs and sellers with expired listings, as they can become a reliable client base.

Chapter 11

Managing the Time Demon

In This Chapter

- ◆ Setting boundaries with your clients
- ◆ Qualifying prospective clients early on
- ◆ Hiring an administrative assistant
- ◆ Effectively dealing with contingencies
- ◆ Working with the closing professional

Controlling time is a constant challenge in the real estate business. The real estate train moves along at a high-speed clip. Not long ago, the sales transaction took sixty to ninety days to travel its many steps to closing. Now that technology has expedited the loan process, closings are taking place in half that time. This situation has caused many real estate agents to lose control of their time. They have let time become their enemy, robbing them of the very freedom and versatility that brought them to the real estate profession.

Don't give in to the time demon. You can't create more time, but you can learn to manage it more efficiently. One way is to master organization and computer technology, the subject of later chapters. In this chapter, we look at identifying the cause of time pressures and how to set up systems so those time pirates do not rock your organized and orderly boat.

Use Your Time Well

The new sales agent is easy prey for poverty consciousness, which incessantly whispers, "You're on commission—the more time you spend, the more money you'll make." Don't give in to it. It is not spending time that will get you there, it is the effective use of time that will. There is so much to learn, a new business to operate, and clientele to cultivate. After about two or three years, your business will have matured some, and you will be on your way to a successful real estate career.

The time to begin building boundaries against the time bandit is when you are first starting out and implementing your work ethic. Set regular hours for yourself and do not work beyond those hours. So many agents become prisoners of their work, schlepping it around everywhere they go. You see them everywhere. They are the ones talking on a cell phone in the middle of the restaurant. This is not good for your self-esteem or for gaining your clients' respect. It's also debilitating to your family and friends if they continually have to play second fiddle to your work.

Act like you have a regular job. Go to the office regularly, and if you want to be successful at maintaining personal time, do not work much more than forty hours a week. Unless you have an unusual time-intensive matter, don't check in again until your regular hours start. Be proactive so that you control your time. Your clients and your peers will respect that you are not a puppet to their whim and call. And your personal life will thrive because it will be first in your book, as it should be.

CAUTION

Caution

Start out your real estate practice with balance. Your personal life has to be sheltered from your work. Otherwise, it will be gobbled up into your practice. Little by little, day-by-day, your personal time will disappear if you don't pay attention to time-management issues.

The Inside Scoop

The National Association of Realtors reports that the typical agent works 43 hours a week.

Don't Be a 24/7 Person

There is no time that is not a good time for real estate. It lives and breathes at all times. It seems to have a life of its own. However, you do not need to be perpetually on call. It is not good business. Some agents try to claim market share by being the most available. Unfortunately, your availability also carries a sign that says, "I am so unproductive or unsuccessful that I have to work all the time." You can be sufficiently available with regular hours. You do not have to be the all-day, all-night real estate store.

Being On-Call for Your Clients

Whether you're in residential or commercial sales, your clients tend to do business with you on their off-hours. They want to get their own work done during regular business hours. You can work out a compromise so that your schedule and your clients' schedules work together.

You will want to work one weekend day, and probably both Saturday and Sunday in the beginning. There's no getting around the fact that residential real estate happens on the weekends in a big way. Also, dedicate a couple of days when you can start later to work later. If you do, you can accommodate clients who want to meet with you after normal business hours. The rest of the week, maintain regular business hours. Put your business hours on your card so clients will know when to contact you.

FYI!

Your clients will continually try to get your schedule to coincide with their *off* schedule. It takes strong determination to reinforce your boundaries repeatedly, but you must. You are a professional and deserve to have your boundaries respected. If you don't respect your time, clients won't respect it either.

The time demons will also tell you that you've got to work sixty hours a week to make a living in the dog-eat-dog real estate world. Don't believe them. The disorganized real estate agent who has failed to adopt healthy work boundaries may need to work sixty hours a week to keep up. You don't have to be that kind of agent. You can be one of the Top Dogs who achieve abundance both financially and personally and have regular work schedules. In fact, you'll only become a Top Dog if you adopt good, healthy work strategies and manage your time effectively.

Beware of High-Maintenance People

You also need to have defined boundaries with clients, especially with potential clients. Always be on the lookout for high-maintenance people (HMPs). I have special antennae trained to detect these time demons. HMPs will suck you dry if you let them. The more you give, the more they want and the less they appreciate you. It's a skirmish that never ends. The new agent, especially, is easy prey for HMPs.

Real estate is often a place where you act as a therapist to soothe and support a client. Budget only a short amount of time for these people, or you will find yourself unable to deal with the rest of your schedule and your other clients. In the real estate business, your time is a precious commodity.

I have met and supported high-maintenance clients. When they call for my services again, I thank them for considering me, but I tell them I have too many clients right now and will not be able to give them the attention they deserve. I then refer them to my referral source for high-maintenance people. I receive the best of both worlds when I receive a referral fee and I do not have to deal with people who keep me on the run.

> **The Inside Scoop**
>
> There is a huge difference between professional courtesy and being taken advantage of. Know the difference. You are not here to please the world; you are here to deliver quality professional services to your clients in a way that supports and serves them.

Once people pass the high-maintenance test, they must be qualified. Are they ready to act or are they just in the information-gathering stage? As part of your public service orientation, you should be willing to give a certain amount of time to people who are researching and shopping. After that, it's time to set your boundary and qualify them by using the checklists set forth in later chapters.

Peer Pressure

Sales has a built-in rush factor. The sales demons realize that excess time encourages indecision, especially when it comes to high-priced real estate. Thus, the real estate sales transaction races on a fast track. The whole real estate industry can be one big pressure cooker. This is one of the major reasons for agent burnout. The unsophisticated agent gives in to this mentality. They interact with peers who perpetuate the rush syndrome and find themselves being pushed along as part of the mad dash to closing.

Anything done from a hurried place is susceptible to error and confusion. There is enough time in this transaction, especially if the steps are taken in an organized, well-thought-out manner. As long as you monitor steps when they need to be performed on both sides of your transactions, not just your side, there will be no reason to rush or to be unreasonably surprised.

In fact, by not rushing through sales transactions, you will stand out among the rest because you will be confident and calm while other agents nervously fidget. While others are trying to keep up in an atmosphere of chaos, your time and energy can be directed to more productive activities.

Hire a Helper

More and more, agents are defeating the time demon by hiring assistants. While transaction coordinators can provide relief, they generally cannot provide the support a busy agent needs. For the high producer, there is nothing like having a good assistant. In fact, the choice to employ an assistant is not only good business sense, it proves to be first-class financial sense. The National Association of Realtors conducted a recent survey, which found that agents who have assistants earn twice as much as those who don't. Those same statistics also show that only one in five agents have an assistant on their team. These agents are the Top Dogs.

Assistants are versed in the real estate transaction and can ease the load considerably. They have become so valuable in the real estate field that there are now courses certifying these professionals. Just as lawyers have certified paralegals to assist them, the agent may have a certified real estate assistant.

The Inside Scoop

The National Association of Realtors provides Real Estate Professional Assistant Certification (REPA), as do many state associations. The two-day course provides an intensive introduction to the real estate business and to the specific ways to support the agent's busy practice. Some highlights of the course are …

- Understanding the business of real estate.
- Knowing what MLS is and being familiar with input forms and reports.
- Knowing how to manage the transaction.
- Understanding the difference between licensed and unlicensed activities.
- Understanding the types of agency representation and disclosures.
- Comprehending key marketing concepts.

Go to www.realtor.org for more information on this course.

You don't have to employ these assistants full time. You can share an assistant with one or more other agents. Your tools to freedom in the real estate sales world are technology and a good assistant. If your assistant is a career real estate assistant, he or she can train you in real estate procedures. These support professionals are one of the most important assets to running a chock-full streamlined practice.

As is described in more detail in Chapter 21, unlicensed assistants cannot do anything that requires a real estate license, such as showing property, explaining a contract or other document to a client, discussing property attributes with a prospect and conducting an open house. But other than that, they can make your life much easier.

An enormous amount of details go into the daily practice of real estate sales. Your assistant can handle most of the administrative functions and coordinate the contacts that need to be made. While your assistant is handling the routine transaction steps and tracking calendar and marketing tasks, you are able to focus on developing new business and listing and selling real estate.

The National Association of Realtors (www.realtor.org) has a checklist of functions that can be performed by an assistant and those that require a real estate license. Simply stated, if an activity is directly related to listing and selling properties, a license is required. When you train your assistant (or he or she trains you) make sure that her duties do not fall into the category of those requiring a license. The distinction can be blurry at times. It makes it a lot easier if you have a handy description of what the assistant can and cannot do for easy reference.

Partnering with Another Agent

This subject was discussed in relation to building your Power Team in Chapter 9, but it is worth mentioning again here since agent partnering can be the ideal solution to the time crunch. For some busy agents, the only way they can feel relaxed enough to enjoy meaningful time off is to know another agent with similar standards is taking a turn at the helm of their ship. Although your assistant can be extremely valuable when it comes to organization, she cannot handle major transaction issues that require the expertise of a licensed agent.

The Inside Scoop

Often it is the physical inspection contingency that causes a transaction to fall apart. It sometimes happens that the buyer obtains inspection reports that say a certain amount of repairs need to be made and the seller refuses to credit the buyer the amount needed to make the repairs. The seller sometimes says the price the client agreed to pay reflects the need for these repairs, refusing to compromise.

The Loan and Inspection Contingencies

The physical inspection and loan contingencies will wrap you around poles a few times if you let them. If you begin each transaction by continually shepherding these contingencies, you will significantly increase the chances that your transaction will close without a visit from the contingency scoundrel.

Keep careful track of these contingencies even if you are on the seller side. Stay in touch with the buyer's agent and repeatedly ask for status reports. By keeping the other agent and your clients on track, you will decrease the likelihood of problems and last-minute issues. When you represent the buyer, take steps toward removing contingencies on the first day of the contingency period. These all-important, sometimes hair-raising contingencies are addressed in depth in Chapter 18.

The Title Contingency

Review of the title report is another buyer contingency that can lead to surprises, cancelled escrows, and their accompanying time pressures. The buyer has a short period of time to review and approve the preliminary title report, or *prelim*. Make sure this report goes to the buyers as early as possible so they have sufficient opportunity to analyze the property's legal criteria.

Title reports contain easements and covenants, conditions and restrictions, and other legal conditions that can drastically affect both the use and value of a property. The buyers need to examine the nature and scope of any such restrictions, which may mean consultation with a professional to obtain advice. The time to do this is before the contingency is removed. The title contingency is addressed in more depth in Chapter 18.

Work with the Closing Professional

The *closing professional* serves as a neutral intermediary facilitating the transaction. In some states, the title company acts in this capacity; in others, attorneys do. They take buyer funds in the form of buyer deposits and lender deposits and distribute them to sellers, lenders, and real estate agents. They give lenders recorded security instruments and give buyers deeds. They handle the paper and money exchange required in the real estate purchase and sale process.

Sometimes the closing professional may wait until the last minute to get everything ready for signing and recording. You can reduce this potential stress builder by staying in close contact with the closing professional, who should be part of your Power Team. Typically the buyer's agent opens *escrow*. But, as with everything else, you want to facilitate all steps of the transaction because the buyer-seller steps are all contingent upon one another. A buyer surprise is a seller surprise.

> **Real Estate Lingo**
>
> The manner in which closings are handled varies depending on your location. In some areas, the **closing professional** is an attorney who also conducts title search. In others, escrow and title companies perform these functions. The choice of a closing professional is at the discretion of the buyer in purchase and sale transactions.

Early on make sure the closing professional has all the information required to close out the transaction. Call a week ahead of closing and ask for an *estimated closing statement*. This will cause the closer to finalize the details of the transaction and complete anything not yet finished.

Real Estate Lingo

Escrow is the independent third party that holds the funds and distributes them according to buyer and seller instructions and processes and prepares the transaction documents. Depending upon your location, escrow is either an escrow company or a closing attorney.

An **estimated closing statement** is one of the last steps the closing professional performs in a transaction. It is a detailed accounting of buyer and seller debits and credits in the transaction. Once the parties approve of the estimated statement, the final closing statement is prepared prior to closing on the transaction.

The Least You Need to Know

- If you do not set boundaries with your clients and associates, your personal life will be swallowed up by your business.

- If you do not qualify potential clients early on, you will be run ragged by shoppers and high-maintenance people.

- Hiring an administrative assistant or partnering with another agent could be your answer for beating the time crunch.

- Physical inspection and loan and title review contingencies should be carefully monitored throughout the transaction, even if you are representing the seller.

- Work closely with the closing professional from the very beginning of the transaction to ensure an organized and orderly closing.

12

Computer Technology

In This Chapter

- ◆ Using technology to streamline your business
- ◆ Reviewing the hardware you will need
- ◆ Reviewing the functions your software must perform
- ◆ Accessing the Internet
- ◆ Utilizing the multiple listing service

Technology is so important to success in real estate sales these days that it warrants an entire chapter. You can get along without becoming a technology wiz, but you will not be able to tap your peak performance unless you make technology the cornerstone of your business. I have two recommendations for you to achieve real estate business goals: First, use all the tools available, and second, always go the extra mile. In this day and age, the tools available to the real estate profession spell c-o-m-p-u-t-e-r with a capital *C*.

In the real estate sales business, technology is required not just because it has become a business standard, but because technology is a lifeline. Agents must have real-time access to the multiple listing service. The challenge for the active agent is that we are highly portable. Agents need to conduct business from various locations—a regular office, a home office, a client's home, and anywhere in the field. The only answer is for you to become computer savvy.

This chapter covers the hardware and software recommended to get your high-tech real estate practice in gear. The next chapter shows you how to organize your technology and duplicate it at home, in your vehicle, and elsewhere.

No More Alibis

After you get your real estate license, your new mantra becomes "Be organized." There are so many details in real estate sales that you cannot afford the luxury of being disorganized for a moment. To be a Top Dog, you must embrace technology and recognize it as an essential ingredient of your business. Technology efficiently tracks an enormous amount of contacts, details, communications, and scheduling in addition to the multiple listing service's thousands of listings.

It's true that many old-timers are incredibly successful without the use of technology. When they built their business model, technology was not what it is today. In this age of advanced technology, especially in the fast-paced real estate world, you must make technology an extension of yourself to be a peak performer. There is just no getting around it. The alibi that you are not computer literate or that the computer just doesn't appeal to you will not work any longer. While the telephone can give a client the personal touch, today's business also requires documentation and timeliness that is only met with technology.

<table>
<tr><td>

The Inside Scoop

An acronym for technology that works for anti-technology people is Terrific Extra Chance to Heighten Natural Organization and Leverage Optimum Gains for You. When technology is seen in this light, it opens the mind.

</td><td>

As a sophisticated agent you require technology to perform a multitude of functions. You prepare your contract documents on computer, not by hand. Managing your leads and prospects through a contact-management program such as Microsoft Outlook or Top Producer is essential for you to fully canvas your market. You also require a calendar program to diary important contract dates and dates to follow up with leads. E-mail and interaction with the MLS is mandatory.

</td></tr>
</table>

Your High-Tech System

In the high-tech model this book advocates, your laptop will travel with you to all locations except in the field (and even then, only if laptop access is inconvenient), where you will use your handheld organizer. Computer technology has become so advanced that some lock-box keys now operate through handheld organizers. With a computer at your fingertips in your many locations, business will travel with you everywhere you go. This, you will find, affords the ultimate freedom and flexibility—one reason you chose this job.

Now you can sit at the coffee shop and review the multiple listing database you uploaded to your handheld organizer that morning. Or make business calls with your cell phone and schedule appointments on your handheld organizer, which you will upload to your calendar and contacts database on your laptop when you *synchronize*. You can even send and receive e-mail with your wireless technology.

Real Estate Lingo

When you **synchronize** your databases, you usually use a docking station connected to your computer and a software program that comes packaged with your portable device. Information such as contacts or calendar entries are compared on the two devices and any new entries or modified entries are added or updated. The result is that both the device and the computer have the same information.

You will find that a sizeable portion of the real estate industry is not yet as high-tech as I suggest, but if you want to be on the cutting edge and a peak performer, heed these steps. Don't let your peers get to you when they tease you about your technology entourage. They're just jealous.

FYI!

I was the first lawyer in my area to use a computer at trial and in deposition. In those days they were called portable computers, and at 25 pounds each, they weren't intended for a lap. It was intimidating to my adversaries since I was able to access documents with a click while they shuffled through thousands of papers. When I was a traveling real estate mediator, I put settlement agreements together on my laptop, printed them out on my portable printer and walked out of the mediation with signed agreements. I am a strong advocate of technology because it gives you a gigantic advantage over the rest of the pack.

The Hardware You Will Need

Before you purchase any computer hardware, do the research. Don't rely on the salespeople. Make sure the literature for everything you buy confirms what the salesperson says. I have a cabinet full of interesting technological devices that were not compatible with my other technology, or didn't do what the salesperson said they would do. The following list is the suggested basic technology you will need in your new life as a mobile real estate professional:

- Laptop computer
- Cell phone
- Handheld organizer
- Digital camera
- Printer, copier, scanner, and fax machine, or an all-in-one unit with all those functions

If you are going to be high-tech, ask all the questions and confirm all the answers before you buy. It is easier to do this in advance than to worry about connectivity, synchronization, or a host of other issues after you have made the investment.

Laptop

The office you join will probably provide a desktop computer for your use, but use your laptop instead so your information will follow you wherever you go. In this manner, you will be far more flexible, which is one of the reasons you came to real estate to begin with. When you purchase your laptop, get the best you can afford. Your supplemental drives need to be easily accessible, not interchangeable. If you will also use a desktop, make sure your laptop has a networking card so you can easily network the two computers to synchronize their information and back them up. You will also want to be able to synchronize with your handheld organizer.

The Inside Scoop

You will have your laptop in the field with you, so you want to make sure its casing is well protected and will withstand being carted around. Buy a well-padded briefcase for it. Computers can be dropped and need the protection. I cannot stress this enough, having learned from experience. You pay a price for the freedom of portability if you don't build in the appropriate safeguards.

You want a good size screen and quality display so when you show clients properties they can see a clear visual picture. You will be able to cut down on driving and showing time if you introduce your clients to prospective properties by computer and if they display almost as well as being on site. Many agents just print out listings for client preview. These properties look far more visually appealing on the computer screen. I use my laptop extensively in the field, which sometimes brings me outdoors.

If you plan to use your computer outdoors, make sure you have a screen protector to reduce the glare.

If you plan to use your laptop when there is no electricity, make sure you have extensive battery power capacity. If you plan to scan, you will need a scanner interface or USB (universal serial bus) port and a printer port for printing. For infrared connection you will need an infrared interface.

> **The Inside Scoop**
>
> Sit down with a basic computer book like *The Complete Idiot's Guide to Computer Basics* so you can understand the basic terminology and concepts of computer networking.

Cell Phone

You will need a *cell phone*. Because you often use your cell phone when driving, make sure it has voice recognition so you can program it to dial for you when you speak a certain name. Install some form of hands-free capability so you can drive with both hands and talk with the use of a headset or microphone. You can also receive and send e-mail and access the Internet with your cell phone, but because the screen is so small and capacity is limited, you will likely want to conduct these activities on your handheld organizer or laptop.

> **Real Estate Lingo**
>
> I use the terms **cell phone** and wireless phone interchangeably. In the not-so-distant future there will probably be one device that will make phone calls and hold a good contact database. At the time of this writing, cell phones are good for telephone calls and handheld organizers and PCs are good for information. But neither is very good at both telephone and database management. Until we get there, you will be a two-device person.

Handheld Organizer

A handheld organizer allows you to bring your address book, calendar, contacts, and multiple listing data everywhere you go. These devices may also have wireless and dialup Internet access, depending upon the device and its accessory features. You network your handheld organizer with your laptop and synchronize the two databases back and forth and with the MLS with the use of a docking station. This synchronization process is discussed in the next chapter.

If I have any choice at all about which computer device to use, I choose my laptop. I bring it to meetings everywhere I go. I work much better with the size of its screen and keyboard and its processing power. Although the handhelds have large-sized keyboards you can attach as an add-on and expansion cards for additional memory, there is only so much you can do with a hand-sized device. So yes, I am the person you've seen at the hairdresser's sitting under the dryer with a laptop perched in front of me.

> **FYI!**
>
> Most cameras come with their own photo software. This software allows you to tweak the picture until it achieves the look you are after by adding more light, centering the picture, enlarging it, giving it more color, and making the property look more appealing. Get to know the software application so you can produce the best-looking photos.

Digital Camera

You will need a digital camera to take pictures of the properties you list. There is a variety to choose from. Some can be purchased as accessories to your handheld organizer. To open the picture on your computer, you need the software application that relates to the digital image.

You will use your photos for your marketing materials and to include with your listings on the multiple listing service and on your website. You can also e-mail your digital photos to interested buyers. Multiple listing services now have the capability to show a large portfolio of pictures of a property. You can also take your own slide show, or hire one of the many companies that prepare virtual slide shows for you.

Printer, Copier, Scanner, and Fax

Your office usually provides this equipment for use at the office. So you need to provide for home and in the field. If you do not already have this equipment, you might choose to get a printer, scanner, copier, and fax or an all-in-one. Your research may indicate that the more features, the more susceptible the device is to problems. Take a look at consumer reports and make your own evaluation.

I recommend that you have your own fax machine with a dedicated line at the office to ensure that your faxes come directly to you and that the line is available to you at all times. Even more important, with your own fax line, when you leave the office, you can forward your faxes to your home fax machine. You don't even need a fax machine to receive faxes anymore. You just sign up with a company that gives you a special e-fax number. Faxes are then forwarded to your e-fax number where they are converted to e-mail format and sent to your e-mail address. You can also send faxes by e-mail in the same way. In this manner you can be truly portable as you send and receive e-mail, voice mail, and faxes at any location.

Having a color printer is an asset in the highly visual real estate business where color is the norm. If you plan on building a vehicle office, you will want a portable printer that will connect to either your laptop or handheld device by cable or infrared port. You might also want to consider a portable scanner if scanning in the field is important to you.

I couldn't live without a scanner. I conduct business primarily by computer technology and strive to be paperless. The scanner turns my paper products into an image that I then store on my computer to complete my transaction database and to e-mail to others involved in my transactions.

In this manner, I am paperless in my transactions, with the exception of the documents that need signatures. We are still stuck with hard copies for obtaining signatures on documents until such time as digital signatures are authenticated in real estate transactions.

As you go along, you can evaluate how important a scanner is for your particular needs. I find e-mailing of documents to be a handy alternative to faxing, especially since clients often have e-mail but don't have a fax machine. I will do just about anything to not have to transmit documents by snail mail.

The Software You Will Need

You want your operation to become a high-level multitasking operation through the efficient use of computer programs. While this chapter describes the programs, the next chapter shows you how to integrate and organize them so they work together. The software functions you will need are …

- Contact, e-mail, and calendar management
- Word processing
- Accounting and check writing
- Website administration
- Internet access
- Multiple listing entries and searches
- Security (for backups and virus protection)

You are probably familiar with many of these applications and will only need training in a few areas. Your goal is to use and manage your applications in such a way that these tasks are easy and compatible. Open one program and you're ready to write a letter. Open another and send an e-mail or fax. There is no need to duplicate information between programs since this information is in your contact database, which can be accessed for the rest of your programs.

Contact, E-mail, Fax, and Calendar

One program usually handles all of these indispensable functions. This type of program is the foundation of your practice. It transforms the agent-juggling act into one efficient and highly organized system. I use Microsoft Outlook because it interacts well with the rest of the Microsoft Office programs I use. Many agents use Top Producer. There are other options as well. Just make sure that the program you use is also able to be used on your handheld organizer or is compatible with it.

Learn how to use all the features of these programs. They will make your life much easier. Once you input a person's or company's contact information, you never have to do it again as long as you know how to access it from different programs. If you want to send someone an e-mail, just click on his or her e-mail address. A fax calls for a click on their fax number. If you want to send a letter by snail mail, your contact program address book provides their address for the letter in your word processing program. Your database on your laptop and handheld will synchronize with one another so they both have information entered on either device.

FYI!

Make sure you specify your return address and signature line in your e-mail setup. This should include your full name, company name, address, telephone, fax, e-mail, and web address. Provide a link to your website. Also include a brief mission statement or specialty motto if you have developed one. I colorize my name and use a font that looks like handwriting for my signature. It almost looks like I have personally signed the message.

Your training will include learning how to attach files of all types to e-mails and faxes. For instance, your contracts and other forms are most likely on the computer. Instead of being limited by the paper shuffle (printing out documents and transmitting them by fax, by mail, or by hand, and receiving them back in the same manner), you are able to attach these documents to an e-mail or fax and send them with a click of your computer.

You can also attach pictures, other e-mails, and address book pages. By using an attachment to e-mail instead of inputting directly into the e-mail, formatting is better retained and transmission may be faster. There are all kinds of tricks of the trade that will make your computer experience much easier and more productive. Take the time to get some training and spend some time with each of the features of your contact management program.

Chapter 14 shows you how your contacts database can be managed in a highly effective way. It shows you how to input contacts so they are categorized in easily searchable ways and so that targeted marketing products are sent to those contacts.

Word Processing

The most universally used word processing program is Microsoft Word. We all need to prepare letters and other documents from scratch or modify existing documents. These may be sent by e-mail, fax, or snail mail, or can be used as your own notes. You will use your word processing program to create all of these documents. Because documents may be many pages long, the formatting functions of a good word processing program are essential. I use my word processing program as my base program where I enter notes as I move through my day. These notes are then either saved as word processed files or copied into other programs.

Caution

Because everyone is worried about viruses, you want to let your e-mail recipient know the attachment is virus free. Be sure you set up your virus checking program to scan all incoming and outgoing messages.

The Inside Scoop

The office that you are affiliated with may provide or recommend a word processing program, and possibly a contact program. While you may not go along with that choice, you want to know that your applications can work with those used by other people in the office.

Accounting and Check Writing

Many agents still write checks by hand and then spend at least a week organizing, categorizing, and totaling receipts for tax purposes. There is no reason to live in the dark ages any longer. Technology provides tools to make these activities easy.

Use an accounting and check-writing software program. These programs automatically itemize your deductions as you write checks. You will also keep track of your trust account and separately itemize client deposits. With these accounting programs, preparation for filing your taxes becomes simple. All expenses are tracked under the correct deduction category as you pay them; then, at tax time a report shows each category, all expenses in that category, and a total for those expenses. Always think as a small business owner should: Does this payment qualify as an expense? Which category does it fall under?

> **The Inside Scoop**
>
> A good accountant is a handy asset! Your accountant may recommend an accounting package and may be able to take information on computer media and use that effectively. He or she will also advise you of deduction categories and levels of deductions in each category that are under the IRS "red flag" level.

Pay for everything by check or business credit card. When you pay your credit card bill, take a moment to itemize each expense into the correct category. When you write your checks each billing interval, you just pull up the contact information for that vendor. There is no need to input that vendor information again as it is already there. All you do is change the amount of the payment if it differs from the time before. Handy window envelopes allow the vendor name and address printed on the check to be seen through the window for mailing purposes.

Website

If you plan to have your own website and administer it yourself, you will need training in website-administration applications. There are a few excellent programs to choose from. The advantage to administering your own site is that you can keep it up-to-date, thereby providing current information and ensuring that the Internet search engines find your site more readily. There are other keys toward getting a high ranking in a search, but that is the topic of many books and several sites on the Internet.

> **The Inside Scoop**
>
> For those unique question-intensive listings, you can refer agents and interested purchasers to your website. Include comparables, a photo gallery, a plot map, use and zoning information, property history, and statistics. Make sure everything they need is at their fingertips. Your time can then be spent in more productive areas instead of responding to a never-ending barrage of questions about the property.

With these applications you can both design and administer your site. There are many people ready to create a site for you these days. Have someone else design it and implement it initially while you or an assistant do the ongoing updating of it. The software application makes site administration easy as long as you receive a little training either on your own or through the program's tutorial. I can change information on my website in just a minute. I open my program, open the file I want to change, make the change, upload it to my website (a click that takes a second), open the website on the Internet—

and there it is. Each time I make a change, I am astonished at how easy worldwide marketing has become.

I had a unique listing recently that had Internet marketing appeal. We dropped it into my website, and I began receiving inquiry e-mails within hours, some from other states and other countries. If you practice in a highly desirable area, it makes sense to have web presence for your listings. If you administer your site yourself, new listings can be added easily and quickly.

Your website can also serve as an activity and information center for your markets. Clients know to check my website regularly for changes to seminar dates and times. They know I continually add information that may be of interest to them. If you place listings on your site, you want those listings to be current and complete. This can be a marketing tool to encourage sellers to list with you.

FYI!

You can also include hidden pages on your site that are only accessible by those who know the exact page address. In other words, the site does not give access to these pages unless their specific address is typed into the browser. I use these hidden pages to broadcast status reports on my transactions, accessible only by my *Power Team* and the clients involved.

In summary, if you want Internet searches to bring you a market, you should have a website and update it regularly. If you want clients and their referrals to include your site in their resource center, let them know by updating your site often and keeping it interesting.

Security (Backups and Virus Protection)

This section should have a big warning sign that says: "If you rely on computer technology, you must have a backup and an antivirus system in place". Because your computer contains your real estate world, you must safeguard its information.

Virus protection is easy. Make sure you have virus protection software, such as Norton AntiVirus, installed on each computer, and that each is updated at least weekly. Backing up takes a little more work.

Caution

If you think laptop "crash" and "loss" are a remote risk, think again. I have been a victim of both. On a plane, someone else picked up my computer and left me his. I never saw the computer again. I have also crashed more than one hard drive by knocking my computer around too much. Consider yourself warned.

The convenience of having a portable computer has its own downside: As it is transported from place to place, it becomes susceptible to crash and loss. Always back up your information to another location that does not travel with you.

In my practice, I have multiple computers that are networked together. One computer acts as a server that all information is backed up to. If you have just one computer or have no network capability, you will have to use writable CDs, floppy disks, Zip disks, or tapes as your backup medium. Consult a professional or a technology-savvy friend if these processes and terms are unfamiliar to you. Whatever you do, don't ignore backups!

Backup utilities come bundled with the latest Microsoft operating system as part of its highly accessible system tools or can be purchased separately from other vendors. Some backup utilities are included with writable hardware like CD writers and Zip drives. It just takes a few clicks to initiate a backup. You can set the back up to occur automatically with just a few more clicks. One week is the minimum time to elapse between backups. I back up only my documents, since my software is available and filed away.

The Internet

Everyone needs access to the Internet these days. If you have e-mail connectivity, you also have Internet access. The Internet is an amazing source of information and tools. Of course, you have to consider the reliability of the source depending on the type of information you find. The Internet can be a multi-purpose tool, useful for gathering information and for marketing your services and advertising your client's listings.

To connect to the Internet, you need the service of an *Internet service provider (ISP)*. You can choose a dialup connection (and optimally a high-speed connection such as DSL or cable) or wireless. You will have to connect to the Internet in order to get your e-mail, get to the MLS listings, or get information from other websites.

Real Estate Lingo

An **Internet service provider** (ISP) is a company that sells you connectivity to the Internet. This service also comes with one or more e-mail addresses.

Make sure you understand your Internet browser and its capabilities so you can make the most of the world of information available through Internet access. The Internet is quickly becoming the place where much marketing takes place. Keep abreast of what the Internet offers. It changes daily. Its potential is unlimited.

Multiple Listing Service

The multiple listing service (MLS) is a membership-only website. The MLS site includes many sophisticated features that allow you to perform complex searches for properties for sale or rent and to locate comparables. There are also prospect matching functions that allow you to automate e-mails of new listings to prospects without even touching your computer. Your prospect receives a full-color display of new listings without any continuing effort on your part.

There are also tax records to search and important statistics to access. Most MLS programs also include desktop art features for professional creation of flyers, brochures, and other marketing materials. Make sure you receive thorough training in the use of this service. You will receive some training through your office, but you should also sign up for some courses through either your local board or the multiple listing service itself. Agents often underutilize computer technology. As you can see, this would be a big mistake for you.

Connectivity

Since you will have multiple locations where you access information, it is necessary to understand computer connectivity for e-mail, fax, and Internet access. This means knowing how to track your Internet service provider's local access numbers and change your access to conform to that number. You will want to know how to make these changes on the devices that will travel with you: your laptop and your handheld organizer. If you do not want to gain this information yourself, then locate a good consultant or friend who is savvy in connectivity.

FYI!

You may have occasion to use a program like PC Anywhere to dial into another computer to obtain its files. I have a desktop at home and another at my office, and a laptop and handheld organizer that travel with me. I use PC Anywhere between the computers to access and update files. I also synchronize via a network, my laptop computer, my assistant's desktop computer, and my desktop computers whenever I am in the office.

You will want to synchronize data throughout all of your devices, which involves having the right hardware and software. Some handhelds have software applications that will not "sync" with the applications used on your laptop. Do not purchase these devices. Get those that are compatible with the applications you use on your computer.

The answer to full integration is twofold. First, make sure that each computer device you purchase is fully compatible with your contact and calendar applications. Second, make sure your computers have the right ports so they can physically network with your other computers so you can exchange information between computers. Again, if you don't understand the issues involved in making these devices compatible with each other, consult a friend or technically savvy person who can help you.

Obtaining Computer Training

For some programs you will require hands-on training, for others online instruction will do, and for others self-instruction will suffice. It all depends on your level of interest and discipline. You will probably use a combination of these sources. Most software programs have handy tutorials that step you through the basic processes. Some classroom training is advisable for the programs you will use most often.

FYI!

I encourage you to become a certified E-Pro, an Internet mastery certification offered through the National Association of Realtors. This course, called E-Pro, is offered online and confers the E-Pro certification which can be used after your name. This program was designed to help you thrive and compete in the world of online real estate. This is a partial course description as described on the NAR's website, www.realtor.org:

- **Getting Connected**—Getting connected is more than going online, it is about creating an Internet presence.

- **E-mail, a new way to communicate and a new way to market**—Master your e-mail software, using it as a tool to communicate before, during, and after the transaction. Learn great risk reduction and marketing techniques.

- **World Wide Web**—Learn the obvious and the subtle advantages a web-marketing plan can have. Create your own Internet Listing Presentation content. Use the WWW to publish information valuable to your prospects as well as your clients. Do your homework before you "buy" a website or pay for an "exclusive territory." Do search engines help?

- **Tying it all together**—Bring the aspects of ancillary technology such as PDAs, digital cameras, virtual tours, and MLS systems to the attention of the e-PRO.

Training you will need is available everywhere, even on the Internet. Since technology is such a large part of the agent's life, the local, state, and national real estate boards are increasingly making computer training available. Colleges, junior colleges, adult education through high schools, and private companies also provide this training.

The Least You Need to Know

◆ Technology is the key to an organized, highly efficient real estate practice.

◆ A laptop computer, cell phone, color printer, copier, and fax machine are essential equipment, while a handheld organizer is optional but highly recommended.

◆ Software functions must cover contact, e-mail and calendar handling, accounting, word processing, MLS, and Internet.

◆ You need to access the Internet to get your e-mail, to use the MLS, and to search for information.

◆ The MLS has many services that can make your work easier, such as the ability to perform a detailed search of listings and other critical information.

Part 4

Putting It All Together

Now that you have built your business, it's time to put it all together. As they say in the interior design business, it's time to furnish and accessorize. This is the section that teaches you how to take a good business plan and make it a master plan. The key elements consist of the following:

- Becoming a master of organization

- Building a *Referral Stream System*

- Following *The New Ideal*

- Making a Winning Listing Presentation

A Master of Organization

In This Chapter

- ◆ You can administer your business from anywhere, if you bring technology with you
- ◆ Coordinate information on your computer and handheld organizer
- ◆ Use your calendar program efficiently
- ◆ Know how your various computer programs work together
- ◆ Set up your home office

This chapter covers organization and efficiency. Once you have your computer technology, your business plan, and your marketing plan in place, the next step is to efficiently integrate them all. Again, it begins with a capital *C* for *computer*. Whereas the previous chapter addressed computer technology from a product selection and training standpoint, this chapter looks at technology from an organizational perspective.

E-mail, cell phones, and fax machines are the technologies that should serve as your communication core. This chapter shows you how to most efficiently use and integrate your computer technology and bring it with you everywhere you go—office, home office, vehicle, and anywhere in the field.

Make Your Computer Your Business Partner

Times have changed, especially where technology is concerned. If you want to move into Top Dog status in the real estate field, you *must* make your computer a top priority, and you *must* become computer savvy. There's just no two ways about this. We have too many technologically competent people entering the field for anyone who wants to claim market share to ignore the benefits of technology any longer.

Agents fight this state of reality, claiming that real estate is a people business that cannot be replaced by impersonal technology. The fact is that technology is not here to *replace* the personal touch; it is here to allow you to be more productive and efficient in order to give you more time to interact with clients and build relationships.

Not everyone has the desire to become a Top Dog, but if you do, organization is essential, and technology provides the key. There are three steps to achieving this goal:

1. Get the right computer programs.

2. Use these computer programs for *all* your business.

3. Bring your computer, either laptop or handheld, everywhere you go during business hours.

Wean Yourself Off Paper

As described in previous chapters, a good contact management program which organizes your contacts, e-mail, and calendar is a must. The trick is not just knowing how to use it, but using it faithfully. Wean yourself off of paper. Make yourself use a computer for everything. I accomplished this by removing pens from my surroundings. I felt as if I was giving up smoking again. But it worked.

After about three weeks, computer entry becomes automatic for calendaring, lists of tasks, and contact information. Since we spend so much time in the field, your handheld organizer is indispensable, but you've got to use it. The transition from pen to computer entry shouldn't require drastic measures; just don't let a pen get in the way.

Of course, the computer efficiency plan will not work for you unless you establish e-mail as a method of supplementing contact with clients, other agents, and peers. Nearly everyone has e-mail these days. Just train them to use it. Once they see the immediate benefits of instant communication and delivery of information, they will be converts. I have no trouble whatsoever mentoring my groups into using e-mail for transactions, and most people who are not as e-mail–based as I am are flabbergasted at the resulting increase in productivity and interaction.

This fact is borne out by a survey the National Association of Realtors conducted recently that indicates that buyers and sellers who receive status reports by e-mail are the most satisfied with their agents because communication is more frequent. You will be met with opposition from many people, but hang in there. It is worth it.

Become a Computer Multitasker

To achieve high performance, you must also become a computer multitasker. It is only through complete familiarity with your computer programs that you will achieve your highest efficiency. Obtain the training that pulls all of your applications together in a unified manner. You should be able to sit at your computer and seamlessly click away as you write letters from scratch, modify real estate forms and documents, e-mail, fax, scan, search the Internet, update your contacts, keep up with your accounting, and calendar your reminders and appointments.

 FYI! _____

I feel like Ms. Spock on my computer as I run several programs, simultaneously multitasking between them all. To do this, you need to know which program performs the functions you require and have the ability to use that function well. This ability only comes through experience, but when it comes, you know you have discovered the most efficient way of doing business. It's as if one day the light bulb comes on and after that, you are a lean, mean, computerized machine.

For instance, you're preparing a listing agreement. You receive an e-mail confirming an appointment. With one little click you reply to the e-mail. You open your calendar and diary the meeting within a matter of seconds. You open the multiple listing service to search for properties for that client. You e-mail your clients the listings you feel may interest them. You open your calculator program to determine the mortgage payment they will make. You get some information on loan rates from the Internet, and then copy that and paste it into an e-mail. Now, you return to the listing agreement you were preparing. You and your laptop become an efficient central office no matter where you are.

Bring Your Database Everywhere You Go

To become a Top Dog in the portable real estate business, you must train yourself to bring your database everywhere you go. I know you're saying, "But nobody else does." It is true that most agents have not partnered with technology to the extent this book suggests. So why should you? Because if you don't, you will not be the Top Dog you want to be as technology sweeps the real estate business over the next five years. The Top Dogs will be those using technology to claim market share and to service market share. With that said, let me illustrate the advantage of making technology portable.

Most busy agents spend at least two hours a day performing administrative tasks, even if they have an assistant. With the right technology at your fingertips, you can easily handle these chores as you step through your day. Can you imagine having two hours a day more than your competitors have? The answer is to have your laptop or handheld with you at all times.

The Inside Scoop

In my car or in the field where inputting information is inconvenient or dangerous, I use the voice recorder built into my handheld to record information requiring notation. For instance, if I need to make an entry while driving and talking on my cell phone, I activate the voice recorder on my handheld and repeat the message. The recorder easily plays back for retrieval of information. When I arrive at my destination, I enter important information into my database.

Inefficiency and disorganization so often result from having information on your computer in one place while you are at another location. For instance, you've just returned to the office from a day (without your computer) in the field, delivering a listing presentation and meeting with various vendors and potential clients. You have a listing to input, dates to calendar from contacts you made in the field, new client information to enter, and so on. There are faxes that have been received and e-mails and voice messages to pore through. You're stuck in office administration mode for a few hours.

This is not the case for the high-tech agent who goes home from the listing presentation to spend quality time with his family. He has minimal voice mail to return since he had his cell phone with him and received most calls.

At the listing presentation, he used his laptop as a visual aid (see Chapter 16), so when he signed his clients up, he entered their contact information into his database. He also completed and submitted the listing to the multiple listing service while with his clients, enabling them to respond to property-specific questions. He had his digital camera and took pictures and uploaded them when entering the listing on the MLS. He also installed a lock box and explained its security features in order to alleviate his new client's concerns over allowing agents access to their home. Instead of requiring several return visits to take pictures, install a lock box, and obtain information for the listing, the high-tech agent accomplished these tasks on the spot when the listing was received.

During the rest of his time in the field, calendar dates and contact information were entered on his handheld instead of on scraps of paper to be entered later. His faxes were automatically forwarded to his home. When he arrives home, instead of several hours of administration, he has a few faxes and some e-mail to review. Who would you rather be? The high-tech agent home with his family having administrated his day throughout the day, or the low-tech agent stuck at the office still administrating the details?

Even if you have an assistant administrating the office for you, it increases office productivity if you organize and administrate your time in the field. In this manner, there is little time spent transmitting information to your assistant later; just initiate the synchronization program on your computer and your information is transferred to your assistant's computer.

Becoming a Calendar Wizard

Full use of your computer calendar is essential to maximum productivity in the real estate field. The business just moves too fast and there are too many details and people to rely on memory or scraps of paper. Even more important is the fact that transactions are deadline driven, and if deadlines are not met, the consequences are extreme.

Some real estate offices still train agents and support staff to use hand-written calendaring systems. I urge you to do it all on computer. If your office insists on using hand-written forms, check with your manager to see whether a computer-entered profile for each transaction will suffice. If not, still use computer entry as your primary tracking method while you conform to office policy using the written method.

For matters that need advanced planning, such as a *contingency release*, I enter the date for both the date of the release and a few days before the release. Everything that needs to be accomplished at a specific date or time goes on my

Real Estate Lingo

A **contingency release** occurs when a contingency is released, either by satisfaction or waiver. There is a specified time period for this to happen. The agent prepares a release of contingency, which is signed by the buyer. If the contingency is not released within this time frame, the transaction most often terminates without penalty.

calendar. Allocate specific hours for prospecting and marketing and put them on your appointment calendar; then adhere to them as if they are actual appointments. You can set your calendar to provide a reminder for each item's entry. The reminder appears on your computer screen at the lead time you specify.

> **FYI!**
>
> In most calendar programs, you can ask to be reminded of appointments and tasks. These reminders have a pop-up window and can produce a sound to notify you. You can specify how much time you want the reminder to occur before the appointment or task start-time. For example, you can receive a warning 30 minutes before the scheduled time that you are to meet with a client. The hand-held devices also notify you, so if you're in the field you will be alerted if your hand-held is on. These notifications have saved me from many embarrassing moments.

Keep Track of Your Tasks

It is also important to calendar items on your daily task list in your calendar. On my task list I include every single thing I need to do, and I mean *everything*. Your calendar program should have an area for tasks, which is separate from time-specific items on each calendar date. As you complete your tasks, cross them off; as more appear, immediately put them on the list.

Print Out Your Calendar the Day Before

Especially in the fast-paced real estate business, the only way you can have an organized, self-directed day is to begin with a clear desk and an organized agenda. Before you leave either your home office or away-from-home office for the day, clear off your desk entirely and print out your schedule for the next day. It should be the only thing sitting on your desk when you begin the day. I have one calendar at home, one at the office, and one in my car. It should be full if you follow the steps recommended in this book.

So many agents are running through their days instead of running their days. The real estate business is a flurry of activity. It is possible to just show up and be madly busy for an entire day. This is what many real estate agents do. They are frantic because they do not follow an agenda.

By printing out your schedule for the next day at the end of your workday, you have time to think about what your next day will be. Planning ahead like this allows you to subconsciously formulate plans for the next day's activities, and when the calendar delves them out you are ready to respond with well-thought-out actions. By managing your time in this manner, you can run a highly efficient, seamless business that will not run you.

FYI!

Your calendaring program tracks your transactions and reminds you when a task is to be performed. When you need to know the calendar dates for a transaction, just enter the name of the client in the calendar search field and it automatically assembles all calendar and task entries in one convenient transaction profile. I e-mail my transaction profile to my clients and Power Team members as it changes or I post it on my website's hidden page so they can track transactions with me.

Organizing Your Computer Files

When you enter the high-tech world, you need a filing cabinet. Of course, it's on your computer. Although the other steps in this chapter are mandatory for the high achieving agent, this step is optional. Personally, I couldn't live without my computer filing cabinet, but I utilize computer technology more than most of my peers. For those of you who want to achieve a good measure of computerized file management, this section and the next are meant for you.

I open a new computer folder for each client and file everything relating to that client in this folder. This includes e-mail I send and receive, contracts, letters, and spreadsheets that relate to the client. The multiple listings I enter or retrieve for my clients go in their folder. Since I also scan hard copies of documents if they are not already on my computer, my client computer file includes the entire transaction.

Instead of dealing with paper throughout the transaction, which can be inconvenient and time-consuming, I make computer data my primary source of information and my traveling data center. I still have a paper file containing signed copies and originals of documents for each transaction, which is retained by my transaction coordinator. But the day-in and day-out activities of my business are conducted according to my handy easy-to-retrieve computer database. Once you make the transition away from paper, you will find that having everything literally at your fingertips makes organization something that just falls into place—all on your computer.

Maintaining Your Paper Files

You still want to retain paper files for transactions for the following reasons:

◆ Your office will probably require it.

◆ Although backing up is reliable, there is still concern that both the storage files and the primary files may be susceptible to crash.

◆ Some transactions still require the use of originals when the parties do not stipulate the use of copies in lieu of originals.

◆ Many people still do not use computer technology to the extent recommended in this book. You will therefore continue to receive many documents in hard copy.

In most of my transactions, I have the parties stipulate that signed copies of documents transmitted by fax or PDF file have the same effect as originals, thereby avoiding the need for transmittal of originals, which can really slow things down. If you decide to use this stipulation in your transaction, make sure you clear procedure with your office manager in advance.

> **The Inside Scoop**
>
> I include the following term in the offers I prepare: "The parties agree that signed documents transmitted by facsimile or PDF file constitute originals for all purposes in this transaction."

In both law and real estate, the use of originals is deeply engrained. Some people of the *old school* refuse to adopt new ways of conducting business. In those transactions we still use originals and labor under the inconvenience of transmitting originals back and forth between the contracting parties. For these transactions, hard copy files rule.

Synchronizing and Backing Up Data

Daily, either at the office or home, you will need to synchronize your equipment and back up your data. With synchronization, entries made on one computer should appear on the other. The synchronization process is more sophisticated than uploading and downloading information because of its ability to determine what has been added most recently on either device and duplicating that information on the other, all in one easy step. If you have an assistant, you need to synchronize with him or her as well. You will also need to synchronize your handheld organizer with the MLS to update any listings that have changed or been added since you last synchronized.

Utilize a docking station and software that synchronizes your laptop with your handheld and vice versa so both devices contain up-to-date information. For laptop to desktop, if you use both, a network cable achieves the same result. And backup of one fully synchronized computer, which was addressed in the prior chapter, is essential.

FYI!

Your handheld will not have the capacity to download all MLS listings, although it should easily hold thousands of them. Download only those that define a specific market. Storage of recently downloaded listings on your handheld is not as good as obtaining real-time information, but it is far better than having nothing at all when you are in the field and unable to obtain direct access to the MLS database.

Build these steps into your schedule on a daily basis. I perform these tasks at home at the end of each day. All I do is integrate my computers with their docking stations or networking cables and hit a few buttons to synchronize, download, and back up. As I wind down from the day, these functions occur on their own. As long as you've set these features up correctly, the process is simple and fully automated. If your system isn't seamless, hire a computer consultant to work out the quirks.

Establishing Your Home Office

In all likelihood you will set up an office in your home. It all depends on your habits and the benefits your away-from-home office provides, but you may find that you spend more time working from your home than from your office. One of the main reasons for choosing real estate is the flexibility, and having a home office provides flexibility in spades. You have to be careful, though, as the homey home office can be a big threat to a solid work ethic and self-discipline. Distractions are everywhere.

Caution

If you choose to work at home any quantity of time, treat it like an outside office. If you don't, your personal life will become your work life and everyone, including you, will resent it. The real estate business by its very nature is personal and social. As such, it is almost impossible to separate it from your family life unless you build in boundaries from day one. Begin with your home office. Make it as separate as possible from the rest of your home.

Build in specific times when you work. Treat your home office just as you would your away-from-home office. Set it up like an office and build in all the high-tech creature comforts to make it a true business operation. Have a station for your laptop. Get a color printer, scanner, copier, and fax, or an all-in-one device. Make it an efficient, professional place to work.

Be disciplined. When you walk from your home space to your business, act as if you have driven to the office. Get dressed for the office and bring your office mindset with you. Don't lollygag in your slippers and robe. If you do, you will make your home office a part of your family life, and you will not be able to separate the two. Your efficiency in both business and personal matters will become impaired because you will not be totally focused on either one.

Transforming Your Home Office

The home office challenge is high on the list of agent obstacles to productivity. It comes second to controlling your time. For this, you must master self-discipline. It is always the case in life that our biggest pleasures can become our biggest pains.

Early on in my split-office routine (some time was spent at home; some was spent at the office), I observed that I was a completely different worker at home. I was not as thorough, efficient, or intelligent as I was at the office. When I examined the cause, I realized that I had failed to bring the essential qualities to my home office that made my regular office so productive.

I allowed too much of a relaxed, comfy environment to permeate my home office. My home office was kind of an office and kind of a retreat. When I was in it, I was therefore kind of a worker and kind of not a worker. I came to name it limbo land before it received its transformation because it was in limbo. A lot of agents and other professionals who sometimes work at home suffer from limbo land syndrome.

In no time at all, limbo land was transformed into a comfortable, aesthetically pleasing, highly productive space through careful evaluation and implementation of a plan I call commercial transformation. Commercial transformation is a process that duplicates your away-from-home office in your home office with one little twist—it's in your home.

Commercial Transformation

The commercial transformation process is comprehensive. You want to duplicate both the physical and emotional characteristics that make you succeed at the office. At the same time, you want to retain the characteristics about being home that drew you to a profession that allowed you to work from home. It's a fine line, but the process of commercial transformation will help.

For my commercial transformation, the following sections show how my report card ended up.

FYI!

This is how it's done. Spend one day at your office doing all the things you do. Make a list of what is in your office that includes the following:

◆ The equipment you use

◆ The furnishings and utilities you use

◆ Placement and accessibility that make you productive

◆ The success mindsets you hold

Home Office Equipment

Both my home printer and fax machine needed an upgrade. My phone did not have headset or speakerphone capacity, so I upgraded it. My computer monitor needed to be upgraded to a larger size with a more pleasing display. With these upgrades, my home office duplicated my away-from-home office equipment.

The Inside Scoop

You can connect your laptop to a full-size monitor for easy viewing. I use a full-size monitor both at home and at the office. It saves me neck and eye strain.

Furnishings and Accessibility

As for furnishings, several changes were required. My desk required ergonomic fitting so the keyboard sat in my top drawer. I needed better accessibility to my files, so I had the built-ins rearranged. I made some accessibility changes by reorganizing my desk for easier access to everyday supplies. I actually duplicated the organization I use at the office.

Although I have always been organized at the office, I never really carried commercial organization to my home office. It made a huge difference in work efficiency. Then I relegated my personal home files to a separate area, making my office primarily my efficient home real estate office.

Real Estate Lingo

Feng shui means "wind and water". and is the ancient Chinese science of balancing the elements within the environment. I recommend reading *The Complete Idiot's Guide to Feng Shui* by Elizabeth Moran to learn more about this subject, which has become relevant to the real estate field.

Finally, I changed the whole *feng shui* arrangement of my office furniture. While I still have a clear view of the yard below, my office is more *inner* directed than *outer* directed. It points more toward productivity than gardening. I moved the dog bed farther away from my immediate desk area so access to equipment is easier and my desire to commune with my pup is more subdued. It is important to access your immediate space and reduce its distractions. I also placed the seating in my office in such a way that it does not invite family members to sit down and gab. Now it says, "This is an efficient real estate office. Stay out unless you are an animal or have real estate to sell."

A Successful Mindset

With these physical changes in place, it was much easier to adopt the mental mindset that takes place when I walk over the threshold to my regular office. I now produce as well at home as I do at my traditional office. I still allow my home office to give me great pleasure because I get to be with the dog and have a beautiful view of my yard, but these steps have transformed my home office into a productive environment. I have no more excuses for doing less than the highly competent job I do at the office.

The self-discipline required to make the home office as successful as your other office takes a commitment to exercise rigorous willpower, but the rewards of flexibility and freedom that mark your career will be well worth the work.

Setting Up a Vehicle Office

There are an increasing number of agents with handy offices set up in their vehicles prepared to print out offers, more property flyers, or anything they may need in the field. With SUVs leading the way as a vehicle of choice and portability built into technology, it is now possible to bring your office everywhere you go. Why not have the technology on board when your client decides she must make an offer? Take her up on it, prepare the paperwork, and print it out right on the spot. The high tech solution is a marked improvement to preparing a written offer on the hood of your car as we did not so long ago.

> **The Inside Scoop**
>
> SUVs come with a full array of options for use and convenience. Some also have space and adjacency plans to suit high-tech motorists. If you plan to use your SUV as an office, look into manufacturer options before you have the outfitting performed.

I know agents whose luxurious leather interior SUVs make comfortable offices in the back seat. A handy tray folds down where they sit their laptop, a portable printer prints out their contracts, and wireless Internet and e-mail allows them to send and receive e-mail and multiple listing information. They sit their clients in their luxurious portable offices and fold down the other handy tray for client signing. One even has a mini-refrigerator, which you might think is going too far.

For those of us who relish convenience and like to work, the vehicle office is the perfect solution to utter portability. In my case, I often work from my RV. I can sit in the middle of the woods or on the beach in my RV and conduct business or write books, as I am doing right now.

Working Anywhere in the Field

You can now do everything in the field that you can do in the office. Receipt of faxes used to be a problem but now that we have e-fax services, there are no real obstacles other than the limitations of wireless technology. A landline is preferable to wireless, but it's nice to know wireless is available when you're in a pinch.

For postal mail, we have priority service so even originals can find you as long as you know where you will be. We will know that we've made it to a whole new level of flexibility when the priority mail carriers contact us by e-mail to let us know they are close to shipping so we can redirect packages to the location we have arrived at. I wouldn't be surprised if this convenience isn't available in the very near future.

You may not choose to be as computer capable and portable as I am, but it's comforting to know that technology is there to assist you if you do choose to be a high-tech portable lean mean real estate machine.

The Least You Need to Know

- ◆ You can store documents in a folder on your computer devoted to a specific client, and you can retain a paper file for that client with your transaction coordinator.

- ◆ If you utilize the technology at your disposal, you can eliminate catch-up administrative tasks that need to be done daily.

- ◆ A good calendaring program helps you organize your day and track transaction deadlines, tasks, appointments, and time for prospecting.

- ◆ Various computer devices need to be synchronized so they each contain the most current information.

- ◆ Your home office, your field locations, and your vehicle can all be set up for efficient office use.

Chapter 14

Building a Referral Stream System

In This Chapter

- Building your Referral Stream database
- Learning the basics of database management
- Planning for use of a handheld organizer
- Choosing your client gifts wisely
- Planning your regular mailer and utilizing a newsletter

Back in the olden days, the Rolodex system was considered high-tech. It was a mess. The best way to achieve any level of organization was to stuff someone's business card in the file alphabetically. There was little room to include important information about the person, so you usually ended up scribbling all over the card. The result was that neither the hand-written notes nor the preprinted matter could be read.

In those days we had an excuse for clutter. Now we don't. With the simplified database management systems we have at our fingertips, anyone can be organized. In fact, in the real estate business where the never-ending parade of names and details are the backbone of your business, a foolproof system is a must. The best way I know of is to utilize computer-based contact management. Regardless, many agents are still fighting computer technology.

This chapter shows you how to build your contacts database into a *Referral Stream System* that will turn your business into a circle of abundance. It's all based on three easy steps — set up, input, and processing. For every input, there is an output and from that output there is a return in the form of an ongoing stream of referrals.

Meeting People and Keeping Their Information

Real estate is a people business. It's just plain and simple. You need to know everyone's name and a little bit of information about them. The people (contacts) you will keep track of in your database consist of service providers (peers and Power Team members), new and old clients (as distinguished from prospects), and prospects (people you'd like to have as clients). In the *Referral Stream System* you are about to build, each contact receives one or more marketing products. Here's an example: My next-door-neighbors are entered in my contacts database and categorized to receive a regular mailer and a holiday greeting.

The Inside Scoop

As a people business, real estate is also a gift-based and thanks-based business. Appreciation and celebration are as much a part of the business as commissions and properties. If you set up your business in an organized, computer-based fashion as described in this chapter, you will grow into a referral-based business in no time. Although people think it's who you know, the secret is really how organized you are about the people you get to know.

If you work forty hours a week in the manner described in this book, keep an organized up-to-date contacts database, and follow the *Referral Stream System* to a tee, you will never have to prospect after the first five years of your business. This is known as the *Referral Stream System* because that's exactly how it works. Contacts are entered in your system, they receive gifts and mailers from you, and they give you a steady stream of business.

Keeping Organized and Caretaking

If you step into the mindset of good organization, which I described in the previous chapter, vigilant caretaking of your database becomes one of the primary steps to creating professional and financial abundance. It is important to remember, though, that your contacts database has to go everywhere with you. That's why a smaller, more portable device, like a handheld organizer, is essential. Get used to having this device with you and use it.

The Referral Stream model is based on the premise that every qualified person you come in contact with becomes a relationship you will have for the next 20 years. As such, they end up in your database under easily searchable criteria and on a list to receive one thing or another from you for the rest of your career.

Sounds like a big commitment, doesn't it, treating everyone as if you will know them for the next two decades? Actually, it's the only way to build a business that *will* last for twenty years. With this enduring point of view, your business becomes a flourishing hub of activity because what you give out comes back to you many times over. And you will be giving out a lot, both in terms of service and appreciation. This model is a highly organized, efficient system that makes you unforgettable because you go out of your way for people and you appreciate them. The system is simple and doesn't take much time, and the reward is abundance for the rest of your career.

The plan is built in three easy steps:

1. Setup

2. Input

3. Processing

FYI!

I use Microsoft Outlook for contact management, but other programs keep contacts as well, such as ACT (spelled as ACT!) and Top Producer. I use Outlook because it is packaged with my other office programs and it provides the basic level of contact database management I need. These programs allow you to index each contact under any number of categories, either preset or customized. All you do is check the category you want to apply to a contact.

FYI!

Although multilevel marketing has a bad reputation, it is an excellent business model. In a sense, this type of contact management is multilevel marketing, which occurs within your contacts database based on the categories you set up. Every input receives an automated mailer. You meet a qualified person. You input them and assign them a category. Each category receives an output. The more people you meet and input, the bigger your network becomes.

Step 1–Setup

The categories you will need to set up in your contacts program follow. Feel free to substitute categories:

- ◆ Gift certificates for referrals
- ◆ Buyer gifts
- ◆ Seller gifts
- ◆ Regular mailers
- ◆ Nice to Have Met You cards for prospects (NTHMYs)
- ◆ Holiday cards
- ◆ Birthday greetings

You set these categories up in your contacts database, such as Outlook. In Outlook, you click the Category button on the bottom of the general contact page. Other programs have a similar feature. Then, when you enter a contact, you select the output you want them to receive. It all happens on the contact entry page described in Step 2, the "Input" step.

Gift Certificates for Referrals

Anyone who refers someone who becomes a client goes on the gift certificate list, which you print out and process monthly. A referral source is usually already in the contacts database, but if not, you should enter the contact.

> **The Inside Scoop**
>
> We have an account with an Internet merchandiser and our gift certificates are all sent by our vendor. Just pick a product you like, set up an account with the vendor, and when it comes time to order a gift certificate, all you do is give the vendor your client's delivery information.

Buyer Gifts

For this example, buyers receive personalized engraved brass door plates. A local company prepares these in a matter of days. Clients love this personalized gift which greets them every time they walk through the door of the house they bought. The gift is a nice gesture as well as a constant reminder of you.

Seller Gifts

My seller gifts are a lovely plant and chocolates presented together. These gifts are easy and my clients love them. I have a local vendor who delivers them. Sometimes the chocolates are truffles; sometimes they're chocolate chip cookies. My vendor makes the choice. They're always something special.

Regular Mailers

You should have some type of a regular mailing that goes out to all present, past, and prospective clients and key professionals. A classy newsletter with information about the market and the properties you have listed and sold is always the best choice. However, you don't need to reinvent the wheel by composing your own newsletter. Companies do this for you. They have a set format and information that they personalize with your name and logo. It only looks like you've spent days creating it.

 FYI!

While using local vendors is important to support your community, so is convenience. If you cannot easily locate a local vendor, just go to the Internet and locate a vendor with a product you like. My company orders everything from the Internet and we have never, and I mean never, had a vendor not send a product.

The expense of having the newsletter prepared is a factor to consider. When you add postage and a long mailing list, it can get a bit pricey. Since your mailers go out four times a year, the cost of creating and assembling your mailer, both in terms of time and money, can be in the high hundreds of dollars and several hours. If you feel that the expense of a newsletter is not yet warranted, still mail something quarterly that looks nice. Always keep in mind that *Market* is your middle name. You become your best mover and shaker when you consistently let people know you are moving and shaking.

The Inside Scoop

To find companies that prepare personalized real estate newsletters, do an Internet search for "real estate marketing newsletter vendors," or a variation of that. Better yet, send your clients a beautiful customized magazine (without advertising) with your compliments. Recently, I was able to break into a hard-to-get market with this type of high-end product. Go to hbdmagazine.com for a sample.

For the agent specializing in a certain neighborhood or market, describing properties sold or for sale is an excellent marketing theme. For example, one agent continually mails lists of properties sold and sale prices in the neighborhood where I live. It gets my attention because I have a high interest in the value of my home, as we all do. To the novice, it appears as if this agent has personally sold all of the described properties. There is no misrepresentation. The agent didn't say she sold these properties, they are just described as properties sold in the neighborhood. This is a very good marketing mailer. I would not be surprised if soon every property on her mailing list is her own listing.

Nice to Have Met You Cards (NTHMYs)

A NTHMY follow-up card or e-mail should be sent to all potential clients, whether you gave them a formal seller or buyer presentation (discussed in later chapters) or just discussed their real estate needs. People appreciate good manners. You want each prospect to receive your message right after you meet with them.

In my business, NTHMYs are not handled by category selection in contacts. You can handle them that way if you choose and for this reason they are included as a category. I like to process them immediately so I handle them on a priority basis. When I schedule an appointment with prospects, I immediately enter them on my calendar for the day after the appointment to send a card. I never leave it to memory. I have e-mail and regular mail NTHMYs. I grab the one that applies when my calendar sends my reminder, include a brief personal greeting, and it's done.

When I enter my NTHMY contact, sometimes I include them in the regular mailer category and sometimes I don't. It all depends on how much I want a relationship with that prospect for the next twenty years. Always think in terms of longevity. That's what makes this model so successful. When a prospect turns into a buyer or seller, they are added to the appropriate buyer or seller gift category. If they were not already targeted for a regular mailer, an entry is made to add them.

FYI!

Last year our holiday mailing consisted of a card containing a CD of Christmas classics with a picture of me and my dog dressed in fancy red and green attire on the label. I go all out for Christmas, and look for something that will stand out from other agents. You don't have to go to the same expense, but do take care selecting whatever you choose to represent you.

Holiday Cards

We only do one mailing of holiday cards each year at Christmas time. Just about every buyer, seller, prospect, and regular business contact is on the list. A simple card to wish these people well will do. I generally go with a generic message like "Seasons Greetings" or "Happy Holidays", as some people do not observe this occasion as Christmas.

Birthday Greetings

Anyone whose birthday was filled out in the contacts detail page under *birthday* should receive an e-mailed birthday card on their birthday when they come up on the calendar. If there is no e-mail address, cards should be sent by mail. You don't even have to perform a category search to send your birthday cards since the contact management program automatically displays each birthday entered on your calendar for that date. My company has one standard birthday card that is used for a year, and then we switch to a new one for the next year.

The Inside Scoop

Do a search on the Internet for birthday e-cards. Most can be sent free of charge. You may need a real card as well, for those people who do not have an e-mail address or those special people you want to greet more personally with postal delivery. In these high-tech times, people often feel more appreciated when you take the extra time to send a greeting through the mail.

Step 2—Input

Here's an example of how this works. At the Chamber of Commerce meeting, I met Bill, a mortgage broker. I had my handheld organizer with me. I find that just the process of entering contact information can bring about lively conversation. I was impressed with Bill and how he conducted himself. We exchanged cards and I said, "Bill, I want to make sure I have your information in my database. Do you mind if I enter you right now and ask you a few more questions?" People love the opportunity to speak about themselves. They are also quite impressed with your level of organization and computer competence. It took me two minutes of fun conversation to enter the information I need for Bill into my handheld organizer.

Real estate is a people business, and you don't want to detract from its social quality. In the beginning, entering data can be clumsy and impersonal. Hang in there; it's worth it. Because you are already a multitasking real estate professional, you'll soon be a pro at inputting information and making lively conversation at the same time.

The information I enter includes the following:

- Name
- Address
- Telephone
- Fax
- E-mail

- ◆ Profession

- ◆ Birthday

- ◆ Notes, such as "Chamber of Commerce, in business for 20 years."

- ◆ Categories, such as "newsletter" or "holiday card"

Simple. I made nine brief entries in the fields described in this list. In Outlook, these entries appear on the general and detail pages for a contact. Because I spent two minutes entering Bill's information, he will automatically come up on my newsletter mailing list and my holiday card list. He will also appear on my calendar on his birthday so we can send him a birthday card. I will also be able to send him an e-mail or fax by just clicking a button.

> ### The Inside Scoop
>
> To locate a contact in a certain profession, in Microsoft Outlook, go to Tools, Advanced Find, Advanced, Field, Personal fields, Profession. Other contact programs have similar search capabilities.

I will be able to access him for mortgage information and to send him clients without even recalling his name. Because I entered his profession as mortgage broker, he comes up under an advanced search for "mortgage broker" under the field "Profession" along with all the mortgage brokers in my database.

When Bill called me a few months later, I didn't remember him. I could, however, search for his name (which took just a few seconds), and I could instantly see how I came into contact with him and all the important information about him. Quick and easy retrieval of information is invaluable, especially when your contacts database is brimming. On this call from Bill, he mentioned his wife by name, and so I added his wife's name to his contact information.

People love to be remembered and appreciated, especially in a service-oriented industry like real estate. Bill will be part of my business for all the years to come because I took two minutes to include him in my database. Since our initial meeting not two years ago, Bill has referred six people who became clients.

Step 3—Processing

Step 3, Processing, is the final step before the Referral Stream begins to take hold. The gift department processes gifts monthly while the snail-mail department performs its processing at varying intervals. The processing department at my office is my assistant who looks a lot like Mrs. Santa on processing day.

The Gift Department

The gift department in my office processes the following gifts monthly:

- ◆ Gift certificates for referrals
- ◆ Buyer gifts
- ◆ Seller gifts

The gift department does everything by e-mail. Because gifting in these categories occurs monthly, we just use the fourth Friday of every month for gift certificates, buyer gifts, and seller gifts categories. On that day, we click a button and receive contact information for anyone coming under those categories with each category run separately.

For gift certificates, we go directly to the Internet vendor we have selected for gift certificates and enter the recipient name and address. It takes a minute per person.

For buyer and seller gifts, we e-mail the contacts coming within those categories to our respective vendors who include a nice thank-you card from us with their deliveries.

> **The Inside Scoop**
>
> The Internet vendor will send either an e-mail gift certificate or a paper gift certificate. They handle the mailing. All we need to do is select from e-mail delivery or regular mail delivery, and supply the recipient address. Oh yes, I forgot: We also have to pay for this certificate. We, of course, use the business credit card because this is a deductible expense.

The Snail-Mail Department

Now to the snail-mail department. This department handles the following categories at the intervals specified:

- ◆ Regular mailers
- ◆ NTHMY cards
- ◆ Holiday cards
- ◆ Birthday cards if recipients are not regular e-mail users

For a regular mailer, if your choice is a newsletter, most likely you have signed up with a real estate newsletter publisher and every quarter you receive the shipment you request. These arrive automatically once you're on their quarterly list. Most of these companies will also mail the newsletters for you. For other mailers, how your mailing is handled is a matter of time and money depending on how long your mailing list is. Your mailing list is produced by calling up all contacts that come under your regular mailer category.

> **FYI!**
>
> If you send a personalized newsletter, consider having the publisher do your mailing. All you need to do is e-mail your contact list to the publisher. If you do the mailing in-house, it is fairly easy to print out labels for all contacts within a specific category. The labels get slapped on, postage or bulk mail is applied, and that's it. You can easily and quickly head up the mailing department in your early days and sit around for a few hours with your family enjoying a little time together growing your business.

In my company, for holiday cards we use a service or my assistant does them. We calendar a month and a half ahead of time for ordering the cards. NTHMYs and birthday cards are sent by snail mail or e-mail on the day they come up on the calendar.

Reviewing the Referral Stream

Bill, the sample mortgage broker, illustrates what happens when you enter a contact into your database. So far you haven't seen the stream of referrals resulting from the *Referral Stream System*. Here is an example of a seller. Carol and James sold their vacation home with my help. After they received their seller gift from us, they continued to appear on the holiday card and regular mailer list.

Carol and James referred eleven people over the next seven years, three of whom ended up as buyers and two as sellers. Three of the other referrals did not become clients, but they referred clients which resulted in two more purchases. The remaining three have not culminated in any business or prospects. One of these three is still on our quarterly mailer list.

> **The Inside Scoop**
>
> We also added Carol and James to the gift certificate category when a client was referred by them. By showing our appreciation, they will continue to remember us whenever anyone mentions real estate.

The three buyers Carol and James referred have resulted in fourteen referrals, which have resulted in five sales. One was a repeat sale. The two sellers they referred resulted in two purchases since they both purchased when they sold and seven referrals which have resulted in two sales. You can see the result of doing a good job for Carol and James and keeping in touch with them via the *Referral Stream System*. Just taking it to the third level I have described and no further brought in thirteen purchases or sales, which at an average 3 percent commission for properties worth $250,000, resulted in commissions of $97,500.

Was it worth spending the time to run the *Referral Stream System* to send gifts, holiday cards, gift certificates, and quarterly newsletters to Carol and James and the same to the other twelve clients to earn $97,500? I would estimate that to earn this referral income stream of $97,500, the time spent inputting contacts or automating my system was three hours and the cost of gifts and mailers was about $2200. Of course, that doesn't include the time it took to service listings and find buyer homes, but it shows that the *Referral Stream System* is well worth the time and money.

> **Caution**
>
> If you share your commission with an office, your commissions will naturally be reduced accordingly.

Examining the Philosophy

When you do a good job for people, they remember you, but only for a little while. When you do a good job for people and give them a gift, they remember you a little longer. When you do a good job for them, give them a gift, and continually stay in touch, they remember you forever. That's the philosophy of the *Referral Stream System*. And it works.

The system is based on principles of psychology and sociology. You show people your competence, and they remember you in the competence sector of their brains. You give them a gift and let them know you appreciate them, and you are also remembered in the nice person sector. When you continually remind them of you, you reactivate the places in which your memory is stored. With Carol and James, I was in two areas, which were activated five times a year with my quarterly mailer and our Christmas cards, not including gift certificates they received. I was therefore on their minds whenever they thought about real estate.

Tips on Making the System Work

Don't be cheap with your gifts. Remember, you will know these people for at least twenty more years. You are an important part of their lives when you assist them with their transactions, and they contribute to your financial abundance through the commissions they pay you.

Choosing recipients wisely is another important step. Make sure the people you add to your *Referral Stream System* are qualified. Establish a definition of your own as to who is qualified. Buyer, seller, and prospect checklists for qualification are presented in later chapters. Good common sense and the ability to recognize the difference between qualified people and non-qualified ones is essential to making your model work well. If you aren't discerning, you could end up spending too much time inputting contacts or too much money on gifts or mailings. If you follow the suggested criteria, your database contacts will all be qualified and your time and money will be justified since the result will be an enviable referral stream.

The Inside Scoop

This efficient plan won't work if the gift department spends too much time shopping, shipping, or shuttling. That means choosing your products well and setting them up for automatic delivery. You need to work with reliable and efficient vendors who can receive your orders by e-mail and deliver those orders to your clients. In this way, your vendors become your shipping department. Otherwise, your new job will be managing the processing department. With a full client base, our processing takes no more than two hours a month. We have more important things to do than process gifts and mailers.

A final note is, why spend your time cold-calling, which no one enjoys? Why not spend it setting up a good marketing system and working the system? You still need to get out there, greet your market, and put contacts into your system. But once you've got them in the system, you can keep them if you stay on top of your system. I guarantee it.

The Least You Need to Know

- The *Referral Stream System* is built on the premise that for every input there is an automated output.

- If you choose your gifts and mailers carefully, your recipients will appreciate your taste and generosity and will remember you.

- The *Referral Stream System* must be vigilantly followed both in terms of input of contacts and processing of gifts and mailers.

- The success of the *Referral Stream System* lies in its ability to get your name and your goodwill to recipients on a regular basis over the long term.

- Consider use of a mailing service for your regular mailers and holiday cards.

Chapter 15

The New Ideal

In This Chapter

- ◆ The New Ideal in representing your clients
- ◆ Sales pitches are a thing of the past
- ◆ Understanding your fiduciary duty to your client
- ◆ Your client's endless decisions
- ◆ Extending the New Ideal to your peers

In other real estate sales books, this would be the chapter on sales. In this book, it's on dealing with your client and peers in a more authentic, professional manner. It presents a *New Ideal* for the services agents render their clients and the way agents treat their clients and one another.

During the last two decades, the hard sell was the standard for real estate and how real estate agents represented their clients. As a result, the real estate sales profession has entered this new century with a reputation that requires serious bolstering.

The New Ideal presented in this book is about bringing the real estate profession up a level so that we are treated as the professionals we deserve to be and our clients receive the quality service they always deserved.

The Times, They Are a-Changin'

Times have changed, but some agents still use the same old high-pressure sales techniques advocated by sales trainers. The style of agents who fancy-talk their clients with sales scripts and other trickster routines is outdated and certainly not in pace with our sophisticated and savvy modern-day real estate clients. Nor does it fulfill the agency obligations agents have to clients.

Real estate buyers and sellers no longer want to be assaulted by sales gimmicks of yesteryear. They ask their real estate legal representatives to pressure them less and treat them more like respected clients in need of reliable guidance. They want to be treated intelligently and honestly, not as though they can be tricked. Sincere and willing agents want to be thought of as more professional. However, we have not yet bridged the gap between pushy salesperson and professional representative.

> ### The Inside Scoop
>
> The National Association of Realtors reports that only 40 percent of sellers used the agent who assisted them with the sale of their previous home for their most recent purchase. This statistic alone shows that real estate consumers are dissatisfied with the representation they currently receive.

The problem isn't only client dissatisfaction. Legal issues exist. The use of sales techniques practiced on clients does not legally satisfy your fiduciary duty to a client. The law gives one important legal directive to agents while outdated sales training techniques give another. They are in conflict.

If you follow *The New Ideal* set in this book and put the interests of your clients ahead of your financial success, you will find legal, moral, and financial satisfaction in abundance. You will be rewarded with commissions, referrals, and your clients' high regard. In addition, your clients will receive the fiduciary representation the law always said they would have.

Performing Our Fiduciary Duty

A fiduciary duty is the legal duty an agent owes his or her client in a real estate transaction. Exactly what is this important relationship that all real estate agents should aspire to maintain with clients? A fiduciary acts on behalf of his client with the utmost of care, integrity, honesty, confidentiality, and loyalty. Your mission is to take all steps with your client's best interest in mind. You are your client's trusted advocate.

This is the highest duty the law imposes. The fiduciary relationship is therefore the most important legal relationship any two people can have. It is a relationship built on the highest of trust where the agent is designated the legal caretaker of his client. It is actually more consequential than marriage because the fiduciary relationship legally requires one to act in the other's best interest; in marriage, the obligation is only moral (and for some couples, it's not even that). Even the lawyer-client relationship does not meet the very high standards legally imposed on real estate agents.

Recognizing the Sales Scripts

Some sales trainers compare the real estate agent-client relationship to hunting. The correlation goes like this:

> When you go hunting, when would you load your gun—when you see the rabbit or before you start walking? If you wait until the rabbit appears, by the time you get your gun loaded, it's certain to have scampered off.

You are instructed to treat your client as the rabbit you are stalking, to hold your unsuspecting rabbit in your focus, and continually berate him or her with sales scripts. The purpose isn't really to kill the client; it's to push him or her to your only objective: closing on a deal.

Motivational sales trainers describe clients as "sitting on the fence" when they are faced with concern and indecision. They tell you this is the time to hit 'em with a script. Pressure does it. Get 'em while they're down.

 FYI!

If your client isn't ready to sign a listing, sales trainers instruct you to hit her with the following:

> Are you sure you can afford to wait? You never know when the market is going to begin its downward spiral. I have seen too many clients wait just long enough to miss a good market and have to sell at a much lower price.

If the client isn't sure whether to make an offer, trainers use fear again:

> This property has attracted a lot of interest since it hit the market. I hate to see you lose it. Nice properties like this don't come along very often. In fact, when I spoke with the listing agent this morning, I think she mentioned something about expecting an offer later today.

This canned script has nothing to do with the property. It is quite effective, though, in getting client buyers to sign on the dotted line.

There are hundreds of sales scripts for every occasion. Some are tailored to be delivered in particular rooms of a house. Some work in any room. One is the very sad story of your last client who waited and lost the home they loved. They never bought another. There wasn't another one like the one they lost. The well-trained agent is able to deliver these lies with sincerity and emotion, thereby instigating the emotion of concern in the wavering buyer.

Agents are often instructed to hide blank offers in a notepad they carry around so they can pull one out just as they are ready to strike their unsuspecting buyer client with the closing script. There isn't time to open your briefcase and take an offer out. You've got to strike quickly.

Some trainers teach you that you must drive your buyer clients to properties. One reason is to maintain control. The other is to condition them by the careful delivery of sales scripts while you have them in your car. There are scripts about getting them in your car so you can feed them these scripts. For the challenging situation when there are too many buyers to get in your car, the answer is to scoop up the children and take them in your car. This ploy is called "Kidnapping the Kids." The parents are guaranteed to show up when you have their children, and you can work on the impressionable kids in your car.

> **Caution**
>
> Stay away from sales gimmicks. If you were trained with them, think before you speak. If it's a sales script, replace it with a genuine desire to facilitate what your client needs and wants.

The sales script is aimed at one thing and one thing only: inducing pressure and fear in clients. These scripts are professionally designed to work these two human emotions to motivate the unsuspecting client. And they do work. They cause buyers to buy when they should pause and evaluate. They cause sellers to sell when another course of action might serve them better. The result is the demoralization of a profession that should be revered as one that discharges the highest legal and ethical obligation to its clientele.

Participating in the Transformation

The rabbit-hunting analogy and the kidnap-the-kids routine blatantly depict the grave need for a transformation of the real estate sales profession. The sales script may have had its place years ago when the real estate industry was still in its infancy. Now that real estate has matured into a multibillion dollar industry and a most popular investment choice, the time has come to overhaul the foundation of the agent-client relationship.

You've come to a profession that is held in low esteem. On the ladder of disrespect, real estate agents come just above used-car salesmen. You therefore have an image problem to overcome, and *The New Ideal* is your tool. The first step is to look more closely at the fiduciary relationship you establish with your client and the legal obligation it imposes.

When does the fiduciary relationship begin and end? It begins the first moment you have contact with the person who becomes your client all the way through discharge of your fiduciary obligation. The person to whom you are pitching sales gimmicks in your listing presentation is the person with whom you are forming a fiduciary relationship. How can you, in good and legal conscience, serve this potential client with anything less than bona fide goodwill and good real estate practice? We look at how in the following sections.

Dropping the Hard Sell

Real estate does not require the hard sell. Nor do your services. However, you are often told that you must master your sales skills and apply them expertly for anyone to hire your services. I disagree. I believe that you have a professional service to render but no product to hard-sell.

Real estate trainers often analogize real estate sales with sales of other products, such as computers, cars, and cellular phones. They talk apples and oranges. In product sales you need to talk up your product in comparison to another product. Product sales are competition driven, for instance, comparing an IBM to a Dell computer. You answer the question of why your product is better than theirs. In product sales you must be one up on your competition and a salesperson in every sense of the word.

But real estate sales are different. You are not direct-selling a product. You work with listings on a centralized database through which real estate sells itself with your skilled representation. You offer your professional representation to a client who has real estate to buy or sell. The way to do this isn't with sales pitches; it is through the delivery of quality professional services.

FYI!

You don't hear doctors or other professionals walking around saying they want to sell their services. "Hey, fella, how about a nice kidney transplant?" Doctors, accountants, and other professionals are facilitators of services. Real estate agents, too, are facilitators of purchases and sales of real estate. Why, then, are real estate agents pushed to become master salespeople?

Demand for Agent Services

The statistics on real estate appreciation are compelling, and become even more so when tax benefits are considered. Over the past two decades real estate has become the top investment choice for a growing segment of society. Everybody needs a home, many people need real estate investments, and others need real estate for their businesses. Real estate is in high demand, especially since the stock market has proven unpredictable. There is more need for an agent's services than ever before due to the increased demand for real estate.

The ever-increasing complexity of the real estate transaction also means increased need for agent services. The routine purchase and sales transaction has transformed into a complex, multistage operation. Property disclosures become more complicated every year, as do the number of details and players involved in a real estate transaction.

In a single transaction, an agent may deal with as many as 35 people. Agents work with people and computers; they complete contract documents, coordinate professionals, and review complex disclosures and reports; and they use psychology, analysis, and other people skills. Agents deal with valuable and coveted assets, sometimes in the million-dollar range. In addition, agents must navigate their clients through all these transactions during high times of stress and in very brief timeframes.

Given the breadth and depth of what agents handle, it doesn't make sense to perceive them as salespeople. The real job is for agents to adopt a new mindset. We must provide quality, professional services to our clients, not to get their listings or sign on their purchases, but because we are their fiduciary representatives. If you make your client's interest more important than your own, you will attract and keep far more clients than the master salesperson. You will also be meeting your legal obligation.

Appreciating the Client's Decisions

Clients are making the biggest decisions of their lives and may be making the largest financial investment they have ever handled. That alone makes clients vulnerable to the most nerve-racking reasons for indecision. Equally as mind-boggling is the fact that the home purchaser is trying to satisfy the personal and emotional needs of his entire family. Home buyers must evaluate their most basic human needs affecting how they live and where they live. The investment property buyer is investing money into what she hopes is a valuable investment for her and her family.

These days there is also another layer of analysis a buyer must make. How will they hold title? Should they have a living trust, and what about a *family limited partnership*?

With an investment property, should they utilize *asset protection* and form a *limited-liability company* to hold title?

Real Estate Lingo

Asset protection refers to the sheltering of assets from excessive taxation and lawsuit-taking by the use of irrevocable living trusts, family limited partnerships, house trusts, and limited liability companies, to name a few.

A **family-limited partnership** is a specially designed limited partnership consisting of one or more general partners and one or more limited partners, which can provide asset protection from personal liability and discount valuation for estate tax purposes.

A **limited-liability company** affords its members limited liability similar to shareholders of a corporation and pass-through taxation similar to a sole-proprietorship or partnership. It can provide asset protection and discount valuation for estate tax purposes.

The following is a partial list of decisions clients face when purchasing a home or an investment property:

Decisions About a Home Purchase

- Is this the right home for our family?

- Can we afford this home? What are our financing options?

- Will this home be easy to sell when we are ready to sell?

- Is this the best home for the price?

- Will the commute to and from work be difficult?

- Are there good schools and other children in the neighborhood?

- Is the structure of this home sound? Are there any repairs we will need to make?

- Is there room for a garden? What is the weather like?

- Is it in an earthquake or flood zone? Will I be able to get enough insurance?

- What will the expenses be for utilities and repairs?

- Have we been careful enough with the inspections? Are there any hidden problems?

- Are DSL, cable, and satellite available here?

- Where are the property boundaries? Are there easements affecting this home?

- Is there development nearby that will threaten our privacy and property values?

- Is this a safe neighborhood?

- How should the title be stated?

Decisions About an Investment Property Purchase

- Will its income justify its expense?

- What are its tax deductions?

- Will *depreciation* represent a good deduction for my portfolio?

- Can I take any *passive losses*?

- Can I *exchange* tax free into this property? Can I exchange out of this property?

Real Estate Lingo _____

Depreciation is the allocation of the cost of an improvement over the life of the asset in the form of a tax deduction.

Passive loss is a loss in excess of income on a rental property.

Exchange is trading a business or investment property or properties for others to avoid taxation of profits.

- What is my tax basis if I exchange into this property?

- Would I be better off just putting my hard-earned money in the stock market?

- What is the rental market for this property?

- What are the terms of the existing leases on this property?

- Can I increase the rents for the existing tenants?

- Can I occupy any of the property?

♦ Would I be better off creating a limited liability company and taking title in its name?

♦ Will insurance cover me in the event of a lawsuit?

As the purchaser's agent, you will often be involved in your client's deliberations when considering these vital issues. As their advocate, always be aware of the consequences of the decisions that face them. It is only through this awareness that you can best discharge your obligation to support their best interest in the transaction.

Supporting Clients

You will find yourself involved in client deliberations or decision-making. In the course of transactions, some clients attempt to second-guess themselves and try to undo what they have done. I am never surprised when clients turn around and head in the other direction. As their advocate, you want to take away the stress and give your clients the space and support they need to make well-informed decisions. The very last thing they need is their trusted agent feeding them scripts intended to move them to buy or sell irrespective of their needs.

FYI!

If your clients lean in favor of terminating a transaction, suggest they see an attorney. Do not try to strong-arm clients with threats of a potential lawsuit from the other party or that they are breaking the contract. Some agents even go so far as to tell their clients that they have earned their commission and they intend to enforce their commission rights against them. Don't turn your back on your clients, especially in a time of high stress when your clients need your support the most. There are legal rights; and then there is personal integrity and fiduciary responsibility.

Replacing the Scripts

When you're having an interaction with a client or potential client and you don't know what to say, just be honest and put their interest first. Your client interactions are just that—conversations between two people, one of whom has a fiduciary relationship with another. If you don't know an answer, say you don't know. If you do know an answer and your interest conflicts with theirs, choose your client's interest.

Here are some typical client questions followed by a typical sales-trainer script and what the agent following *The New Ideal* might say. It is quite telling to compare the difference in flavor between the scripted response and *The New Ideal* response:

Question 1: "Won't you reduce your commission?"

Script: "Which services do you want me to cut, marketing or listing?"

The New Ideal **response**: "This is what we charge to give you the very best service. If we charged less, we would have to give you less. We don't do that."

Question 2: "Another agent said he would list my property at a higher price."

Script: "The truth is that many agents will tell you anything, especially a listing price not justified by the market, to get you to sign on with them."

The New Ideal **response**: "The listing price I suggest is based on a detailed and careful analysis of the market based on the comparables I shared with you. A higher price is not supported. I feel it would be a disservice to you to list the property at a higher price."

Question 3: "We would like a shorter listing term."

Script: "It takes a good six months to sell a home. If we didn't give this six months, I could not do a good job for you."

The Inside Scoop

When you are responding to a client question, try to keep in mind the principle of "Do unto others as you would have them do unto you."

The New Ideal **response**: "Whatever term makes you most comfortable is fine with me as long as we start with an initial term that gives me a good chance to fully market your property. We can always extend after that if it doesn't sell and you are happy with my services."

Question 4: "We want to think it over."

Script: "Are you sure you can afford to wait? You never know when the market will go south. The market is good now. That's all we know."

The New Ideal **response**: "Sure. Take your time. Your choice of agent to sell your valuable asset is very important. I don't plan to be away so contact me when you're ready, and I will stay in touch. In the interim, review my package and give me a call if I can answer any questions for you."

Question 5: "We are thinking about renting our property out instead of selling it."

Script: "Recently I spent time with an agent who rented his home in this area. … [long story] … so instead of receiving rent, he had to hire an attorney, file a lawsuit, and refurbish the property. It all cost him $12,000 in addition to the rent he lost." (This is not a true story, but it is the script you are urged to give.)

The New Ideal **response**: "Our database also includes rental prices. I can provide you with some rental figures for the area if you like so you can further analyze this option. It's all up to you. Whatever you want is right for me."

Relating to the Competition

The problem hasn't just been the relationships between agents and clients. We need to transform the way we treat our fellow agents as well. As we change our client relationship from salesperson to facilitator, we must also change the competitive way we treat our peers. Competitiveness is part of sales mentality. It is not a part of professionalism and high integrity.

Competition consciousness goes hand in hand with high-pressure sales. It takes fear of others pulling ahead of you to fuel your motivation. The result is the real estate field becomes a back-biting, dog-eat-dog industry full of agents willing to do just about anything to get business. This attitude does not speak highly of the profession, and it takes its toll on the relationship between agents. *The New Ideal*, therefore, also extends to upgrading the way we treat our fellow agents.

Real Estate Lingo

There are two definitions of a professional: (a) One who is worthy of high standards; (b) One who practices a profession for his or her livelihood. The real estate agent with *The New Ideal* fits both definitions.

Predicting the Result

If you follow the steps in this book, you have chosen real estate sales as your profession because you are willing to discharge your legal obligation to clients in a professional way. You are genuinely interested in helping people find their next home, office, or investment property that will serve them through the upcoming years. There's really no good reason why you should strong arm someone into hiring you. You're good at what you do. You enjoy doing what you're doing. People need your service.

Find your clients through successful marketing described in the chapters on marketing. Genuinely and intelligently offer them your professional services to represent them in their purchase or sale. Let them know you are not part of the old soft shuffle. Define the fiduciary obligation you have to them and commit to your willingness to fulfill it.

Realize that real estate is in high demand, as are your services. Discard salesmanship and competitive attitudes as you embrace *The New Ideal*. The natural result of practicing this type of high-integrity professionalism is that you will gain market share and you will feel a pride that will permeate your professional life. Hopefully, someday soon sales mentality will be a thing of the past in real estate sales. You will be on the cutting edge and clients will naturally gravitate your way because you are part of this *New Ideal*. High integrity and competence draw people like a magnet. It is an unbeatable combination.

The Least You Need to Know

- ◆ The hard-sell tactic puts you in the same category as the slick, used-car salesman.

- ◆ The law has decreed that you have a powerful fiduciary relationship with your clients.

- ◆ Buying and selling property are complex transactions and require that the client make many difficult, important decisions.

- ◆ Acting with high integrity and putting the client's interest first results in a good conscience, an excellent reputation, and a stream of referrals.

- ◆ Treating your fellow peers with respect instead of competitive disregard will improve your relationship with peers and clients alike.

Chapter 16

A Winning Listing Presentation

In This Chapter

- Qualifying potential sellers
- Putting your listing package together
- Making the listing presentation
- Conducting the comparative market analysis
- Using the listing agreement and sample net sheet

This chapter is about qualifying your seller prospect and making your listing presentation. Qualifying the seller is essential to cutting down on the time you spend with a seller prospect. After you qualify your seller, prepare your listing package, make your presentation, and have the seller sign a listing agreement.

The components of your listing package are of vital importance because they set the stage for your listing presentation. This chapter describes each document that should be included in your listing package and exactly

---

how you should present the listing package. The following chapter is on representing the seller after you receive the listing. Chapter 18 covers representing the buyer, and Chapter 19 addresses what to do when you are asked to represent both the buyer and the seller.

Qualifying Sellers

Time is a most precious commodity. If you don't have a clear plan in mind in the real estate field, you can easily end up spending too much of your time with potential clients who are not ready to buy or sell. You want to help them, and you understand that it takes time to prepare to buy or sell. However, your income depends on commissions.

Client inquisition is my terminology for the process of a potential client taking up far too much of my time just learning about real estate. The only way you can control your time is by setting boundaries. To do this, you must qualify your potential clients early on. If they don't qualify, you can certainly assist them, but at least you will know where they stand so you can gauge your time accordingly.

Let's walk through the steps of the important qualification process. Assume that through successful application of your marketing skills and your *Referral Stream System*, you are in communication with a seller prospect. Now what do you do? If your prospects are not in a seller state of mind, it will not behoove you to dedicate large quantities of time and energy to them. There is no such thing as a perfect client, but you can come close to finding one by qualifying your potential sellers. If they qualify, you give them the full-blown listing presentation. If not, put them on your list of prospects to receive mailers.

Here is a list of questions to ask of your seller prospect. These questions will serve both to qualify a seller and to get helpful information for preparation of your listing package:

1. When do you plan to move?

2. How soon do you want to list your property for sale?

3. After you list it for sale, how long do you anticipate it will take to close on a sale?

4. How much do you think your property is worth?

5. How did you arrive at this value?

6. If this is a home you intend to replace, have you begun to look at other homes? Have you found any you are interested in? What is the price range of your replacement home?

7. If the property in question is not your primary home, do you intend to buy another property?

8. How far are you in the agent-interviewing process?

9. What is the most important factor you will consider in choosing to list your property with one agent over another?

10. (Include this question if you feel the prospect is qualified.) Can you give me the amount you owe on the property so I may prepare some figures for you as part of my listing presentation?

11. (If warranted) When can I come by to see your property and give you a brief listing presentation?

12. (If warranted) May I bring my professional stager with me? She is a wiz at deciding what steps, if any, should be taken to get the top price for your property. (Professional staging is covered in the next chapter.)

> **The Inside Scoop**
>
> Qualifying your clients is probably one of the most important time-saving steps you can take. After you have done this about 15 times, the process will come naturally to you. In the beginning, a checklist approach helps.

If your potential seller is ready to list the property within the next 60 days or so, you will know it from the answers you obtain through this qualification process. If the seller is ready, you can take the next step, which is preparing your listing package.

Listing Presentations

The sales trainers make a listing presentation sound like you're auditioning for a part in a Hollywood movie. They suggest you spend two hours selling your potential client on yourself. The big to-do is all very contrived, dramatic, and unprofessional. They give you yet another inventory of fancy scripts to spew forth in order to bring the big one in for a close.

 FYI!

The National Association of Realtors reports that sellers of homes typically interviewed just one agent before selecting the agent who ultimately sold their home.

Let's put away the script and begin anew in an entirely different way. Remember, it is a fiduciary relationship of the utmost trust and confidence we are building here, not selling a horse. The listing package you prepare will form the basis of your presentation, so let's take a look at what that package should consist of.

But first, let me suggest that you bring your professional stager along to your listing presentation when warranted. Your stager should be prepared to conduct an onsite analysis of the property and recommend prelisting steps that will enhance the marketability of the property. I find that clients are quite impressed when a stager is brought to the listing presentation. You will have to make the judgment call for the area in which you practice and the property to be listed.

Your Listing Package

In real estate, looks are important. When preparing your listing package, make it look good. Use nice paper and a good color printer. The seller will assess your marketing abilities by the presentation of the documents in your listing package. Make the very most of this opportunity.

Every listing presentation is worth giving your all with intelligent, well-delivered information and an earnest desire to help. The listing package you prepare will serve as your calling card. The seller will review it many times over. It will be compared with other listing packages. If it is good, you may be assured it will receive the review of many eyes.

I suggest your presentation package consist of the following, either bound or neatly organized in a professional preprinted folder and in the following order:

FYI!

In my area of the country where prices are off the charts, high-end offices put together 35-page, full-color, glossy, bound listing packages. They are no less than works of fine art and literature. Very impressive.

- Current market trends page and marketing plan
- Your office and personal bio and mission statement
- Your most recent mailer
- Comparative market analysis in full color
- Sample net sheet
- Your agency disclosure form and a sample listing agreement

Your listing package will make your listing presentation simple because it will be your guide to exactly what you cover during the presentation. Have a copy for yourself and one for your client so you can review these documents together. If your stager has analyzed the property in advance of your presentation, include your stager's recommendations and cost estimate. Your listing presentation should be no longer than one half to three quarters of an hour. Bring your laptop computer so you can show your prospect exactly how a new listing appears on the MLS (multiple listing service).

Provide a Current Market Trends Page and Marketing Plan

Include a page on current market trends. This should be colorful and include graphs showing statistics that will be important to this seller. Don't just pull these figures. Explain them to your prospective sellers.

FYI!

Important statistics your market trends page should include are:

- ◆ Number of properties listed in the same category as the seller
- ◆ Average list price for the properties listed in the same category
- ◆ Average days on the market until closing
- ◆ Average list price compared to sale price
- ◆ Your or your company's statistics in comparison

In your marketing plan, tell the seller exactly how you intend to undertake the job at hand. Describe the *broker's open*, the frequency at which you will hold *open houses*, newspaper advertising and frequency, lock box use, and other marketing methods you will use. Detail the features of the property that you will highlight in your marketing. If you plan to feature the property on a website, or give it a website of its own, describe your plan. Let them know you have really thought about this, because you have thought about it.

Real Estate Lingo

The **broker's open** is the property showing for the agent community as opposed to the **open house** which is for the public.

Prepare Your Bio and Mission Statement

Clients want to know who you are almost as much as what you will do for them. They are interviewing you for the important job of selling their valued asset. Include a mission statement that distinguishes your services from the rest of the pack.

Include information about the company you work for, but keep it to a minimum if you personally have an impressive listing history to show. If not, include the company's listing and sales statistics, but also include information about yourself.

If you do have an impressive history, list current and past listings. Include client contact information (if those clients have given you permission). Attach letters your clients have written thanking you for your help.

> ### The Inside Scoop
>
> People often shy away from talking about themselves, especially boasting about their past successes. If this is the case for you, your inclination will be to leave the reading of your bio to the seller. Don't. Make sure you cover your bio in your oral listing presentation. Although sellers often review listing packages after presentation, you can't rely on that. Why blow this important opportunity by leaving out what may be the most important factor to the seller? If you have multiple transactions under your belt, you may want to have a separate bio aimed for the seller, and one directed at the buyers.

I keep clients' complimentary letters in a file called Testimonials. These letters are added to my website and my resumé. Keep your bio to one page if possible, excluding attachments. Make it look professional by using standard resumé format and impressive by using classic fonts. Include some color. Depending on your bio, it can be the most important component of your listing package.

Include Your Mailer in the Listing Presentation Package

Include your most recent marketing mailer with your listing package. Some agents have a mailer covering a variety of topics. If you have one tailored to the steps in a transaction or the services you will provide to the seller, include that. If you have a newsletter, include your last one. If you give free seminars, include your schedule.

Real Estate Lingo

A **CMA**, or **comparative market analysis**, is a summary of comparable properties in the area that have sold recently, generally in the last six months. Comparable properties are those with similar numbers of bedrooms and bathrooms, square footage, and lot size. This report, which is akin to a mini-appraisal, includes color photos of the comparable properties and recommends a listing price.

Comparative Market Analysis

Multiple listing programs allow you to prepare a professional looking *comparative market analysis (CMA)* of a property with the click of a few buttons. You can personalize these reports to include your potential client's name, address, and other identifying data. Better yet, use Top Producer or some other real estate marketing program and you will impress your clients all the more.

The CMA states your recommended list price for the property. Print out a full copy of the comparable properties your package lists. The comparable listings serve as backup for your rec-ommendation. These reports are incredibly useful for discussing the property value in a scientific, objective manner. Sellers can be highly charged over price, feeling their property, especially their home, is worth far more than the market will bear.

One of the many useful functions of the CMA is to flush out seller price issues early on. Always be prepared for a seller to have a dream price far greater than the current market price. There is a fine line between alienating a seller in love with his property and presenting an objective view of the market. Make sure you never belittle the seller's point of view or his property. People's homes come high up on their list of emotional importance. You don't want to step on any emotional toes.

Prepare the Sample Net Sheet

This document helps the seller understand how much the closing costs will run and how much they will net from the sale. It deducts loan payoff, commission, and other estimated closing costs from the recommended sales price. This simple document should be completed at your listing presentation unless the seller has provided you with loan payoff figures in advance.

It is at this point that your knowledge of tax law comes in handy, not to render tax advice, but because you want to show the seller that you are competent and aware of sale ramifications. Depending on the tax law at the time, your client may have taxable gain requiring some analysis as to how to reduce or defer it. Of course, you don't actually want to render tax advice; however, because you are savvy enough to raise such issues, the seller will be impressed by both your integrity and your knowledge.

Listen to Your Clients

Before you discuss the listing agreement, give your prospects a chance to voice their concerns, issues, and thoughts. Ask them whether they would like to change anything about your plan. Inquire as to whether there is anything you left out. They know their property better than anyone else, and their thoughts and comments are valuable.

Ask them whether anything about the sale process you have suggested makes them feel uncomfortable, because the plan can be tailored to meet their needs. They are the bosses. Are there any family issues you should consider? It is only through enlist-ing them into your plan that the sale of their property will evolve into a team en-deavor, the most satisfying feeling for you and your client alike.

Include Your Agency Disclosure and a Listing Agreement

Include your Agency Disclosure form and a *listing agreement* as the last documents in your package. You will have made a thorough, impressive presentation, followed up with the agency disclosure and listing agreement that will cement your relationship with this seller.

Real Estate Lingo

The **listing agreement** is the contract between the seller and broker. It outlines what the agent will do for the seller and how much the broker will be paid. It also includes the price the property will be listed at and how long the listing will last. Listing agreements are usually exclusive rights to sell, meaning that the broker gets paid regardless of who brings in the buyer.

The Inside Scoop

Most multiple listing software allows you to enter a listing in the form without uploading it into the database until later. This allows you to assemble the required information without the necessity of uploading until you're ready to present your new listing.

When you get to the listing agreement in your package, ask the sellers whether they are ready to sign the agreement now, or should you just step through it and they can think about it. (The listing agreement is discussed more fully in Chapter 19.) If your prospect is ready to sign, follow the high-tech agent's example in Chapter 13. Enter the property on the MLS while you have your clients there to provide you with all the detailed information required. If the light is right, take your digital photos. You don't have to upload it to the MLS yet, but you'll have all your input work done. I have my stager take the photographs. She does her magic, and then she stages each photo she takes. She has a better eye for just the right shot.

If your prospects are not ready to sign up with you, tell them to take their time. There is no urgency. Real estate transactions are rushed along far too quickly. Our clients' number-one complaint is that the process becomes a mad dash to the finish. Let your potential clients know that you feel this way, if you do, and that you believe that planning and good coordination can take the crisis mode out of the real estate transaction.

Utilizing Technology to Instill Trust

A laptop is indispensable at listing presentations. The MLS database can be used to justify the listing price you recommend and to gain seller trust. Potential clients appreciate seeing how the MLS is set up and how their property will be featured on it. They trust your CMA statistics more if they are able to see them on the computer. They also tend to trust you more because you have chosen to share the coveted database that most agents jealously guard. (There is no rule against showing listings to your clients. You just can't let them access the database without your supervision or let them view confidential remarks.)

Do not skip this step. It may not seem like an important step to you, but it provides a real advantage in gaining client trust. Remember, you're dealing with what is possibly their most valuable asset. They want to see exactly how you come up with the value you assign. Emotionally, they want to be included and informed about the list price you recommend, and you accomplish this by sharing your database with them.

> **The Inside Scoop**
>
> Existing homes sales were 5.3 million in the United States in 2002.

If you have a website for your listings, pull up a current or previous listing on your laptop. Show them that this is what their listing will look like on your website. They will be impressed with your marketing abilities and your intent to utilize high technology marketing methods in addition to those traditionally used.

Allow for Rejection

Although your affirmation will be that this client will list with you, don't be discouraged if this doesn't happen. The seller needs to go through the very important process of agent interview and selection. We make a lot of money from selling properties. Listing presentations that don't pan out are just one of the costs of doing business.

Think of them as a public service. They are a part of what agents do, not just to get the listing, but as a service to owners in the community. If your presentation was thorough, and it was if you followed this format, you gave the seller valuable time and information, and it will come back to you. Good service always brings a priceless return.

The Least You Need to Know

- ◆ Time is precious, so qualify your potential seller clients before you invest too much time with them.

- ◆ In your listing presentation, provide information about yourself, an analysis of comparable properties and the market, and a recommended listing price.

- ◆ Evaluating and presenting current market trends lets you and your prospect gauge the market together.

- ◆ Let your prospect know exactly how you intend to market their property, including any Internet exposure.

- ◆ Sharing information from the MLS with your client gives you an advantage over your competition.

Part 5

The Parts of a Transaction

This chapter looks at the residential real estate transaction from the following multiple perspectives:

- ◆ Representing the seller
- ◆ Representing the buyer
- ◆ Using the transaction documents

As you'll learn in this section, representing the seller and buyer involve very different approaches to the real estate sales transaction. Each representation has its unique steps and issues. This part of the book takes a close look at the steps involved in client representation and concludes with a quasi-legal analysis of the transaction documents so you may more professionally guide your clients through transactions.

Chapter 17

Representing the Seller

In This Chapter

- ◆ Staging the property for sale
- ◆ Listing on the MLS
- ◆ Conducting the broker's open house
- ◆ Conducting the open house for the public
- ◆ Handling multiple offers

Congratulations. Your listing presentation was successful. This chapter covers all the steps you will take on behalf of your seller client from signing the listing agreement to closing on the sale. Before showcasing your new listing, you want to perform a marketability assessment of the home. Should a professional stager be hired? Are there seller disclosure issues? Should inspection reports be obtained? Are there title issues that may arise?

Once you have performed your assessment and readied the property for the market, you can feature it on the multiple listing service (MLS), show it to your fellow agents at the broker's open house, and then show it at the public open house. When an offer is received, you will undertake the all-important process of reviewing the offer with your client and responding. Once you're in contract, careful facilitation through closing becomes

Real Estate Lingo

The **listing agent** acts for the seller according to the terms of the listing agreement. The selling agent brings in the successful buyer. If the listing agent also acts as the selling agent, he is acting as a dual agent.

FYI!

My stager offers a basic staging flat-fee package. The flat-fee structure is more acceptable to the seller wary of hidden selling expenses. You, too, can sit down with your stager and come up with flat-fee basic plans that meet the needs of standard homes.

your most important job. This chapter assumes you have a signed listing agreement and you are now officially representing the seller as the *listing agent*.

Professional Staging

Where prices warrant presale expense, properties are often professionally staged before they go on the market. We make a major production out of getting a home ready for its coming-out party. Staging the property to achieve optimum visual appeal is often the very first step you will take. I believe that staging should precede every home showing, even in less-expensive markets; thus, Chapter 22 is devoted to this important topic.

In that chapter, I suggest that you pay for basic staging as part of your listing services. Even if you decide that fronting the cost isn't for you, I still encourage you to highly recommend this process to your sellers. You don't have to spend hundreds or even thousands on the process, but it can make big difference in both a home's listing price and its market appeal.

Evaluating Property Problems

The second step of your marketability assessment is to determine potential property issues and address them. Are there property conditions that may cause concern to a buyer? The days of buyer beware are over. Sellers have to disclose any problems they are aware of relating to the property. Some offices have a policy of staying away from seller disclosure issues. My policy is it's better to encourage full and complete disclosure and find out about any potential problems early on. Believe me, if the buyer decides to sue the seller later for failure to disclose, you will be named in the lawsuit as well. Head it off early. Handle it now.

Seller disclosures are discussed in more depth in Chapter 19; be sure to review this chapter. Although a seller's written disclosures are often not due until after an offer is accepted, a good practice is to have the seller complete these disclosure forms now. The questions in these forms are targeted at flushing out property defects, and these are the very conditions you want to pinpoint early on.

One way to handle property defects is to hire a professional inspection company to identify the problems and have them repaired before listing the property on the MLS. In most states, the seller has to disclose this inspection and its report to a buyer in contract, so consider that issue as well. Depending on what the report says and the extent of the repairs recommended, the seller can either make the repairs or not.

At least the seller will be informed of conditions when the buyers have their inspection done. The seller will be prepared to deal with these issues. It is wise to have one company perform the inspection and another company perform the repairs. In this manner, your inspection will be an unbiased opinion unmotivated by a tendency to recommend unnecessary and costly repairs.

> **Caution**
>
> One question on a typical disclosure statement is, "Are there any conditions you have not described that materially affect the value and desirability of the property to a buyer?" In other words, if there isn't a question that specifically addresses a condition, there's a catch-all place to include it.

One more condition to assess before the conclusion of your marketability analysis is title. Is the seller aware of any unusual conditions of title that may cause a prudent buyer concern? If you feel title issues may exist, order a preliminary title report or abstract of title as soon as you receive the listing.

Are there easements in favor of neighboring property? Are nonconforming uses being made of the property? Are there any boundary problems—for example, is half of their backyard actually the neighbor's property? Are there *set-back* problems with the side deck? Are there any improvements made without permits?

The time to tackle these problems is now for two reasons. First, the seller has to disclose these issues. Second, you can set a plan in place to either address these issues when they come up or head them off entirely.

> **Real Estate Lingo**
>
> A **set-back** requirement is established by zoning law or agreement between neighbors as to how far an improvement might be situated from a certain marker.

These are your problems as well as your client's problems. These are the types of issues that cause an otherwise highly marketable property to become stale and undervalued. If the property doesn't sell, you will not have done your best for your client and you will have spent what will ultimately be a great deal of time getting nowhere. The listing will expire with unsatisfied clients and no income in your pocket. Be proactive. Address these issues in the beginning and encourage your clients to take the steps their consultants suggest to make the property as marketable as possible.

Listing on the MLS

Now that premarketing steps are complete, you're ready to service your new listing. When the property is ready to be previewed, advise your office of the listing and place it on the multiple listing service (MLS). Upload as many digital pictures of the property as your listing service will allow or set up a *virtual tour* shoot.

When your listing is entered in the MLS, it will show up as a new listing on what is referred to as the *Hot Sheet*. This is your listing's most important day on the market as agents feast their eyes on the hit parade of new properties.

Real Estate Lingo

A **virtual tour** is a depiction of a property as if it were photographed with a video camera. It takes you through the property as if you are viewing it in person. You can do this yourself with your digital camera or hire a firm to do it. Check with your local association for referrals.

The listing is then automatically matched up with agent profiling in a process called *prospect matching*. For example, Agent B has a client who is interested in a three-bedroom, two-bath home in a certain town with a view of the water. He enters this criterion into the multiple listing and asks for notification when a new property matching it comes on the market. This new listing matches, and the multiple listing program automatically notifies him of this new listing.

Hosting the Broker's Open House

When you enter your listing in the MLS, you choose a date—generally a few days to a week later—for the broker's open house. On that date, the agents working in the area of your listing tour the property. It's always a good idea to *host* your broker's open house by serving refreshments to your peers. The broker's open house is the second most important step in your listing's marketing program.

If your listing was well-received when it was entered on the MLS, agents have already brought their clients to see the property by the time you hold the broker's open house. Agents can be very quick when they believe a new listing is hot and they have client interest. They don't want to dilly-dally until the broker's open house, where the world of agents will converge upon this unsuspecting property and bring in lots of competition.

Agents sometimes ask those who show up for the broker's open house to fill out a suggested listing price form. If the client has pressured you into listing the property at above market value, these forms completed by fellow agents can go a long way in helping convince the seller that the price should come down. If agents feel the price is too high, so will their clients. They may not even show the property to a potential buyer because of its price.

FYI! _____

If the market is hot, you may want to consider listing the property but not installing a lock box or allowing a showing until after the broker's open house has been held. In this manner you make room for more competitive bidding since all brokers will see the property at the same time. This will allow your client to receive an offer resulting from full-market exposure.

The agents touring your listing are your gateway to buyers. The vast majority of listings are sold by other agents. Each of these agents leaves the broker's open house and broadcasts news of this new listing to their offices and their network of qualified buyers. It is only after the broker's open house that your listing has been fully marketed to the local real estate community.

Holding the Open House for the Public

When you entered your listing with the MLS you also selected an *open house* date. The open house is the agent's way of inviting the public to preview a home listed for sale. This event you advertise in the local newspaper. Although it has been advertised to the agents on the MLS, the agents are not really your market for this event. The public is. You also advertise the open house in the local paper and attach an *open Sunday* rider to your sign. Another good idea is to send postcards to the surrounding neighbors, inviting them to drop by an hour earlier than the general public for a personalized tour of the house.

The open house brings people who are looking to buy or who may be about to sell. Buyers and sellers often frequent open houses before they are ready for their own purchase or sale. They want to see how it's done and what it's all about. The old adage is a property doesn't sell at an open house. This is true. But your *services* do sell at an open house. Especially because your middle name is *Market*.

Real Estate Lingo _____

The **open house** is just what it sounds like. The house is opened to interested buyers to tour. Buyers are notified by newspaper advertising, well-posted signs, and sometimes by agent mailers.

At the open house you are showcasing yourself just as much as your client's property. People will ask your opinion about the market and inquire about your experience. It's your time to shine and to generously assist visitors with their real estate issues. It becomes your time to stand out, although first and foremost the feature of the day is selling your client's home.

Many agents say open houses are a waste of time. Their experience is that the crowds aren't interested in buying; for the most part, they are just getting an education. And if someone becomes interested, they make an offer through their own agent, not through the listing agent. I thoroughly disagree with this philosophy. I think an open house is everything but a waste of time. I refer to it as a goldmine.

Everyone who comes to the open house is a potential client. They are not just there for the refreshments, unless you're serving shrimp and champagne. They have come out of genuine interest in this home or they are interested in the sale process because they will soon become involved in it as a buyer or seller. What more can an agent ask for?

When you think of the amount of cold calling and prospecting agents do to turn up one live potential client, why would the open house that brings them to your very door be considered a waste of time? It's a jackpot. I know agents with similar thoughts who will handle open houses for other agents gratis just to have potential clients appear before their very eyes.

Your Open House Checklist

Here is the step-by-step process to follow when conducting your open house for the public:

1. Mail a notice to the neighbors. The customer service department at your favorite title company will be happy to compile a list for you and even provide you with mailing labels. You want to mail to the 50 neighbors that are closest to your client's home. Send them a notice telling them that you have listed the home at your client's address and invite them to come to the open house. Remember to invite them to a special "for neighbors only" preview of the home, one hour before the general public is to show up. Some agents will even follow this up with a Saturday face-to-face visit with the neighbors, reminding them about tomorrow's open house. This system is prospecting at its very best.

   Neighbors also make valuable sources of future potential sellers. Even if the neighbors have no interest of their own, you will have introduced yourself by your mailer. If they come to the open house, you will have a chance to meet them in person. Meeting potential clients when you are in the course of doing an impressive job for another client is the best possible introduction of all.

> **FYI!**
>
> Neighbors are an excellent source of buyers. They might have watched the house for years, hoping it would come up for sale. They might have relatives or friends who would like to live close by. They may want to purchase the property as a good investment that they can keep their eye on. Familiarity is a property owner's best friend. Some people will do anything to stay in their neighborhood, even move across the street. They know the neighborhood and its services and conveniences. So when it is time to upgrade, they already know where they want to be.

2. Invite your buyer and seller prospects to your open house. This is a good way to allow people you've been prospecting to see you at work. It will give your seller prospects a good idea of what they can expect for an open house of their home. Your buyer prospects might even be interested in this home. Your prospects will be impressed, and their rating of you can't help but go up.

3. Signage. If the home is in a high-traffic area, make sure your open house is posted in as many areas as possible. Do this days in advance for post-driven signage. On the day of the open house make sure your directional signs direct them to the home from all busy thoroughfares. Don't just depend on an address to get them there. Guide them in with nice-looking signs well posted from point one to point ten and all the points in between.

4. Office preparation. Your open-house supplies should include the following:

   ◆ An ample supply of marketing flyers for the property, along with its plot map

   ◆ A review copy of advance inspection reports that give the property a good report

   ◆ A guest book for people in attendance to sign

   ◆ Your bio and mission statement

   ◆ Your business cards

   ◆ Comparables supporting the listing price

> **The Inside Scoop**
>
> Every handout should have your name and contact information on it. Provide pens for guests who want to make notes. If it is a hot property, hire another person to assist with the greetings and train that person to set up intros to you when appropriate.

5. Set up your traveling office in the property. Before your clients leave, ask them whether you can use their phone jack for your laptop. Set up your laptop so you can access the MLS. You want access if the opportunity arises to search listings for potential clients, to review new listings if there is a lull in the day, or to send and receive e-mail. Make sure your property flyers and marketing materials are placed in an accessible location. Have your guest book in the same vicinity.

6. Ready the property for visitors. Make sure the property is ready for the open house by following these pointers:

   ◆ The sellers, their children, and their animals should be gone for the day, and their valuables and prescription medications should be locked up.

   ◆ Display fresh flowers, install some air fresheners, light a nice-smelling candle, and put on soothing music.

   ◆ Make sure the temperature is right. If not, put on more heat or air conditioning. If the weather permits, light a fire.

   ◆ Keep the front and back doors open for easy access if the weather permits. Open all the drapes. Turn every light in the house on. Everything should be bright and cheery.

The Inside Scoop

The smell of fresh-baked cookies can add to a feeling of warmth and home. Some agents bake cookies in the kitchen oven and offer them to guests. Others use a frozen apple pie generously sprinkled with sugar and cinnamon and set on a low temperature to flavor the air with aromas that remind the prospective buyers of home and family. There are many ways to make a property appealing to each of the senses.

Greeting Buyers

When people arrive, introduce yourself, ask them their names, and find out whether they are neighbors. Ask them to sign your guest book. Give them a property flyer and graciously invite them to show themselves around and take as much time as they want. Invite them to ask you any questions they may have about the property or about the real estate market. Then leave them alone.

Before they leave, if they have not spoken with you again, connect with them and engage in simple, friendly conversation. Ask them questions you would ask anyone coming to an open house, such as, "Where do you live? How long have you been looking? Are you selling a home of your own?" If they are neighbors, the questions will be different. Just be friendly and interested. You won't have the look of dollar signs in your eyes; you will have the look of genuine interest instead.

Tell them you would be happy to assist them with any real estate matter they may have now or in the future. You're not being pushy. You're just being honest and sincere. Give them your card and your bio. On the back of your bio you may want to include a personal mission statement. For instance, if you have followed the steps in this book, you will be an agent with a *New Ideal*. Your mission statement should reflect your desire to meet your fiduciary duty by making your client's interest more important than anything else. It should address how you will support their personal decisions even if they conflict with your own.

If it feels appropriate, ask their opinion of the house. Ask what features met their needs and which did not. If it appears that this house simply did not fill their needs, ask whether you can show them some listings on your laptop if they are not already working with an agent. Since you will have your laptop set up and accessible, you can easily input the criteria for the home they are interested in and in minutes have listings that fit their criteria. Tell them you would be willing to meet with them in the next week and show them these properties. You do not want to spend more than a half hour with each prospect. Your main purpose is to sell your client's home, and responding to property-specific inquiries is your primary objective.

In the course of a three-hour open house, most agents who conduct themselves according to this chapter have a handful of new prospects. If you prepare for and handle your open house in a first-rate manner, you will have a built-in prospect bank that continually refills with each open house you give.

Responding to the Offer

You receive a call from a buyer's agent advising that she has an offer on a property you have listed. If she asks to personally present the offer to your client, thank her for the opportunity but respectfully decline. For the reasons set forth in the next chapter, it is not in your client's best interest for the buyer's agent to personally appeal to their emotions.

Don't attempt to convert the buyer's agent to *The New Ideal*, which discourages sales tactics like the ones the buyer's agent proposes to practice on your sellers. *The New Ideal* will take hold over time; until it does, this agent is just doing the job as she knows it for her client. Once you have the offer, present it to your clients in person. Don't try to do it over the telephone.

Real Estate Lingo

The **net proceeds sheet** helps the seller understand what their closing costs will be and how much they will net from the sale. It deducts loan payoff, commission, and other estimated closing costs from the sales price.

At your office, complete a seller's *net proceeds sheet* based on the purchase price. Also, review your file and prepare a summary of the listing showing how many days it has been on the market and how many offers have been made; compare that to your MLS statistics for average days on the market before sale. You want to assess whether this listing has received its market or whether there is more yet to come. If you are past the average days on the market, the offer should be considered more seriously since this listing has reached its peak.

Chapter 19 describes in detail the written agency disclosures you have made to your client and the terms of the offer that will be of the greatest importance to them. Use it as a guide as you review the offer with your clients. Have an extra copy of the buyer's offer for all clients and yourself to review. Go through each and every term and the significance of each to your client. If you are now representing both parties to the transaction, you should amend your agency disclosure that describes whether you are acting on behalf of the buyer only or on behalf of both the buyer and seller.

Real Estate Lingo

A **counteroffer** is a response to an offer that changes or adds some terms.

If there is a term your client is not comfortable with, prepare a *counteroffer*. You should respond to all offers since you have an interested buyer in hand. It makes sense to work with that buyer in arriving at mutually agreeable terms if you can. Any term can be changed. There is no downside to making a counter offer since the seller can always accept a different offer anytime before the counteroffer is accepted.

Handling Multiple Offers

If you're in a fast market, you must be prepared to encounter and respond to multiple offers. Value is one thing, but in a fast market of rapidly appreciating property where there's just not enough to go around, value has little relation to what an interested buyer is willing to pay. This is the concept of supply and demand at its extreme. When there is little supply but high demand, value becomes quite relative. In such a market, knowing how to handle multiple offers is essential to giving your clients the full representation they are due.

If this type of market beckons to you, meet it with a good plan in place. There's nothing like a good bidding war to get the old adrenalin going. You've got to plan for it and work it to make the most out of this ideal situation. First, set a date for all offers to be submitted and specify the date on your listing with the MLS. If the market is hot and the property is attractive, make sure the word gets out telling agents to submit their client's *highest and best* offer since you are expecting quite a bit of competition. Review all offers before responding to any. Once this process has played itself out, you should have the best offer the market will bear.

Now you are ready to accept an offer. You can always accept the others in backup positions in case the first contract falls out of escrow for some reason. It takes skill and experience to handle a bidding war effectively. In my area, the bidding war process results in offers $200,000 and more above fair market. If this ideal market presents itself to you and you do not yet have the experience to artfully bring the process through its stages, bring in another agent who does. It is well worth having a capable team on hand to allow this process to render the maximum possible reward for both you and your clients.

Facilitating the Transaction to Closing

As the seller's agent, your main job after an offer is accepted is to facilitate seller disclosures and monitor the buyer's performance. Once disclosures are made, your job is to ensure that the buyer removes his contingencies in a timely manner. It is always best to prepare your seller for later bargaining when the buyer removes his physical inspection contingency. It is at this juncture that the seller should be prepared for yet another negotiation since the buyer sometimes conditions contingency removal on a seller credit to address required repairs.

You want to continually track all steps of the transaction to ensure continued progression toward closing. Although the loan contingency is not your client's, you want to stay in close contact with the buyer's agent to ensure that the loan is progressing toward closing. About a week before closing make sure the settlement statement addressed in Chapter 19 is correct and the lender documents are in or at least ordered.

FYI!

The old way of handling contingencies was to do everything you could to get the contingency removed. A step closer to closing was the primary goal. In your new professional role according to *The New Ideal*, your only sales script is, "What is the best possible action for my client?" For example, if the buyer wants your client to credit back an amount that doesn't make sense to the seller, support your client in terminating the purchase agreement. There's no fancy footwork to do, just support your client's decision.

Make sure that all closing documentation has been prepared and no other documents are required. A buyer surprise or a title company surprise is a seller surprise. The only way to increase the odds of the transaction closing without problems is by staying on top of each stage of the transaction, whether it requires action on your part or not.

Dealing with a Stale Listing

A listing gets stale if it stays on the market without moving longer than other comparable properties. A home gets its most exposure in its first few weeks on the market. Upon obtaining the listing, you began marketing it directly to potential buyers and to other agents who may bring in buyers. You submitted the home to the MLS, announced it in your office, held a broker's tour, contacted your potential buyer list and agents who may have waiting buyers, held open houses, and submitted advertisements to the local newspaper. Your listing enjoyed its wave of marketing without receiving an offer.

A listing becomes stale for three reasons:

- It is overpriced.
- It has condition problems.
- The market is slow.

If other properties within your listing's price range are moving, the property is the problem, not the market. Your listing is either overpriced or it suffers from a condition problem. If it is overpriced, take it off the market for a time and pop it back on the market at a lower price, or just reduce the price without taking it off the market. Depending on your choice, it will either be shown as a new listing again or a price reduction, and will be priced more in line with the market. You will want to set up another broker's open house if the price has come down enough, because there is a whole new buyer's market to which it will appeal the second time around.

If your clients refuse to come down on the listing price, suggest that they provide a buyer incentive such as *seller financing*, *lease-option*, or *equity sharing*. They need to increase their market by offering an advantage to compensate for the higher than market price. If they refuse an incentive, either release them from their listing agreement with the permission of your office or don't renew their listing when it expires.

If the property itself has condition problems, take it off the market, address the problems, and then reintroduce it to its market with a facelift. If the property has access problems, shows poorly, or needs repair, take steps to address these problems.

Sometimes a property just needs minor reconstruction or clearing out of clutter and sprucing up. Taking these steps can make a big difference in how the market responds to your listing. Once conditions have been addressed, put the listing back on the market advising that it has been cleared or renovated. It will come out as a new listing and if the conditions are adequately addressed, it will now receive its market.

Real Estate Lingo

With **seller financing**, the seller agrees to make a loan to a buyer who may not otherwise qualify for a loan or who wants to avoid lender loan costs.

A **lease option** allows the buyer to occupy the property with a right to buy it at a later date. It allows a buyer who is not ready to purchase to occupy the property, have a right to purchase it, and to get ready to purchase it.

Through **seller equity sharing** the seller stays on title for a percentage interest in the property (usually to the extent of the down payment or a portion of it), the buyer does not have to come up with the down payment (or portion of it the seller leaves in), and the seller cashes out the remainder of his interest with the new loan proceeds and receives the amount of his retained equity and his percentage of appreciation at the end of term (often five to seven years). This is an ideal way for a principal residence seller to reduce his tax basis and begin an investment portfolio since his ownership interest become his investment property.

Overpricing a listing is like gambling with a valuable asset. If you are very lucky, you might snag a buyer at a price higher than the property's value. Then, you are faced with the buyer discovering his mistake and backing out during the contingency period. If your luck holds and the buyer releases his contingencies, the problem then becomes one of lender appraisal since the property will most likely fail to justify the sale price. If you are not so lucky, your listing will sit, get stale, get a reputation as a house that is impossible to sell, and leave buyers wondering what is wrong with it.

Always remember that if the price is low enough, its market will come. In other words, a low enough price will cure any problem. You can only rely on market comparables if your property is in comparable condition to other similar properties. If it is not, the price must be reduced to bring it its market.

Reporting to Your Clients

The first complaint clients have about agents is the pressure tactics they use. Second is the lack of contact. Once you have a client's listing, frequent, consistent contact is essential. Always keep in mind that you are in the business for more than making the commission at the end of the road. You are here to benefit your clients throughout their transaction, making it the best possible experience for both of you. Treat them like family and they will treat you the same.

> **The Inside Scoop**
>
> Sellers decide if they want to accept offers contingent upon finding a new home. Buyers can also make offers contingent upon selling their home.

Most often your seller also needs to buy another property. In fact, the National Association of Realtors reports that 84 percent of repeat homebuyers nationwide sold their previous home at the same time they purchased their new home. These two transactions therefore should occur in tandem as much as possible. The seller needs to know what is going on even if nothing is going on. They want to know they are on your mind.

Although the commission you will make should never be a gauge of the services you will give to a client, it is a consideration. These clients are significant contributors to your financial support. Why not give them everything you've got to give? If you have nothing to report, tell them so every few days.

Take advantage of the simplicity of e-mail communication. The vast majority of your clients have e-mail these days. They may not check it consistently, but if you tell them you will keep them advised in this manner, they will. As you update their listing, change their marketing materials, or advertise their property, e-mail a copy to your client. They will feel in the loop and well served. Clients who were reluctant or adamantly opposed to using e-mail as a supplemental communication method often overcome their hesitancies within a few short clicks.

The Least You Need to Know

- Use a professional stager to give a property its optimum eye-appeal in order to be sold quickly and at its highest price.

- The MLS listing will include a date for the broker's open house and the open house for the public.

- Use the open house to market your services as well as the property itself.

- You should understand the contract terms and be prepared to discuss each with your client when an offer is made.

- Present a purchase offer in person if at all possible.

Chapter 18

Representing the Buyer

In This Chapter

- ◆ Qualifying a prospective buyer
- ◆ Making your presentation to a buyer
- ◆ Touring properties with buyers
- ◆ The offer, the counteroffer, and where you go from here
- ◆ Taking the transaction through closing

This chapter is about representing the buyer. It begins with a buyer prospect whom you qualify for readiness to purchase. When your prospect is qualified, you deliver your buyer presentation. This presentation does not result in a signed agreement with your buyer, the way it did with the seller, but it does establish your relationship as this buyer's agent. After the two of you commit to the job at hand, you begin the process of touring properties and ultimately making an offer to purchase.

Later in this chapter, we look at the most important offer terms and how they should be handled with your client. Some states have forms that define transaction terms. This form can be a useful tool for explaining terms to your clients. Opening escrow is the next step followed by performance of the all-important loan and physical inspection contingencies.

At closing, you want to be with your client when he confronts the huge stack of documents to sign.

Qualifying the Buyer

Before you start searching for listings and driving prospects around to tour properties, you want to qualify them, just as you do your sellers. Showing properties to clients takes a lot of time and energy. Before you make this investment, you want to determine whether your potential clients are ready or close to ready to buy, both emotionally and financially.

> ### The Inside Scoop
>
> In the spirit of generosity and cooperation, you may choose to do some MLS prospecting for non-qualified clients. This would consist of giving them some property listings that fit their criteria. The chances are, when these people are more motivated, they will come back to you both because you were sharp enough to know they weren't ready and kind enough to share listings with them anyway.

Here is a checklist of issues to discuss with prospective buyers in order to qualify them:

1. How long have you been looking for a property and how many properties have you seen?

2. Do you have a preapproval letter from a lender? (If the answer is no, the buyer will need to get that prior to shopping for a new home.)

3. Are you a first-time buyer?

4. Have you worked with other agents in looking for a home? If yes, have you already connected with an agent you feel comfortable with to help you find the home of your dreams?

5. If you own a home, when do you plan to sell it? Have you listed it? Have you interviewed agents to list it?

6. (If they own a home) Do you intend to find a home you want before you put your home on the market? If so, how do you intend to handle a situation where you need to close on the new home before your existing home sells? Have you discussed a *bridge loan* with your lender?

Real Estate Lingo

A **bridge loan** is a short-term loan made in expectation of permanent longer-term loan. Also known as a swing loan.

7. What is the biggest obstacle to finding the property you want?

8. What is wrong with the homes you have seen thus far?

9. What qualities do you feel are important in the agent you will choose to represent your interests?

10. If you find a home through my services, are you willing to place the listing of your home with me if you are pleased with my services?

11. If we were to find the perfect home today, are you ready to make an offer?

It is only through discussing the previous set of issues that you can know your prospect's level of motivation. It makes no sense to cart people around to properties for sale if they are not ready to sign on the dotted line, or at least, if they are not reasonably close to buying.

Presenting to the Buyer

After you have qualified the buyer, you will prepare your buyer package, which should include:

♦ A sample listing

♦ A sample preapproval letter

♦ Your office and personal bio and mission statement

♦ List of transaction steps and standards

Caution

Each step in a transaction is very important. Missing one can break the contract due to the time constraints. So share this with your potential clients, understand it, and develop a method of tracking and following up to keep everything on schedule.

Print out a full-color buyer's listing from the multiple listing service as an example of how a property is listed. Point out the categories and explain how you use specific criteria under each of these to select properties that match their needs. For example, show them a sample three-bedroom, two-bath home with a pool. If they desire each of those characteristics, this property will show up as a match in your search of the MLS. This illustration shows them that the more specific they are in their criteria, the more likely a matching property will fit their needs.

On your computer show them how a search is performed and how you are alerted when a property match occurs. As I've mentioned before, agents are far too guarded with the MLS. Clients are highly interested in this service that is off limits to them and appreciate your introducing them to how it works. There's nothing in the MLS rules prohibiting client review as long as you are the one doing the showing and do not show clients the confidential remarks.

If your prospects do not yet have loan *preapproval*, advise them that this will be the first step on their home-buying agenda. Only with that in their possession will they be taken to look at properties. No buyer offer is seriously considered without a preapproval letter. The preapproval process will also tell them the loan amount for which they can qualify. With this important financial step taken in advance, they can focus on finding the right property within their budget instead of finding a property they are uncertain they can afford.

List of Transaction Steps and Standards

Have a list of the standard transaction steps, what will be expected of the buyers during the transaction, and which transaction fees are customarily paid by the buyers. Even if the buyers have purchased many times before, it always comes as a surprise to realize just how complicated the real estate transaction is. Most people purchased real estate when the transaction was far less cumbersome. This list helps buyers understand the course their purchase will travel and the need to have an agent by their side who really understands the process and will protect their interests. The agent who explains the process simply and straightforwardly stands out to them. This step will also cut down on surprises later if the transaction takes unexpected twists and turns.

FYI!

It is a wise idea to interview inspectors long before you need them, and add those who are reliable and professional to your personal referral list. One or two will already be on your *Power Team*. You will want to review some sample reports, talk to some previous clients, and have assurances of availability and price. You place your reputation on the line every time you make a referral, and yet this is part of your service. So pick a team that will work with you and for you.

When you describe the physical inspection contingency, let them know that you will guide them to inspectors who will assess the condition of the property for them. You will review their experts' reports with them and decide whether a seller credit should be given or if perhaps the transaction should be terminated. Tell them that you will support the right course of action for them, whatever that may be, because you are part of *The New Ideal*.

Listen to the Buyer

The final step of your buyer meeting is to discuss two primary issues with your potential clients: First, what they want in an agent; and second, what they want in the property they are looking for. Always use your best active-listening skills while at the same time making it perfectly clear that you will find them the home they want within 30 days as long as they are specific about their needs. They have to do their part of the job which is to know what they need and agree on it. If you have a husband and wife who have different needs tell them to call you later when they are in agreement. Then bid them adieu.

Once this presentation has concluded you will know whether you and your prospects are a match. If you are, commit to one another. In most states, there is no formal agreement entered into with the buyer. The commitment is more of a moral one where you agree to help them find the right home and they agree to work with you in doing so.

Touring Buyers

In selecting properties to match your clients' needs, make sure you use the purchase price listed in your clients' loan preapproval letter. Before you tour your clients, make sure you preview properties. There should be no surprises when you arrive at a property; if you have not previewed a property, there will invariably be conditions you are unprepared to address. Do not make this mistake.

At the property, give your clients all the space and time they need to really get a feel for the home. Tour them through and answer any questions they may have, but don't crowd them. Nationwide, the typical search takes seven weeks during which the buyer visits 10 homes before they buy. If your typical buyers are Internet searchers, it takes them only four weeks and six homes.

> **The Inside Scoop**
>
> Take your clients in your car with you if at all possible. It makes for much better personal rapport and is far more convenient. You have probably been to the properties you're showing your clients, so you know how to get there. You also want to point out the neighborhood features along the way.

Reporting to Your Client

When you are prospecting for buyers, let them know the results of your daily search. Even if there are no new properties meeting their criteria, report that to them. The only way to keep clients happy is to frequently let them know you are working for them and looking out for their best interests.

> **FYI!**
>
> If you train your clients to receive communication by e-mail, it just takes a click of their e-mail address to send them a listing if a new one is found or advise them that there are no new properties meeting their requirements. There just is no reason whatsoever to miss checking in with your client at least every few days.

A recent survey by the National Association of Realtors reports that communication is the key to homebuyer satisfaction. The survey states that Internet buyers were contacted by their real estate agent every 4.3 days, while traditional buyers were contacted every 6.5 days. More frequent communication resulted in a higher degree of satisfaction among Internet buyers; 90 percent claimed to be very satisfied with their agent as opposed to 32 percent of traditional buyers. The main reason for Internet buyers' satisfaction was that their agent was "always quick to respond." In contrast, the main reason expressed by traditional buyers for their dissatisfaction was the lack of communication from their agent.

Preparing the Offer

When your clients find a property they are prepared to make an offer on, the old sales trainers tell you to sit them down immediately at the property, pull out the offer you've got hidden in your notepad, and go for it. Don't give 'em a second to start second-guessing themselves. If you do, you'll lose 'em. This is Smoking Gun script No. 44.

> **FYI!**
>
> As reported by the National Association of Realtors, repeat homebuyers needed only four weeks to sell their existing home. More than half of repeat homebuyers began their home search before they placed their existing home on the market.

The agent with a *New Ideal* is not pushing his clients to make impulsive decisions. Drive your clients back to your office and prepare the offer in a professional setting. There is no rush other than the normal time consideration in making the offer before someone else does. For those occasions when clients are in their own rush, and in some hot markets there is good reason to be, bring out your technology and let 'er rip. For the agent whose other middle name starts with a C, computer technology is the name of the game. The savvy agent has her laptop and printer stored in her car for just this type of occasion.

The next chapter describes in detail the required written agency disclosures you will make and the terms of the offer that you will now prepare. Use it as a guide as you put your client's offer together. Go through each and every term and the significance of each to your client.

It is entirely possible that your client's offer will be responded to by the sellers with a *counteroffer*. Always prepare your clients for this possibility so that when a counter is received, they are not unduly disappointed. It is just another step in the purchase process.

Offer Presentation

For agents still practicing salesmanship standards, presenting the offer involves setting the stage for a Hollywood soap opera. Many sales trainers advocate the sales pitch method—you've got to pitch the sellers so you can sell them on your clients. They instruct you to contact the listing agent and ask to present your offer in person to his or her clients. If the listing agent is crazy enough to let you in the client's door, you sit down with the sellers and use every gimmick in the book to try to get them to accept your client's offer. Bring your client's letter of introduction and a nice glossy picture of them. Oh, heck, why not bring a video tape of them and play it for the sellers. Better yet, bring your clients with you and let them crawl!

> **The Inside Scoop**
>
> Sixty-three percent of buyers said the Internet shortened the search time for their new home. Internet users tended to be younger and purchase more expensive homes than other homebuyers.

For the agent with *The New Ideal*, Hollywood dramatics have no place in the offer presentation process. The sales pitch method is clearly not in the seller's best interest, and both listing and selling agents should refuse to participate in it. The buyer's personal characteristics have nothing to do with whether the seller should accept their offer. The offer and acceptance process is not a social or dramatic engagement; this is a serious business transaction where the sellers should exercise objective judgment based on the terms set forth in the offer.

The Transaction Timeline and Steps

Once your client's offer is accepted, you will prepare your *transaction timeline*. It is now time for you to jump into action on three important fronts:

- Opening escrow

- Obtaining the title report

- Dealing with the contingencies

Opening Escrow

The first step taken after an offer is accepted is to open escrow. Typically this step is taken by the buyer's agent. When you open escrow, you submit your client's purchase

Real Estate Lingo

A **transaction timeline** takes the terms of the purchase agreement and gives them dates, the most important of which are contingency periods and closing date.

deposit and provide the escrow officer or closing attorney (depending on the state you are in) with the relevant details relating to this transaction. You don't have to know what to say. The closing professional will ask you a list of questions and you provide the answers. Other than that, make sure any terms relating to amounts to be paid or credited are related to this professional who will itemize these amounts on the settlement statement.

The closing professional serves as a neutral intermediary facilitating the transaction and ordering title reports and title insurance. This professional takes buyer funds in the form of buyer and lender deposits and distributes them to sellers, lenders, and real estate agents. He gives lenders recorded security instruments and gives buyers deeds. He handles the paper and money exchange required in the real estate purchase and sale process.

FYI!

In some states, attorneys are required to serve as the title examiner and closing agent. In other states, the attorney is typically not a part of the transaction. Instead, the title company prepares the title report. In states where transactions do not require attorney involvement, the buyer is left to review a highly technical report that includes legal descriptions and legal information that often is beyond the understanding of most people.

Obtaining the Title Report

Within a matter of days of opening escrow the preliminary title report or abstract is received, which your client then has a limited number of days to review and approve. Sometimes this requires attorney scrutiny if there are easements and other conditions which limit the use of the property. If an attorney is not handling the closing, make sure you refer your client to one if there are unusual exceptions on the report. For the first several transactions, show the report to your office manager so you may learn what is unusual and what is not.

FYI!

The title report is the legal biography of the property, so to speak. It has three primary components:

- The legal description
- The exceptions
- Title insurance provisions

The title report is of paramount importance because it describes all legal rights and obligations associated with the property. It can be equated with the human's birth certificate, credit report, and life insurance policy. The legal description describes its physical existence, whereas title exceptions list its credit problems. The title insurance pays off if there is a problem with either of these. Thinking of the title in this common sense way can make title issues simple and straightforward.

Although you should not give legal advice, and interpreting these reports *is* giving legal advice, it is important for you to understand these reports. With a basic understanding of title reports, you can head off any title issues that become apparent through your early review. Even trained professionals tend to run the other way rather than attempt to grasp complex title terminology that sounds like language from another planet. Understanding these reports is actually not complicated once you see them in a practical, logical way.

The Legal Description

Each property comes into legal existence through a legal description recorded with the recorder's office of the area where the property is located. Often the property's legal description is expressed by reference to a parcel map such as the following for a client's six-million-dollar home:

All that certain real property situated in the City of Belvedere, County of Marin, State of California, described as follows:

PARCEL 2, as shown upon that certain map entitled, "Parcel Map, Lands of Fred Flintstone, as described in Volume 3296—Official Records, at Page 282, City of Belvedere, Marin County, California," filed for record March 3, 1980, in Volume 17 of Parcel Maps, at Page 87, Marin County Records. EXCEPT-ING ANY portion of the above described property along the shore below the line of natural ordinary high tide and also excepting any artificial accretions to said land waterward of said line of natural ordinary high tide.

Each time the property's legal existence is affected, a document is recorded on that property. These documents add to or subtract from the full rights of the property. For instance, an easement against the property subtracts from the property's rights whereas an easement in favor of the property adds to the property's rights. The following is an example of an easement in favor of a property, which becomes part of the property's legal description:

AN EASEMENT for roadway purposes over the portion of the easement described in Parcel Two in the Deed from Belvedere Land Company to John D. Doe, recorded October 10, 1946, in Book 529 of Official Records, at Page 419, Marin County Records, which lies within the boundaries of Parcel 1, shown upon that certain map entitled, "Parcel Map, Lands of Fred Flintstone, as described in Volume 3296—Official Records, at Page 282, City of Belvedere, Marin County, California," filed for record March 3, 1980, in Volume 17 of Parcel Maps, at Page 87, Marin County Records.

Exceptions to Title

The title report then lists all exceptions to clear title, meaning all financial obligations for which the property serves as security and all physical constraints that restrict the use of the property. For example, the easement described above in favor of one property will be shown as a title exception for the property burdened by the easement.

> ### Real Estate Lingo
> **Mortgages** are used in some states while **deeds of trust** are used in others to secure a lender's interest in a property. The promissory note describes the obligation while the mortgage or deed of trust is recorded on title to show the lender's security interest in the property.

When there is a loan that the property secures, the loan is recorded on the property as a *mortgage* or *deed of trust*, whichever security instrument is used in your state, and is also listed as a title exception. Think of the original legal description of a property as its birth certificate and the rest of the documents that affect the property as its credit report.

Conditions and Restrictions

Title reports sometimes list covenants, conditions, and restrictions (referred to as CC&Rs) that affect the use of the property and may affect its value.

Buyers must thoroughly analyze these constraints to determine whether they are willing to live under them. These restrictions can mandate the nature and extent of improvements that can be made, whether the property may be leased out, how many animals the buyers can have (and their sizes and weights), and a long list of other freedom-inhibiting factors.

CC&Rs can also show up unexpectedly on title when there is no condominium or home owner's association. These restrictions most often come into existence when the original developer creates a subdivision. In the subdivision process, each parcel will have conditions recorded on title to allow the properties to legally reciprocate with and conform to one another. Sometimes owners enter into agreements with adjoining owners and record these agreements on title.

Often the seller who failed to analyze his own title report when he purchased is unaware that there are title restrictions. These may come as a complete surprise to the unsuspecting buyer. The educated and prudent agent who understands these title warning signs can alert his buyer to these issues early on.

Obtaining Title Insurance

Title companies and closing attorneys search title to make sure all rights and obligations affecting a property are set forth in one report for the buyer's review. Title insurance is then issued to the buyer and lender insuring that title confers the ownership rights described in the title report. If a claim is later made that the title report was in error, the title insurer steps in and defends the parties, legally protecting their property interests.

Title insurance has a body of law all of its own, which can benefit your clients if you understand it. Just like any other insurance policy, title insurance policies offer a wide range of coverage. There is basic coverage, extended coverage, gold coverage, platinum coverage, and everything in between.

Some policies provide protection that others do not. The property your client is buying may have unique characteristics that require a special endorsement. For example, if your client is buying a property that was just renovated by the sellers, there may be a potential for *mechanics liens* to be recorded on the property after close of escrow.

> **The Inside Scoop**
>
> Basic coverage does not involve a site inspection by the title company, whereas extended coverage may. A site inspection allows the title insurance to provide coverage for more conditions than the basic policy.

> **Real Estate Lingo**
>
> **Mechanics liens** are recorded liens that contractors and suppliers may record on a property if they have provided services or materials to the property. The property is responsible for the lien amount whether the service was contracted for by the current owner or the prior owner. The assumption is that it benefited the property, so the property is responsible, hence a lien against the property.

Basic title insurance does not ordinarily cover mechanics lien claims without a special endorsement. Your client should be advised to talk to the title insurer about additional coverage. It is only through knowing the types of extra coverage available for title insurance policies, or at least those most customarily used, that you can guide your client to make these important title insurance decisions so they do not become last-minute issues.

Dealing with All-Important Contingencies

Contingencies are conditions that can make the difference between a purchase closing or not. A contract is *conditional* (meaning not yet a binding contract) until its contingencies are released, at which point the contract becomes binding and enforceable. In other words, it's a done deal when the contingencies have all been satisfied or removed. Until then, it is conditional.

> **Real Estate Lingo**
>
> A **conditional** contract is one that has conditions which make the contract non-binding until the conditions are removed. Most often these conditions are loan or physical inspection contingencies, finding a replacement home, or selling a home. If these conditions are not satisfied, the contract terminates without penalty.

Most contingencies are general; some are finely crafted works of legalese. Some say practicing law while others say practicing real estate. The most typical contingencies are the loan and the physical inspection contingencies. You have to plan ahead for these contingencies, carefully monitoring the progress of steps being taken to satisfy these conditions. Until the buyer receives full loan approval from their lender and releases the inspection contingency, the contract is just that: contingent.

The Physical Inspection Contingency

The physical inspection contingency can be a hair-raising experience for you and your client. It takes a lot to perform a medical checkup on a property in a brief timeframe. The condition of the property—all the way from its soil to its roof and then out to its boundaries—requires assessment in order to determine if the property is worth what is being paid. In addition, its feasibility and legality must be analyzed. The feasibility relates to the use that legal zoning allows. Legality is the term that refers to whether improvements have been performed with the correct permits and according to building codes.

During this contingency period the sellers (and the agents in some states) also make their written disclosures of the property's conditions, covered in the next chapter, and often provide the buyer with a pest inspection report. These reports should be carefully analyzed by the buyers and their consultants. Most buyers have a pest control (often ordered by the seller), home, and sometimes roof inspection performed. Others also require a soils inspection, structural inspection, and survey. In most states, these inspections are made at the buyer's expense, with the exception of a seller-provided pest report which is paid for by the seller.

All purchases should include a trip to the local building inspection department to assess the property's zoning and legality. Your client must confirm that all required permits were obtained when improvements were made to the property and that the use of the property conforms to the zoning requirements. In some localities, a city inspection report detailing these matters is a condition of sale. Although the seller's disclosures should detail these conditions, the buyer is prudent to make his own independent analysis since the seller may be unaware of some requirements and less than forthcoming as to others.

> ### The Inside Scoop
>
> There are conventions in each area about who pays for these inspections and mandated local inspections. In some locations, the costs are split; in others, the buyer or seller pays for the inspections. Your office manager will be able to assist you with the customary arrangement for your locale.

Generally, the buyer has a short timeframe within which to complete these inspections. Assume that you are representing the buyers who have 15 days to remove their physical inspection contingency. Get them set up for general building inspections immediately. When the market is busy it often takes a week to 10 days for these professionals to conduct their inspections, and then they must produce a written report. Often recommended repairs need to be analyzed and seller credits need to be negotiated, which may involve hiring a contractor to provide a professional estimate for work to be done.

Fifteen days is therefore a very short period, but the seller wants this period to be brief since this is the contingency when some transactions fall out of contract. Because marketability of the seller's property is impaired during the time a contract is contingent, it is in the best interest of the seller for the inspection contingency to be as brief as possible. It therefore behooves you to move forward with setting up inspections immediately.

> **The Inside Scoop**
>
> If you have an inspector or two on your *Power Team*, offer these names as possible service providers. There is a difference between providing names to select from and choosing the inspector for your client. Hopefully you have done a good job qualifying the members of your *Power Team*, and they will do a quality job for your client.

Allow your clients to choose their own inspectors. If they ask you for recommendations, and they will, give them a few to choose from. I have handled more than one lawsuit by the buyer against her agent because the buyer was unhappy with the inspector's services—and the inspector was referred by the real estate agent. The arm of liability swings wide in real estate transactions because of agency relationships that weave in and around the transaction.

The physical inspection contingency is ready to be released only after the inspections of buyer's choice are performed, the legal analysis has taken place, and the buyer is satisfied with all evaluations. If, based on these many analyses, the buyer feels a credit should be made to the purchase price, this is the time to negotiate its amount. It is during this stage that some contracts terminate because the seller does not want to give the credit the buyer desires, or the buyer decides against purchasing because of facts that come to light during inspection.

The Loan Contingency

The loan contingency is another time-sensitive step. Because the loan can hold up a transaction, make sure you continually check in with the loan broker to ensure that the loan is on track for full *loan approval*. The *loan contingency* typically consists of two stages—preapproval and full approval. Historically, buyer *prequalification* was sufficient as stage one. Times have changed. The modern buyer should be preapproved for the loan, not prequalified, either at the time the offer is made or within a few days of its acceptance.

Once a preapproval letter has issued, loan approval is no longer considered much of a contingency since the buyers are already approved for the loan. The only thing left to approve is the property, which depends on its appraisal and a review of the contract. Typically, neither of these factors presents a problem, but you should continually monitor the loan. Track the date for full loan approval and continue your monitoring thereafter since lenders are famous for last-minute preparation of hundreds of pages of documents requiring review and signing by the buyer. Don't let a last-minute lender spoil the transaction you have taken such care to maintain in a balanced, stress-free manner.

Real Estate Lingo

Loan approval is the full and final process whereby the lender approves of the loan and the property that will secure it.

Loan contingency is the period during which the buyer obtains loan approval. The buyer makes the offer contingent upon obtaining the loan described in the offer. The loan contingency often expires 30 days prior to closing.

In **prequalification,** the lender takes the potential buyers' application and prequalifies them for a loan based on the information provided, but undertakes no confirmation of the buyer's information, as it does in preapproval.

FYI!

A lender takes the potential buyers' application and prequalifies them for a loan based on the information provided, but undertakes no confirmation of the buyer's information. In the preapproval process the lender takes all the confirmation steps it would for full loan approval with the exception of appraisal of the property (since the property has not yet been located). With preapproval, the buyers have already been approved for the type of loan they describe in their offer. Only stage two of loan approval, qualification of the property, remains. Stage two rarely presents a problem as long as there are comparables to confirm the property's value.

Closing

About a week before closing make sure the settlement statement addressed in the next chapter is correct and the lender documents are in or at least ordered. For the buyer, signing of closing documents can be a nightmare. If it were not for the loan documents, closing would be rather simple. The loan documents are sometimes a full inch thick and require numerous signatures. If you want to really understand them, it takes more than an advanced degree.

Because of this, it is important for someone who can explain the closing documents in a clear, concise way to accompany your buyer to the closing. For the buyer side of the transaction, the professional team may consist of one or more of your *Power Team* members. Both your escrow professional and the mortgage broker are well qualified to undertake this task. Since you are the person who has been by your client's side every step of the way, you should also be at their side when they sign the closing documents. It is part of good service and caring about your clients.

> ### The Inside Scoop
>
> A gift such as that recommended in the *Referral Stream System* is a good idea to cement the relationship after the close is complete and the buyers have taken possession of their new property. After all, you have earned a nice commission and have become a trusted advisor to these people.

Acting as a Dual Agent

As soon as you discover that your office will represent both the buyer and seller in a transaction, run the other way. I mean this, but in the real world this is not what is done. The next chapter explores this situation in detail.

The Least You Need to Know

- ◆ Your time is important, so qualify the client first.

- ◆ Know the steps required to make an offer and counteroffer, and understand the complexities in any contract.

- ◆ Understanding the title report can make you a real asset to your client and can head off any potential title issues early on.

- ◆ Stay on top of the loan and physical inspection contingencies.

- ◆ Attend escrow signing with your clients as a matter of professionalism and integrity.

Chapter **19**

Using the Transaction Documents

In This Chapter

- ◆ How do you get familiar with the forms used in real estate?
- ◆ What agency role are you playing in this transaction?
- ◆ What are the terms of the listing agreement and purchase agreement?
- ◆ What are seller disclosures and agent disclosures?
- ◆ Are agents required to undertake their own inspections?

In your prelicensing curriculum and on your exam, the agency relationships and contract documents that will form the basis of your business were covered in part. But these principles are very difficult to grasp without a working foundation. Most licensees just memorize the material without really understanding how these key fundamentals apply to real-life transactions.

Some offices will train you extensively in their sales procedures, legal principles, and contract forms, whereas some will barely touch on these subjects. It is only through working with real transactions that true understanding arises. Although this book can't give you that, it comes close. This chapter introduces you to the transaction forms and how to achieve the most success when working with them.

The Primary Documents

The documents that will become part of your life for your foreseeable future are ...

♦ The listing agreement by which your sellers will employ you.

♦ The agency disclosure that advises the parties of their agency relationship with you.

♦ The purchase agreement.

♦ The seller disclosures and agent disclosures.

♦ The closing settlement statement.

FYI!

Your escrow officer or other closing professional is the best person to step you through the intricacies of settlement statements. These statements can simplify complicated calculations and itemizations and step you through any problem areas.

FYI!

Although commissions are entirely negotiable, they are often ...

♦ 10 percent for raw land.

♦ 6 percent for residential and commercial property.

The Listing Agreement

The listing agreement is the favorite document of agents. It is the contract that gives you the right to sell your client's property and to earn a commission for doing so. Generally, the exclusive right-to-sell listing agreement appoints you as the exclusive agent to sell the property. You earn a commission if the property sells during the term of the listing even if someone else sells it. Sometimes other types of listing agreements are used, but most often you will use the exclusive right to sell.

The most important terms in these agreements are as follows:

♦ The price the property will be listed for

♦ The term of the listing

♦ The amount of commission you will earn

Listing Price

The listing price should be determined by your comparative market analysis (CMA). Often sellers feel their homes are worth more than what the comparables indicate. If you and your client disagree on price, the discrepancy needs to be resolved. In the beginning you will probably want to take any listing, but when you become seasoned you will realize that servicing an overpriced listing is a headache you really don't need. If your seller won't budge, it might be best not to sign him up.

Listing Term

The term of the listing is how long the listing will last. The agent wants a long term and the client wants a short term. If your clients have not worked with you before, they want assurance that you will perform before they give you a long listing term. You can't really blame them, can you?

You will come across sellers who are unhappy with their listing agent's services, but they're stuck in contract for a term that needs to run. Many real estate firms will not let a seller out of a contract based on dissatisfaction with the agent's services. They insist on expiration of the term before the listing is terminated.

Depending on the market, three months could be a listing period that will give you enough time to fully market the listing. If so, agree to a three-month period which can be extended if your client is satisfied with your services. *The New Ideal* presents a new level of trust and integrity where pressure is no longer the name of the game. Instead, give clients a lot of breathing room and they will come back again and again.

The listing agreement also often includes a protection period, which is often 90 days after expiration of the listing. During the protection period, the agent earns a commission if the seller enters into a contract with buyers the agent dealt with during the listing period.

Caution

Many listing agreements have a bolded notice to sellers that commissions are not set by law and are negotiable.

Commission

The commission to be paid on sale is also described in the listing agreement. Although commission standards are observed by agents within a given office, commissions are negotiable. They are not set by law and the agent is given the duty to advise a client of this fact. At the same time, your office probably requires that you charge a certain set commission. It is confusing to advise your client that commissions are negotiable and in the next breath tell them your commission has to be a certain percentage. However, this is what must be done.

Agency Disclosures

As a real estate agent, you have an agency relationship with your client. You are their advisor, and as such you are in a fiduciary relationship with them, meaning you are acting on their behalf in a relationship where you have a duty of trust and loyalty to them.

Agency relationships form the basis of an enormous amount of lawsuits in our already congested court system, primarily because they lend themselves to almost unlimited obligation by the agent. It is therefore vital for you to know the extent of the obligations you are required to perform for your client once you enter into this relationship.

Real estate agency relationships are a constant source of ever-changing legal definition, and you should be aware as definitions continue to change. This can only be done if you continually obtain education in this highly relevant area of the law. Given the magnitude of roles the real estate agent plays in a typical transaction, there is always a fine line to walk between illegally practicing another profession, rendering the service you are required to as your client's agent, and going the extra mile to take care of your client in the most thorough way you can.

FYI!

A sample agency disclosure in California describes the duties of the agent *to his or her client* as a fiduciary duty of utmost care, integrity, honesty, and loyalty. To the other party not a client, the agent has these duties:

- Diligent exercise of reasonable skill and care.

- A duty of honest and fair dealing.

- A duty to disclose all known facts materially affecting the value and desirability of the property that are not known to, or within the diligent attention and observation of, the parties.

You need to know exactly when to keep going and when to stop dead in your tracks. For instance, when reviewing the title report or the seller's disclosures, when do you step over the line and begin practicing law without a license? When discussing the tax ramifications of your client's purchase or sale, when do you step over the line of legal liability into the bailiwick of the tax professional? If you do not want to wear lawsuits as a shadow, you must be able to make this distinction as part of your second nature.

Whose Agent Are You?

There was song by The Who that was popular in the 1970s called "Who Are You?" I suggest the new agent play a variation of this song called, "Whose Agent Are You?" whenever signing an offer. When you begin your representation of any client, you must advise your client whom you represent and obtain your client's written acknowledgment. In most states, an agent cannot act as a dual agent (representing both sides of a transaction) without written consent of all clients. In law this situation is a conflict of interest; in real estate it is described as dual agency. In other states, dual agency is prohibited, having been replaced by designated brokerage or transaction brokerage.

The agency disclosure form legally describes the type of agency you are performing for your client or clients. It is up to the agent to indicate on this form which option relates to the particular agency. Some of the options are as follows:

◆ Seller's agent

◆ Buyer's agent

◆ Disclosed dual agent

◆ Designated agent

The agency disclosure form explains the duties associated with each type of agency relationship. This form is signed by your client during your very first contact with them. If your agency relationship changes at any time during a transaction, you must then issue a new agency disclosure defining your new agency relationship.

Dreaded Dual Agency

Dual agency occurs when the same office represents both parties in a transaction. Some states prohibit an agent from acting as a dual agent while other states allow dual agency but call it something else, such as designated or transactional agency. Even if dual agency is permitted by law, there are many different ways real estate offices respond to fulfilling this precarious role.

Some offices will not allow one agent to represent both sides in a transaction as they believe that although dual agency is not illegal, it is asking for trouble. In those situations, the office manager appoints another agent in the office to act as agent for one of the parties to the transaction. The office itself is acting as a dual agent since the office is brokering both side of the transaction, but when separate agents are designated to represent the clients, potential problems are significantly reduced.

FYI!

A sample agency disclosure in California describes the duties of the *dual agent* to both buyer and seller as:

- A fiduciary duty of utmost care, integrity, honesty, and loyalty.

- Diligent exercise of reasonable skill and care.

- A duty of honest and fair dealing.

- A duty to disclose all known facts materially affecting the value and desirability of the property that are not known to, or within the diligent attention and observation of, the parties.

The Purchase Agreement

The second most important agreement you will use is the purchase agreement. It is the successor to what used to be called the deposit receipt, and in some states purchase agreements are still called deposit receipts. Before we became a society requiring seven-page purchase agreements, we used deposit receipts of less than a page. Even the one-pager was successor to the good old-fashioned handshake, which today means, "How do you do?" where before it meant, "I stake my life on it."

There is no standard form purchase agreement used nationwide. Some offices use the one their state board uses, whereas others use their own forms. In the area where I practice we have our own form, which is used by most offices. It does a very good job of setting and describing the transaction steps. A thorough reading of the purchase agreement you use is absolutely essential. In fact, study it so well you know it verbatim.

Some contract forms are so confusing even the agents do not understand them. It all depends on which form your office requires you to use. If another office is the selling office (the office that brings in the buyer), their contract will be used in the transaction. The contract used is decided on by the office representing the buyer. Therefore you also want to be intimately familiar with any other contract forms that are typically used in the area where you practice. If you do not thoroughly understand the purchase agreement, there is no way your client can. In my locale, there are two forms used. Half of the offices use one, while the other half use another. The competent agent must fully understand and be well versed in the use of both contracts.

After you feel you can almost repeat verbatim and give a legal course in the purchase agreement your office uses, sit down with the office manager or a mentor you have chosen. Step through the discussion you should have with your clients as they are signing these forms and making their choices. The purchase agreement sets up significant legal consequences and includes numerous legal choices. You should be able to concisely and articulately explain each provision to your client while conversing intelligently with them about their specific situation.

> **Caution**
>
> Some purchase agreements protect the agent by stating, "Both parties acknowledge they have not relied on any statements of the real estate agents which are not expressed in this document."

Understanding the Terms

There is an art to stepping through legal forms with a client. There is one way to do it if your client is the buyer and a very different way to do it if you are representing the seller. You should understand which terms are in the contract for whose benefit. You should know what is standard and what is not. You should be aware of other terms that may arise in the purchase or sale transaction. These other terms are only gleaned through experience, which a beginning agent does not have. This is a good time to ask for some guidance from your support team.

If you cannot get this training from your office, find your own training. There are unlimited resources from which to choose. Hire a consultant or an attorney. Go online. Take a real estate course. Go to your local board and review its educational resources. This is essential training. Once you really understand these documents, engage in some phantom transactions. Have your mentor or office manager assign purchases of properties listed on the MLS. These transactions should have differing variables, so that you can experience different buying and selling scenarios.

Prepare the purchase documents and the rest of the documents for these illustrative transactions. Get to the point where you know each term verbatim so that when you are completing these forms with your clients you are knowledgeable. You will need to guide and advise clients as you determine the terms for their transaction, and you will be unable to effectively do this if your face is stuck in the contract trying to decipher it.

> **The Inside Scoop**
>
> In some states, mediation, arbitration, liquidated damages, and other legal-oriented provisions must be stated in bold lettering and initialed immediately below the provision.

For your first few transactions, do what makes you feel most comfortable. You might want to talk with your clients, get an understanding of the terms of their offer, and then complete the offer in private. This way you can really focus on getting the terms right without looking like you don't know what you're doing. When you present the offer to your clients you will have thought out and chosen their options and will be prepared to discuss the terms with them.

Dealing with Legal Terminology

When it comes time to explain legal terminology such as mediation, arbitration, or liquidated damages, have a preprinted definition of these terms for your client's review. I review about 200 transactions a year. More often than I would like to admit, buyers do not choose binding arbitration because agents tell them not to. Agents should not be instructing clients, especially with regard to such important legal decisions. Agents should provide clients with a preprinted definition of arbitration and leave it to clients to decide or consult with their attorney.

> **The Inside Scoop**
>
> Some states have developed forms describing important transaction terms. If your state has, use this form in defining terms for your client. If your state has not developed this form and your office does not have one of their own, you should prepare a document that defines the important terms.

The very best way to handle these decisions is to make your clients aware of them before they are in the offer stage. Give your buyers a copy of the transaction definitions so they may consider these important issues in advance so they may be prepared to make their own important legal choices when the time comes.

The Terms of the Purchase Agreement

The following are the most important terms that should be considered by buyers and sellers:

♦ **Purchase price**. The buyer wants to offer his best price, keeping in mind that if it is a seller's market, he may not get the house he wants if the price is not high enough. The seller should consider when he should counter seeking a higher price than the buyer has offered or accept the price offered for the sake of being in contract.

♦ **Deposits**. Many states use 3 percent of the purchase price as the norm for an initial deposit and increased deposit on a home. The *initial* deposit is paid when the offer is accepted and is often 1 percent of the purchase price. The *increased* deposit is most often tied to buyer's release of contingencies and represents the rest of the preclosing deposit. The seller wants to see the buyer put up a high deposit while the buyer wants to put up as little as possible. Thus, they generally follow the norm.

◆ **Loan contingency.** A preapproval letter conforming to the terms of the loan described should either accompany the offer or be submitted within a few days of acceptance of the offer. Make sure the financing terms specified are terms the buyer is willing to accept and that his or her loan conforms to what the market offers. The seller does not want his property tied up in contract only to see the buyer terminate the contract because he is unable to get the loan described. The timing for release of the loan contingency is important to both the buyer and seller. The seller wants to see the loan contingency released as soon as possible so he knows he's in a binding contract that cannot be cancelled. The lenders usually won't lock a loan for longer than 30 days without extra fees. Thus, the norm for release of loan contingency is 30 days before escrow is to close.

◆ **Physical inspection contingency.** The seller wants to see this contingency removed as soon as possible in order to move one step closer to making the contract unconditional. He also wants to get past the negotiation which sometimes accompanies the buyer's release of this contingency. The buyer, on the other hand, wants to have enough time to perform all the property inspections required, obtain estimates for any repairs required, and negotiate with the seller for a credit to purchase price if necessary. Most contracts try to keep this inspection period to 15 days.

◆ **Purchase of home contingency.** Should sellers counter the buyer's offer with a purchase of home contingency making finding a new home a condition of the sale of their home? Or, should they just build in a rent-back period so they can rent back from the buyers if they have not found their new home or are not ready to close on it by the time this escrow closes?

◆ *Sale of home contingency.* You will have discussions with your buyer clients about whether their offer should include a contingency making the sale of their home a condition of their purchase offer. In a strong seller market, an offer with this type of contingency will have less chance

> ### The Inside Scoop
>
> The usual time for an inspection contingency is 15 days. The usual time for expiration of a loan contingency is 30 days before closing. This may vary by locale and the needs of the parties.

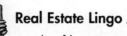

Real Estate Lingo

A **sale of home contingency** makes the buyer's offer conditioned upon their selling their existing home.

of being accepted. Generally it takes less time to sell a house than to locate and buy one, so as long as their offer to purchase has a closing date that accounts for sale of their home, they probably should not include this contingency.

◆ **Closing date.** The best way to analyze the timing of an offer is to prepare your transaction timeline by matching up the contract terms with a calendar. It provides a reality check for both the buyer and seller. Make sure the closing date works for your clients. They may have some needs for an extended closing, a quick closing, or a rent-back situation.

Real Estate Lingo

A **liquidated damages agreement** is a provision in the purchase agreement where the seller retains the buyer's deposit if the buyer *defaults* on the purchase.

Real Estate Lingo

Binding arbitration is a legal process that replaces the court system if the parties so agree in writing.

Mediation is a settlement process that precedes legal proceedings that is often agreed to in the purchase agreement.

◆ **Liquidated damages.** Some purchase agreements contain liquidated damages provisions. In most states, if the parties agree to liquidated damages, the amount of damages available to the seller in any legal action later brought against the buyer who fails to close after releasing contingencies is fixed by the amount agreed to. This provision should be carefully evaluated by both the buyer and seller. This is one provision where a legal definition of exactly what liquidated damages are and the effect they have when a party defaults is absolutely necessary.

◆ **Mediation-Arbitration.** Have a legal definition of exactly what mediation and binding arbitration are and how these choices affect the parties' rights if one party needs to sue the other.

◆ **Additional terms** can be the most difficult to understand and have the most legal significance. Review these carefully and pull in an attorney if needed.

Seller Disclosures

The seller's duty is to advise the buyer of conditions that materially affect the value and desirability of the property to the buyer. This is the legal definition. How does a seller judge what is material or desirable to a buyer he has not met? Most states have Seller Disclosure Statements that attempt to elicit seller information bearing on these issues.

Many areas also have a supplement to the seller disclosure form calling for more information than what is called for on the state-mandated form. One question that often appears on the supplemental form is, "Is there any other condition that affects the value and desirability of the property to the buyer?" This is the catchall that causes the seller to fulfill his disclosure duty and often creates liability for a seller who responds honestly to the rest of the questions but fails to include something that should be described in response to this question.

The problem with the process is that our seller clients need guidance in completing these forms. Failure to disclose is the most common reason buyers sue sellers and their agents. Yet agents are often advised by their offices to stay away from advising their clients on disclosures because this would constitute the illegal practice of law. The end result is the agent often hands her clients the disclosure forms and says, "Complete these and return them to me." End of story. Actually, the story doesn't end there; it often ends in litigation where both the seller and agent are parties.

Caution

In some states, including California, agents are required to perform a visual inspection of the property and report written findings on the seller disclosure forms.

There is a better way. It would be a simple matter for each office to have legal counsel prepare a one-page instruction sheet for sellers to use when completing their very important disclosures. I have included this type of instruction in documents available on my website at www.msullivan.com.

Agent Inspection and Disclosures

Real estate agents have always been responsible for faithfully representing the known conditions of a property. There is now a growing trend across the country to require agents to actually *inspect* a property for visible defects and to *disclose* the results of their inspections to buyers. In some states already both the agent for the buyer and the seller must undertake a visual inspection and report findings on a disclosure form.

In California for example, the agent's visual inspection duty extends to conditions within improvements on the property and on its grounds, as well as environmental conditions. Agents walk around with a Red Flags checklist performing visual inspections that previously were the job of the licensed inspector. Soon this may be the standard nationwide.

In these states where the duty of inspection is being shifted to the agent, there is a balancing act that must be done to fulfill the agent's duty of inspection while taking care not to hold himself or herself out as an expert. There is also an art to completing the agent disclosure form in a way that achieves these dual purposes. Make sure you fully understand the agent inspection and disclosure laws of your state by discussing this very important subject with your office manager or your state real estate association.

The Settlement Statement

The settlement statement reflects each amount charged or credited to the parties in the transaction. It is your obligation to make sure the terms of the purchase agreement are carried out in this statement. Call a week ahead of closing and ask for an estimated settlement statement. This will cause the closing professional to finalize the details of the transaction and complete anything not yet finished. You want to monitor the settlement statement to ensure that all transaction obligations have been expressed correctly. Is the buyer warranty shown as paid by the seller? Are the transaction fees prorated as described in the purchase agreement? Is any credit to the buyer correctly stated? Are there prorations for expenses between buyer and seller in accordance with the closing date? Is your commission calculated correctly?

The Least You Need to Know

- There may be several forms in use for your area that are common in real estate transactions, and you should be fluent in all of them.

- The agency relationship is an obligation that needs to be fully understood by you and your client.

- The listing agreement is a contract between the sellers of a property and the office that will represent them.

- The purchase agreement is complex and involves contingencies and terms that you should thoroughly understand.

- Disclosures are mandated by law to be made by the sellers and sometimes their agents to describe conditions that may materially affect the value and desirability of the property.

Part 6

Becoming a Top Dog

Top Dogs adopt proven methods to stand out in their field, the most popular of which are cutting-edge strategies, giving and getting support, staging listings, and cultivating future income streams.

Top Dogs build destination websites that are rich with promotional content and valuable tools. They seek specialized training and professional designations in order to provide the most skilled and best services possible. You'll see why Top Dogs stage listings and pay for this service and you'll learn that Top Dogs also treat their businesses as a conduit for investment deals, always on the lookout for future income streams.

Chapter 20

Cutting-Edge Top Dogs

In This Chapter

- Building a website and providing special value on it
- Embracing technology with a bricks-and-click business model
- Defining your specialty and claiming it
- Obtaining specialized training
- Getting professional designations

The Top Dog is a particular breed whose ears point and tail wags when opportunity appears. Top Dogs spring into action when they sense advantage and in so doing, emerge as the top movers and shakers in the real estate sales field. This chapter and the rest of this book describe some of the tools and strategies agents use to achieve admission to this unique breed we call the Top Dog.

Real estate sales can earn its top producers a robust income, and this is borne out by NAR's survey showing that top agents nationwide earn a median gross income of $177,400. In high-value areas like California, where the median home price is twice the national median, the median income for Top Dogs is also doubled. But it is not income alone that defines an agent as a Top Dog. There are many other factors, which are explored throughout these remaining chapters.

The Top Dog's Motivation

What motivates the Top Dog? A study of these unique real estate professionals indicate that they are motivated partially by financial reward and partially by a deep desire for professional and personal challenge. Top Dogs say that when they take their place in real estate, they know they have found their calling, at which point they move ahead with confidence and determination. These are some of the steps they take:

- They build a destination website that responds to existing clients and draws new clientele.

- They incorporate technology fully into their business.

- They specialize in a particular market.

- They obtain professional designations and training.

- They practice according to *The New Ideal*.

- They further develop their Personal and Professional Power.

The Inside Scoop
Real estate generates nearly one third, or $2.9 trillion, of the U.S. gross domestic product, and creates jobs for over nine million Americans.

- They get support from assistants and advisors.

- They get support from spiritual practice.

- They stage their listings.

- They build a Referral Stream System.

- They build Future Income Streams.

We've discussed some of these topics already. This chapter focuses on website development, specializing, and obtaining professional designations and training.

Destination Websites

According to a 2002 National Association of Realtors survey, 41 percent of homebuyers use the Internet as an information source in buying a home. In more progressive areas of the country, that number is nearly doubled, making four out of five buyers likely to use the Internet to find a home. Another survey conducted by NAR shows that buyers who use the Internet are also among the most desirable clients, because compared to non-Internet buyers, they ...

- Spend 20–50 percent more on their homes.

- Close their deals in half the time of the average buyer.

- Are more likely to use an agent to buy or sell property.

The Inside Scoop
In 2002, 50 percent of agents had websites. In early 2003, 64 percent of agents had websites. Use of computers now approaches 100 percent, with many using portable laptops. E-mail is used by 94 percent of agents while 85 percent use digital cameras. Use of personal digital assistants is on the rise and 33 percent of agents use five or more technology-based products.

Hearing these statistics, the Top Dog is on full alert, so much so that the vast majority of Top Dogs have their own destination websites to attract Internet buyers and sellers.

Catering to Internet Clients

Before the Internet became popular as a way to find information, products, and services, buyers followed traditional methods of home search: They drove around to look for homes for sale, they used newspaper ads to direct them to properties, and they ultimately hired an agent referred by a friend or family member to find them a home. Internet buyers for the most part discard traditional means and use the Internet to find both properties for sale and agents to represent them. Convenience and information accessibility is often their determining factor when choosing an agent.

Statistics show that on the average, Internet buyers visit six websites to find an agent and eight sites to look at property listings. When they do select an agent, they are motivated and ready to buy. This is the dream client we all hope for and the client the Top Dog sets his aim to secure through being one of the six or eight websites the Internet buyer searches.

A familiar term to all real estate agents is *farming*. Farming is considered the most effective tool for cultivating and identifying prospective clients. The disadvantage to farming is that it takes a lot of effort and expense over a long period of time to capture your market, if you are able to capture it at all.

FYI!

The brass tacks of a farming campaign are obtaining a targeted mailing list of about 250, designing and producing a well-designed mailer, composing hand-written notes, affixing labels and postage, sorting, and making trips to the post office. These mailing campaigns must be repeated on a consistent basis at least quarterly. They are a lot of work and the results are often disappointing when compared to all the effort spent.

The answer for the Top Dog is to do reverse farming. Let your clients come to you via a well-planned destination website on the Internet. With traditional farming you decide what your specialty is, pinpoint 250 people who would be interested in your specialty, and bombard them with your mailer over and over and over. In Internet farming, you decide what your specialty is and put up a website that responds to an Internet search for that specialty—and they find you over, and over and over.

Can you imagine having a market that delivers your message worldwide 24 hours a day, 7 days a week, 365 days of the year, while you sleep, while you lay on the beach in Hawaii, while you take in a movie? Your website is a 24/7 marketing resource of the most unlimited potential as well as a 24/7 resource for your existing clientele. This, coupled with the fact that according to a survey by the National Association of Realtors two thirds of adults nationwide are online, make website marketing a number-one priority for Top Dogs. They lead the pack by making their business model one of bricks and clicks, offering impressive offices for client in-person contact and an enviable Internet presence for cyberspace clientele.

Defining Your Specialty

The secret of Internet farming is to create a specialty that caters to keyword search. For instance, "Back Bay Boston Mass homes for sale buyer's agent" is sufficiently specific for an Internet buyer who is looking for a home in the Back Bay of Boston and wants to be represented by a buyer's agent to locate an agent whose website uses matching keywords. Through a successful web presence, Top Dogs are able to attract any target viewer by designing their websites and its content to do so.

How do you achieve this goal? Identify a small focused group to target and make that your specialty. Or, tackle this the other way around. Take your specialty, if you already have one, and create keywords associated with it, then break those words down into a smaller, more identifiable market. Be the client you want, sit at the computer, and input the description this Internet buyer or seller would use to describe your services.

It could be "retirement homes in a gated community in Sarasota Springs, Florida" or "golf course homes in Palm Desert, California" or "first time buyer homes (your area)" or "lake homes in Sheridan Beach, Indiana". You want to make sure your site will come up in the top ten of the keyword search for both buyers and sellers. For the seller, you may need to also include keywords that attract sellers if they differ from your buyer specialty.

> **The Inside Scoop**
>
> A seller may not search for homes for sale in a certain area. They may instead do a search for "real estate agents in Phoenix, Arizona". Follow the same process you did as the Internet searcher, but this time be the Internet seller.

It is only through acting as the Internet consumer that you will target the right keywords to flow traffic in your direction. This is not the job for your website technologist. Only you can identify the market you want. Once you have the right keywords, it's time to hire a professional to create your site for you.

Creating and Indexing Your Website

Chapter 12 covered how to find web designers. Review that information. In addition, go to sources described in Chapter 21 to find technology support and virtual assistance. If you want to capture Internet clients, as Top Dogs do, you want your site developed by someone who focuses on search engine placement. It is easy enough to take this extra step, which gives you a gateway to Internet clients, but it is one that is often missed by real estate agents when putting up their sites. If your intention is to be amongst the Top Dogs, take the following steps when your website is created and maintained:

- ◆ Identify your specialty with such specificity that you will come up under the top ten of a keyword search for both buyers and sellers.

- ◆ When you hire your website designer, tell him or her that one of your main objectives is search engine placement under those keywords. Make sure the designer focuses on the correct keywords and other types of criteria that will give you the highest prominence within the keywords you have identified.

- ◆ Each time you add a page, give it keywords describing the product or service that page describes.

Using Your Site as a Destination Point

Top Dogs make their sites a destination point, not only for those who use the right keywords but for their home base. "Build it and they will come" was meant for website marketing. When they come, as they will, Top Dogs give them a reason to stay. They treat their visitors well and give them what they are after.

For buyers, Top Dogs provide maps of the area, community information, school information, mortgage information, weather reports, a link to obtain their credit report, and access to the listings on the multiple listing service. But they don't stop there. A common mistake agents

Caution

Don't give in to the urge to just grab a simple website like everyone else has. Most people do that and do not enjoy the Internet traffic that could conceivably replace the need to prospect for clients.

make is to assume that only buyers are looking at their websites. What about sellers or for sale by owners (FSBOs)? They, too, are part of the Internet generation and an important source of business for you.

Top Dogs attract Internet sellers to their sites by offering a free comparative market analysis, free staging services (addressed in Chapter 22), or *seller-only services* where they represent only the seller, thereby avoiding dual agency representation. If you want to attract sellers in a certain town or area, include detailed information about that community's special characteristics. For FSBOs, give them a page or two on your site to assist them with the job ahead. If you draw FSBOs to your site when they begin the job ahead, they will think of you first when they encounter problems and realize that hiring an agent may be their best solution.

Real Estate Lingo

Seller-only services are the single agency representation of the seller only.

As computer and Internet technology continues to take over the mainstream marketplace, more and more people will use the Internet to assist them in the home buying and selling process. Internet consumers are shopping for products and for services on the Internet. Before they list, many sellers surf the net to determine the value of their homes. In this process, they could easily come across your site if it is indexed optimally, and may very well choose to list with you.

When Top Dogs add a new listing to their sites, they make sure its page is indexed correctly for keyword search purposes to come up under keywords that describe the property as specifically as possible. Make sure that each page of your site has its own set of descriptive keywords associated with it. Your listing in Dallas should be indexed under Dallas, whereas another listing in Ft. Worth should be indexed under Ft. Worth. With the intention of your website capturing as much of its market as possible, you should always think in terms of keywords for every addition you make to your site.

Using Your Site in Everyday Business

After you get your domain name, promote it in everything you do. I use mine to post my seminar schedules, to announce job openings, to post transaction status on hidden pages, to provide information about the continually evolving nature of my practice, and to feature my listings.

On other pages hidden on my site, I include transaction reports for each of my pending transactions. Instead of having the approximately ten people involved in each transaction checking in with each other and me by e-mail and phone to determine the status of a transaction, its status is posted on my site at a hidden page that can only be accessed with its specific address. The professionals I work with and my clients enjoy this feature and refer me business just because of the convenience this service provides.

> **FYI!**
>
> My website does multiple duties. I am using it at the moment to find an assistant. My ad in the paper says, "Administrative asst. real estate, see msullivan.com/assistant.html". On that page I have a highly detailed description of both my office and its operations and the position I have open. If I paid for an ad to include these specifics, I would pay for a full-page ad. It's far less expensive and easier to just do it on your website. It also cuts out any applicants who do not have Internet competence. Over the weekend, I rethought my job description and changed it on my website with just a few clicks. I would not have been able to do that with the newspaper ad I had placed.

Some Top Dogs provide concierge services to their clients by creating customized confidential pages on their sites for each new client. On these pages they provide resources that clients may need during their transaction. Contact information for local moving services, utility services, handymen, contactors, auction companies, pest control, and home inspection services and lenders are just a few of the resources provided. Clients appreciate being supported in this very personal way, which goes beyond the typical service provided by agents. Some agents also provide limited in-house support to help clients with their moves, such as calling utility companies to transfer service.

> **The Inside Scoop**
>
> Although you will most likely hire someone to design your site, I suggest that you administer it yourself. It's the only way you can use it to its maximum in your everyday business. If you do not want to deal with uploading and keywording new listings, at the very least make sure your website consultant has the right keywords from you to index each page of your site. Otherwise, your new pages will not be a destination point for Internet keyword searches likely to reach those pages.

Design Your Website Well

Top Dog websites are user friendly and visually appealing, and their content is easy to access. Nobody wants to sit scrolling through pages of text or to wait for a slow page to load. They want to point, click, and be visually entertained while they receive good, quality information. When you hire your designers, make sure they are able to provide not only the graphic and technological expertise to make your site look good and function well, but also have a good understanding of your business needs and whom you intend to be your audience. Although you will provide the keywords, you want your designers to understand your target market so they can design it with your market in mind.

Not only do you want your site to draw people, you want it to represent your interests capably. Demand the same standards of professionalism and content that you would in any material intended to be published worldwide. Your website will become your new business card and your new image. The vast majority of clients who retain my services have been to my website and fully understand exactly what I do before I even meet them. Their first image of me is through my site. If my website were not professional looking and highly informative, some of these clients would not come through my door. And those clients who did not come through my door would not refer the other clients that later did.

E-Mail Productivity and Professionalism

Top Dogs are ready to deliver Internet prospects to their door. Each page of their sites includes an obvious link to send them e-mail. Internet surfers expect an immediate way to get in touch with you to ask about a property or your services. You built it, and they will come if you give them a way to get to you.

> **The Inside Scoop**
>
> Responding to e-mail is where Top Dogs take a leadership role. They have assistants who respond to their e-mail when they are out in the field.

You must also respond quickly to these communications. Internet consumers are accustomed to rapid response. If you do not respond in a brief period of time, 15 minutes for instance, they will move on to the next site which is only a click away. Many agents do not make e-mail a high priority. When you have a destination website that has been carefully designed to capture your market, make sure you are set up to respond to it when it comes.

When you send or respond to e-mail, whether with Internet prospects or your regular business base, make sure your e-mail includes a full signature and address block. It, too, should be professional looking and include all your identifying information. Setting up a signature file is a simple procedure in every e-mail program. The vast majority of agents do not take advantage of this simple option—these are the very same agents who plaster their names and faces in every other conceivable manner, yet fail to capitalize on marketing when it comes to e-mail.

Specialized Training and Professional Designations

Another way the Top Dog achieves his status as a peak performer is through specialized training and professional designations. The Top Dog begins his career highly motivated to be the best, continually striving for cutting-edge strategies to tip the scales in his favor. These peak performers are motivated to go the extra mile, and they often believe that specialized training and designations will deliver them to their own personal finish line.

Broker Licensing

Top Dogs who obtained their broker's licenses felt they were catapulted to a new level of achievement. They gained a freedom in their newfound ability to work on their own which increased their bargaining power with the company they worked for and gave them more of an entrepreneurial frame of mind. Some never left the company they worked with, but their commission split shifted more in their favor. Some started their own offices and either worked alone or employed other agents to work for them.

In most states, agents may become licensed as brokers if they complete additional educational requirements and a period of time actively working as an agent. Each state differs in its requirements. In most states the broker exam is a full day with a break for lunch. The questions are very similar to those on the agent's exam but cover a broader spectrum of subjects. The broker prelicensing courses and examination preparation is handled by the same companies that prepare agents for licensing, as described in Chapters 4 and 5.

FYI!

In the majority of states, licensees must have two years of full-time agent experience and about 90 hours of additional education in order to obtain broker licensing. This is just an average. Check with your state following the guidelines in Chapters 4 and 5 for more specific information.

Specialty Training

Some Top Dogs attribute their success in part to the expertise they gain from course instruction. Julie, whom we met in Chapter 3, felt her expertise in understanding tax issues has brought her a broad range of clients she would not have drawn had she not become a tax wiz. Another Top Dog, Eric, believes that the contract law courses he has taken help him to understand contract provisions and contingencies that contribute to his success. Both of these Top Dogs carefully select the courses they take to fulfill their *continuing education* requirements to advance the particular specialty they have identified. Some Top Dogs I regularly deal with specialize in equity sharing and lease options, which give them yet more ways to put deals together, a clear advantage in the real estate sales field.

Basic tax laws relating to real estate are not difficult to understand. The agent who understands taxation on the sale of a principal residence and on the sale of an investment property takes a leadership stance both among his clients and peers. The current principal residence tax law is simple. It exempts a certain amount of gain depending on whether you are married or not and has time restrictions with respect to residing in the property. That's it. As for exchanging out of an investment property, the tax-free exchange should be understood by every agent, whether residential or commercial. Its rules are also straightforward.

> **Real Estate Lingo**
>
> **Continuing education** is required in most states and in Canada to keep your license active. The number of courses required varies greatly between states and provinces.

Obtaining Professional Designations

The National Association of Realtors reports that agents holding professional designations have incomes that are $27,000 higher than those who do not. Most Top Dogs acquire one or more professional designations as they achieve their success. As part of their carefully orchestrated regime to climb the real estate ladder, they achieve financial reward and professional respect far greater than the norm.

Some Top Dogs feel that their designations brought more respect from their clients and peers, which in turn heightened their creditability and enhanced their professional development. Some feel that the training and study they undertook to obtain their designations gave them more knowledge and tools to use in their business, thereby increasing their potential. All felt that obtaining professional designations is an important career step to take.

> **The Inside Scoop**
>
> The National Association of Realtors (www.realtor.org) offers 15 designations and two certifications. There are other national programs and many state programs in addition. E-Pro is one of the certification programs. This program was featured in Chapter 12 and is recommended by many Top Dogs.

Some designations are conferred by the National Association of Realtors, while some are given at the state and local level. Most of these designations require education, some have experience criteria and some have tests that must be passed. The following list describes some of the more popular designations obtained by Top Dogs:

CRS (Certified Residential Specialist)—The CRS Designation is awarded to agents or brokers who complete advanced training in listing and selling. The CRS Designation is the highest professional designation awarded in the residential sales field. Fewer than 5 percent of all agents and brokers hold the CRS Designation. The designation has educational and experience requirements that must be met.

ABR (Accredited Buyer Representative)—This designation focuses on all aspects of buyer representation. Designees must complete the *REBAC* course, pass the test, and provide documentation of buyer agency experience.

GRI Graduate REALTOR Institute— Many Top Dogs obtain the *GRI* designation early in their careers. The GRI program consists of 92 hours of course instruction and is considered by many as the most comprehensive training program available in the country. GRI is often the first designation agents obtain and becomes the stepping stone to more advanced designations such as the CRS and CCIM.

> **Real Estate Lingo**
>
> **REBAC** stands for Real Estate Buyers Agent Council of the National Association of Realtors, the national association that confers the ABR designation. They can be found at www.rebac.net.

> **The Inside Scoop**
>
> Research shows that sales agents with the GRI designation earn at least 35 percent more than non-GRIs.

CCIM (Certified Commercial Investment Member)—CCIMs are recognized experts in commercial real estate brokerage, leasing, asset management valuation, and investment analysis. This is the designation that Jim, our commercial real estate agent from Chapter 3, obtained. There are extensive course and experience requirements for this designation in addition to an examination that must be passed.

CPM (Certified Property Manager)—Top Dogs in the real estate management sector acquire valuable real estate management skills through educational offerings leading to the CPM designation. CPM members have the competitive edge in real estate management. In Chapter 3 you met Melissa, who obtained another national designation, Master Property Manager (MPM). Thereafter she served on the national board for the National Association of Residential Property Managers (NARPM) for eight years and served as its president one year.

> **Caution**
>
> Only 1 percent of real estate practitioners have obtained the CCIM designation.

LTG (Leadership Training Graduate)—Some Top Dogs who have leadership roles in their communities have obtained the LTG designation. The course-intensive program consists of a curriculum that focuses on career improvement and individual goal attainment, and is designed to advance leadership skills. Only 1 percent of real estate professionals have achieved this designation.

The Least You Need to Know

◆ Top Dogs follow the bricks-and-clicks business model utilizing the Internet for clients and to promote their listings.

◆ Top Dogs regard e-mail correspondence as a top priority to retain Internet-driven prospects and to coordinate with existing clientele.

◆ Your website must be well indexed with keywords to be found in an Internet search.

◆ A specialty will help build your niche and get you discovered on the Internet.

◆ Additional designations will promote your achievements and set you apart from other agents.

Chapter 21

Giving and Getting Support

In This Chapter

- ◆ Performing an entrepreneurial analysis
- ◆ Reviewing the *Principals of Personal and Professional Power*
- ◆ Getting technology support
- ◆ Getting administrative support
- ◆ Obtaining virtual assistance

Top Dogs realize they can't do it alone. They recognize that it is through community and good values that their business and personal lives become rich. They subscribe to the philosophy that abundance results from equal amounts of give and take. When their business signals either a time to grow or a time to give back, they listen with an entrepreneurial ear. They understand that there are different types of support and are able to obtain the appropriate remedy at a given stage. This chapter demonstrates the necessity of adopting an entrepreneurial state of mind from which to consistently fine-tune your business and give it the support it needs.

The Top Dog Plan

As Michael Gerber describes in his book *The E Myth*, the successful small business must achieve and maintain a balance of three essential aspects: the entrepreneur (the visionary), the manager (administrative, practical steps), and the technician (in this context, the real estate professional). Although good values are implicit in any good business plan, many Top Dogs make them a priority by making *Personal and Professional Power* a fourth ingredient that must also be considered as their businesses mature.

> **The Inside Scoop**
>
> Read Michael Gerber's excellent books, *The E Myth* and *The E Myth Revisited*. These books will assist you in setting up your business with an entrepreneurial state of mind.

Top Dogs are wise enough to identify when their business needs to reach its next stage of development. They understand that the signal for growth is also a call for an assessment of their business plan. The difference between the Top Dog and not-so-Top Dog is that the Top Dog performs this essential appraisal before forging ahead to obtain support. The type of support called for depends on which of the four essential business ingredients requires bolstering:

- Is your *Personal and Professional Power* in need of fine tuning?

- Is the call for growth more of an organizational, *administrational* one?

- Does your business plan require an infusion of *entrepreneurial vision*?

- Does the adjustment required involve the real estate *services* you provide?

Top Dogs realize that it takes continual monitoring of these four aspects for their business to achieve optimum success. If one facet gets out of kilter, the business will begin to suffer. The Top Dog is careful to continually observe her business's barometer to ensure that it stays on an even keel.

Hiring a Business Coach

Top Dogs often hire a business coach or consultant to assist them in performing these important business evaluations, especially at the first critical growth stage. This process doesn't necessarily involve a detailed master plan and days of a consultant's time. Your primary goal is to create a forum from which to make this important assessment and to receive support while doing so. A good coach will assist you in making sure that your business vision is realistic, sufficiently comprehensive, and that it matches the support you feel is required.

Now that coaching has become a popular method for entrepreneurs to gain support, you can set up an appointment very similar to how you can obtain psychological support, and hash out your needs in an hour or two. If you have the right business coach, especially one who has a good entrepreneurial vision and a thorough understanding of the real estate business, your decisions will be far better than if you make them on your own.

This initial stage of growth is critical and Top Dogs know that taking time to consult with an advisor and formulate a business plan is time and money well spent. Moving beyond the comfort zone of operating solo is a challenging step to take. Get the help you need to do it so your business will evolve to its full entrepreneurial fruition.

 FYI!

To find a business coach, use those keywords in your Internet search. If you want to sit down with the coach, key in your locale. If you are open to consulting by phone, you can hire someone anywhere. Go to www.msullivan. com for coaching services provided by the author of this book.

Monitoring Personal and Professional Power

Given the importance of technology in the real estate field, the first type of support your business will most likely need is technological support. Top Dogs realize that technology is their ticket to paradise (or at least to Hawaii), yet before forging ahead for a high-tech overhaul, they take a step back to monitor the four aspects of their business in light of the impact technology will have on it.

In so doing, the Top Dog understands that in order for her personal services business to successfully incorporate highly impersonal technology, technology must be delivered with a human touch. It is therefore necessary to first conduct an assessment of *Personal and Professional Power* to ensure that a good measure of passion, humanitarian values, and good ethics are present in her work:

Caution

Statistics tell that within the first year 40 percent of small businesses fail and within the first five years 80 percent more fail. *The E-Myth* developed by author Michael Gerber is based on the idea that your business is nothing more than a reflection of who you are. If your business is to change, as it must to thrive, you must change first.

- ◆ Principle 1: See your work as your passion.

- ◆ Principle 2: Develop a burning desire to succeed.

- ◆ Principle 3: Be an independent thinker.

- ◆ Principle 4: Have a positive attitude.

- ◆ Principle 5: Be self-disciplined.

- ◆ Principle 6: Be ethical.
- ◆ Principle 7: Have good people skills.

Gary Keller and Joe Williams, the founding partners of Keller Williams Realty, are a perfect example of Top Dogs who practice by these principles. In 1983, these two brokers followed a burning desire to succeed by starting their own brokerage. They positively planned for success, and through a practice of good values, specialized training, and cutting-edge business strategies, they persisted to become a new type of real estate provider. With an entrepreneurial state of mind, they continually reached for new ideals making personal ethics, teamwork, and empowerment strategies part of their business philosophy.

The Keller Williams' system evolved with a strong mentorship program whereby new agents are coupled with mentors, and when they become seasoned, they mentor others. They also developed a rather innovative profit sharing program in lieu of traditional broker-agent commission sharing. Both their mentoring and profit sharing programs are examples of giving and receiving as a consistent flow that energizes and vitalizes business. The result has been a win-win approach whereby Keller Williams teams up with their agents in a personally, spiritually, and financially empowering manner.

The result has been a new generation of broker-agent relationships whereby brokers and agents empower one another and mutually share in the profits of their success. Today, Keller Williams is a highly successful, innovative international company with 273 offices and nearly 20,000 agents. Keller Williams's mission statement is now expressed as follows: "To build careers worth having, businesses worth owning, and lives worth living." Their values are described as, "God, family, then business."

One reason for Keller Williams's success is that their business model is based on *The Principles of Personal and Professional Power.* This type of mutuality of relationship brings a more impassioned, humanitarian quality of service as Keller Williams treats its agents as team members and its agents in turn treat their buyers and sellers as team members. Their relationships are marked by a passion and human touch that is rarely seen in a business environment, especially in the competitive real estate world. I have personally had an opportunity to meet an office of these agents. The difference between these people and agents with other offices is dramatic, to say the least.

Although a Keller Williams's enterprise may not be the goal of all Top Dogs, the vision is nevertheless the same. Many Top Dogs are aware that *Personal and*

The Inside Scoop

M. Scott Peck, the author of the best-selling book, *The Road Less Traveled,* defines the incorporation of these more caring vales as the process of achieving spiritual competence.

Professional Power must be the foundation of their business to thrive in a truly impassioned way, and to fully incorporate technology with just the right human touch.

FYI!

Topping the list of the American Dream is owning your own home. Second to this is owning your own business. Because of the small business owner's inability to compete, small business was gobbled up by big business, putting business ownership out of reach for most. Times have changed with recent exponential technological advancement. It is once again possible for the small business to charge ahead as long as technology is its platform. Small business has been given a second chance.

Obtaining Technology Support

Technology support comes under the category of both administration and entrepreneurial vision in the small business model. It is necessary for basic business needs, yet for the Top Dog it is at the core of future marketing and planning strategies. Monica, another Top Dog, demonstrates the plan she followed to merge high technology with her platform of skilled service and *personal and professional power*. She relates her story in her own words:

I realized in the early stages of my career that technology was a major key to success in the real estate sales business. I realized if I used technology wisely, I would be assured of a greater market share. If I did not, I would be out of business in a few years. I bit the bullet, opting for technology. Since I was not particularly technical, I decided that the best use of my time and patience was to hire a technology advisor instead of trying to master technology myself. My local real estate association continually guided me to the latest computer technology, and it seemed like the assortment of high-tech tools was never-ending. It seems like every time I blink, new technology appears.

First the MLS went online. That was an incredible learning curve for me. Then my desk phone became a traveling cell phone and my lock box became computerized. If that wasn't enough, laptop computers began showing up in the field soon followed by even smaller handhelds. Then wireless technology became the craze. Finally, good old reliable cameras became digital, and now my cell phone takes digital pictures. I have been able to keep in step with technology by having a good technology consultant. Each time new technology becomes available, I hire my consultant to coach me on my purchase options and train me in the use of each device. When I got a laptop and began taking it home and in the field to client's homes, my consultant showed me how to connect it to the Internet in each of my locations. When I began using a hand-held, my consultant coached me on its use and its features. I learned how to synchronize it with my laptop and to download the MLS listings each morning so I can access up-to-date information anywhere in the field.

When it comes to technology, I make it a part of my own personal skill set, using it in every facet of my business. I open-mindedly make technology my friend, not just something my hired help use. I also share its benefits with my clients by personalizing web pages for them containing valuable resources. When I hired my first assistant, I pulled in my technology consultant to train her in the various technologies she would be required to use. I continue to hire my consultant on an as-needed basis as I continue to evolve as technology evolves.

> **The Inside Scoop**
>
> In these high-tech times, there are tons of technology gurus who like to show off their skills for free, especially if they are related. Each manufacturer's website also provides free online tools to navigate you through their products. For Palm's personal digital assistant go to www.palm.com to check out their newest models.

Monitor Your Level of Personal Service

Monica and several other Top Dogs stressed the importance of continuing to monitor the personal services aspect of your business as it becomes more and more technology-based. Monica is sensitive to the fact that while technology has its incomparable advantages, bonding with clients and delivering personalized service cannot be over-shadowed. She understands that technology and personal service must be sustained in equal balance.

Some of our Top Dogs shared ways they achieve this balance. For instance, Monica supplements her technology-based communications with a personal call to or an in-person meeting with her active clients at least once a week. She also includes a friendly and warm personal touch in her technology-based communications with clients. Her e-mail messages always include a personalized salutation and an endearing closing such as "have a nice day" or "with all the best," and she often includes a brief message that is personal in nature. She uses e-mail as she would converse with clients by phone. No one ever said our e-mail communications have to be dry and impersonal.

Another Top Dog who administers his own website brings the personal touch to clients through technology-based concierge services. He creates a page on his website for each new client to provide them with handy resources and transaction information. This isn't exactly the personal touch that comes from pounding the flesh, but clients feel nurtured and cared for by this high-tech customized service. One of the big differences between Top Dogs and bottom dogs is the Top Dog responds to change proactively and sensitively, always keeping sight of their number one objective—to provide quality personal and professional services to their clientele.

Website Support

About four years ago, Monica decided that it was time for her to have her own website. Her technology consultant hired a company to design the site and taught Monica how to administer it herself. With the use of website-administration software, Monica is able to upload photos and text and change her website as her business evolves. Another Top Dog who was as high-tech as a church mouse is so thrilled with her ability to administer her site that she gives monthly online seminars for her clientele. Each month she prepares an informative presentation on a topic that will interest her clients and uploads it to her site. Her seminar happens without her as her local and cyberspace clientele receive a generous portion of quality service.

Administrative Assistance

In addition to technical support, your business will eventually need administrative support. Monica's experiences in obtaining administrative assistance can help you decide how to do the same. About four years ago, when Monica's practice reached about 18 transactions a year, her business reached the critical stage that is encountered by all Top Dogs. It was time to move her business to its next stage by hiring support. Her office had a transaction coordinator, but because there are 15 agents in the office, a 15-way share did not provide the support she needed.

FYI!

Here are some quotes of Top Dogs relating to the subject of getting help and support:

Before I had an assistant I did not have a life. Having an assistant allows me to have more balance and more options.

Earning good money and enjoying your work means spending money and getting support. I do both through hiring assistants.

A secretary saves you time, but an assistant generates income. I hired an assistant and doubled my income in the first year and also freed up my time.

Monica had mixed feelings about hiring someone. On one hand, support would be a welcome relief as it would allow her to give her clients better service and would provide her with much-needed personal time. On the other hand, she had heard so much about the problems employees can cause. She was ambivalent, but decided to move beyond her comfort zone and hire someone. Her decision led her to other decisions. Did she want part-time or full-time help? Did she need a licensed assistant or an unlicensed one? Should her assistant work with her at the office or out of the assistant's own home?

Part Time or Full Time?

Monica felt that she could either split an assistant's time with another agent or hire an assistant on her own. If you find yourself at this crossroad, see whether another agent in your office has an assistant who could work for you part time; or see whether someone else in the office could use part-time help. Since Monica's business grew at a fast clip, and would probably continue to do so, she decided to hire a full-time assistant with real estate experience.

Licensed, Unlicensed, and Experienced?

When considering hiring an assistant, a decision that faces all agents is whether to hire a licensed or unlicensed person. The answer to this question will depend on the specific duties you will require of your assistant. If you find that your assistant can help you most by performing activities directly related to listing and selling properties, he or she must be licensed. Some of the duties that can be performed only by a licensed assistant include developing advertising copy, showing property, explaining a contract or other documents to a client, discussing property attributes with a prospect, and conducting an open house. If your assistant will perform only clerical and administrative functions, the assistant will not need to be licensed. Most states also permit unlicensed assistants to access the MLS and lock boxes.

A good candidate for an assistant is a licensed salesperson in your office, relatively new to the business and still struggling. Monica felt that hiring a new agent was only a good short-term solution since the agent would probably reintegrate into his own business after he got the hang of the real estate business. She wanted a long-term solution.

> **The Inside Scoop**
>
> Fifty-two percent of personal assistants to agents are employed part-time and 46 percent of personal assistants are unlicensed.

> **FYI!**
>
> Agents who share assistants recommend that the assistant work full days for each person, such as Mondays and Wednesdays for one and Tuesdays and Thursdays for the other, alternating Fridays. Working half days for each person poses continuity problems.

In Office or Out of Office?

There are factors that will determine the location where your assistant will work. Is there desk space at your office or will you have to accommodate your assistant in your space? Is it important to you that your assistant be considered an independent contractor (IC) instead of an employee? If so, assistants who work out of their homes are more likely to meet IC status than those working out of your office.

If your personal assistant is an independent contractor, he or she is responsible for all tax obligations. If your assistant is an employee, you are responsible for withholding taxes and for paying various taxes and benefits in addition to the salary you pay. In other words, you will pay more if your assistant is considered your employee. Review the IC requirements described in Chapter 7.

The office where Monica worked did not have space for her assistant, so her assistant would have to share Monica's office space, work out of her own home, or work from Monica's home. Monica opted not to share her office space, nor did she want her assistant to work out of Monica's home. It was also important to Monica that her assistant qualify as an IC, which was another vote in favor of her assistant working out of her own home. Monica's decision was to hire an assistant who could work out of her own home, unsupervised by Monica. (These days another option for agents is to hire a *virtual assistant*, which is discussed later in this chapter.)

Monica also wanted to hire an assistant who had her own equipment so that she didn't have to purchase equipment. Her assistant needed to have a relatively new computer, Internet connection and e-mail, a fax machine, a scanner, and a printer.

FYI!

The laws of the real estate licensing body in your state and the policies of your brokerage company will affect who you can hire. From a legal perspective, a license is required by any person who provides information to the general public that could be considered influential in a real estate transaction. For instance, an unlicensed assistant cannot show a client's property or communicate features of a property to consumers.

The Inside Scoop

IC status for an assistant is beneficial to you since it avoids the payment of employee benefits that can be costly.

Real Estate Lingo

A **virtual assistant** is a support professional who provides administrative, creative, or technical services on a contractual basis. Virtual assistants use advanced technological modes of communication and data delivery, which allow them to work remotely.

Creating a Job Description

The best way to go about hiring an assistant is to first create a job description. Identify exactly what you want your assistant to do. Take the time required to get a good idea of every duty that will be performed by your support professional. Then prepare the following:

- A list of tasks you want your assistant to perform
- A list of skills that will be necessary to get those tasks done

A List of Tasks to be Performed

This is the job description Monica now uses for her assistant:

- Print out daily calendars.
- Process new listings and enter them into the MLS.
- Prepare timelines for each pending transaction, calendar all dates and track them.
- Track the progress of listings.
- Update transaction status reports in the computer database and on the website.
- Order appraisals and inspections.
- Track loan approval.
- Schedule listing presentations, open houses, closings, and other appointments.
- Prepare listing presentation packages.
- Prepare buyer presentation packages.
- Place advertisements for listings.
- Photograph listings.

> **The Inside Scoop**
>
> The National Association of Realtors' most recent survey shows that agents with personal assistants earn 2.25 times more than agents who do not. Twenty percent of agents use at least one personal assistant

- Process *Referral Stream System* gifts and mailers.
- Send progress reports to buyers and sellers.
- Coordinate signage and lock boxes for listings.
- Update the website as needed.
- Coordinate closing paperwork.
- Synchronize information between computer databases.

- Make transaction changes in the MLS database.

- Prepare CMAs in the MLS database.

- Perform listing searches in the MLS database.

- Prepare correspondence.

- Pay bills, make deposits, and perform all accounting on the computer.

Specific Skills

The following is a list of skills an assistant would need to accomplish the tasks listed in the previous section:

- Internet browser knowledge

- E-mail proficiency

- Understanding of database management

- Microsoft Word experience

- Knowledge of accounting and check-writing programs

- Knowledge of PowerPoint for buyer/seller presentations and seminars

- Website administration software proficiency

- Good people skills for dealing with clients and vendors

- The ability to multitask and prioritize

- Knowledge of MLS database

- Technological savvy

- Pleasantness

- Willingness to pick up and deliver flowers, newsletters, mail, and so on

How to Find an Assistant

Now that you know what skills you need in your assistant, how do you find this person? First, ask your office manager. Check with other agents in your office. Contact agents at other offices. Contact your local association for their referrals. Better yet, hire a certified real estate professional assistant.

FYI!

The National Association of Realtors provides certification to real estate professional assistants (REPA) following a two-day intensive introduction to the real estate business and to the specific ways they can support agents. The following is a partial course description:

♦ Understand the business of real estate

♦ Know what MLS is and be familiar with input forms and reports

♦ Be familiar with local listing and sales forms

♦ Know how to manage a transaction

♦ Understand the difference between licensed and unlicensed

♦ Understand the types of agency representation and disclosures

♦ Comprehend key marketing concepts

♦ Be familiar with the level of professionalism and ethics expected of assistants

The best way to find someone who has become assistant-certified in your area is to contact one of the sponsors of this certification program listed on the website of the National Association of Realtors. Contact the sponsor for your location and ask them for rosters of people in your area who have obtained certification.

Another option is to have the assistant you hire complete the two-day certification program. When Monica looked for her assistant the REPA certification program was not yet in existence. She placed an ad in the local newspaper, which read: "Real estate transaction coordinator needed, full time, e-mail resume to (her e-mail address)."

She received 25 applicants, interviewed five, and hired one. She conducted skills testing on the computer and all office equipment and on phone answering. She tested for proficiency at software use and database management. Her first assistant did not work out and her current assistant has been with her for nearly four years.

Monica's business did progress to its critical next stage as a result of hiring support. After 18 months her production nearly doubled, and Monica cannot imagine working without the support of an assistant. She is personally happier having someone to share her business with and for the first time since she became licensed, she has the freedom to take vacations and enjoy more personal time.

Money and Benefits

A specified salary plus bonus for each transaction closed is the most common way of paying assistants. You may also want to pay a bonus for each referral your assistant brings into the office. You can also pay benefits, such as medical, dental, and retirement benefits if you choose. The more you give, the more long-term allegiance you get. If appropriate, let your assistant know that he or she can move up from an administrative role to an independent agent if he or she chooses.

When you hire your assistant, don't forget to market to his or her sphere of influence and to give your assistant a referral fee for all business that comes in as a result. Monica's assistant's contacts have brought her several new clients, for whom her assistant has received referral fees. The circle of abundance has therefore reached Monica's assistant as well as Monica, as it should.

> **The Inside Scoop**
>
> If you do hire employees, as opposed to independent contractors, enlist the help of a payroll service to handle payroll calculation, tax deposits, reporting, and benefits.

Obtaining Virtual Assistance

A virtual assistant is someone you find through the Internet. Virtual assistants can carry out many of the tasks of in-person assistants while performing their work in remote locations. They will primarily communicate with you through e-mail or phone. Virtual assistants have their own high-tech equipment and can give you a wide range of support without even setting foot in your door. There are now virtual assistant educators providing certification as Real Estate Support Specialists. One is the International Virtual Assistants Association, www.ivaa.org.

Having a virtual assistant is really not much different from having an assistant who works out of his or her home. Because of the growing demand for real estate assistants, virtual assistants have become quite popular for the active real estate pro. The one ingredient you miss out on by hiring a virtual assistant instead of a local assistant is that you will not benefit from their sphere of influence. You will have to consider whether this fact is important to you.

> **FYI!**
>
> Searching the Internet led me to web pages of a number of real estate support specialists listing the following services:
>
> ◆ Managing your listings
> ◆ Coordinating your closings
> ◆ Developing your web presence
> ◆ Designing polished marketing pieces
> ◆ Updating your MLS and database program
> ◆ Sending post-closing gifts

You gain several benefits from employing virtual assistants. Virtual assistants expand your hiring options since you have a global pool to choose from, and the competitive prices and services that an unlimited marketplace permits. For example, you might not be able to find a reasonably priced, experienced web designer in your area. With cyberspace as your hiring platform, you have highly competitive rates to choose from and can select a professional from virtually anywhere, not confined by the traditional barriers of time and place.

Virtual Assistance Versus Live Assistance

I have hired virtual assistance for website makeovers, programming projects, and for producing promotional materials. Some websites, such as www.eLance.com, act as middlemen and will place your project out for bid. When the bids come in, you are able to choose the one that best fits your budget, and the hiring process begins. Remote work is particularly well suited to projects that are self-contained, such as web design and administration, database management, mailing projects, and developing presentations.

Virtual assistants offer several advantages over an in-office assistant. First, you have no overhead because you do not provide the assistant with space or equipment. Remember, this person is virtual. Second, they are clearly independent contractors who save you the expense of employee taxes and benefits. Third, you can hire virtual assistants on an as-needed, per project basis. Fourth, they are paid between $15 and $135 per hour depending on the type of service you require. As the Top Dog moves her markets and business communications through cyberspace, virtual assistance can be a cost-efficient and productive way of gaining support.

The Inside Scoop
If your virtual or non-virtual assistant works out of remote locations, you can share information with them as if they have a direct network connection with your computer. With software such as PC Anywhere, they can connect to your computer and share files with you and vice versa. With synchronization software, you can also synchronize your assistant's calendar and contacts database with yours and vice versa. There are many services that provide sync capability, including Yahoo.com, which provides this service free of charge.

Receiving Spiritual Support

Some Top Dogs also pursue spiritual support. They find that real estate and its competitive mindset present a constant challenge to staying aligned with inner values and empowering philosophies. Historically, the business world has very little experience of people living from a conscious, empowered state of mind. There is almost an unwritten assumption that to succeed in the professional world one needs to be ruthless.

Many find that ruthlessness is built into real estate almost more than other professions because of its highly competitive, fast-track environment. As *The New Ideal* takes hold, benevolence will begin to replace the lack of compassion in the real estate arena. The profession will become more empowered and integrity-based. For now, we still face ruthlessness more than benevolence.

Many Top Dogs realize that while a strong business model is essential to success, humanitarian values and spiritual competence are the seeds to deeper, more everlasting rewards. They sense that their work has meaning in relation to the whole, allowing their work to bring them closer to mankind. They realize that as they evolve personally, so does society.

> **FYI!**
>
> M. Scott Peck describes in *The Road Less Traveled*, "As we evolve as individuals, so do we cause our society to evolve. Evolving as individuals, we carry humanity on our backs. And so humanity evolves."

It is the unique Top Dog that feels, "My work is my life and my life is my work." She feeds a yearning for relationship with the world, allowing her business to become a conduit for the life she wishes to live, a visible manifestation of who she is and what she believes. I understand this type of Top Dog because I am one. My business has always been a major source of my connection to humanity, a place in which I engage mankind with the most earnest of my potential. Our small service businesses can become a place where the world becomes a handy size, where we can have a little piece of humanity for ourselves.

Most people with a humanitarian yearning have a spiritual practice that continually rejuvenates them and their business. Your spiritual practice may be based in gratitude and prayer. Some use a practice of meditation. Others seek religion and its community. Whatever your practice, it can provide a pipeline to a source of increased vitality and a greater sense of welfare and benevolence. It can be the reason why you get up each morning feeling the world just can't get any better.

Giving Support Through Mentorship

Many Top Dogs had mentors who helped in one way or another to guide them along their professional paths. When some Top Dogs reach a certain level of professional achievement, they often recognize the need to give back. The process of giving back adheres to *The Principles of Personal and Professional Power*. Sometimes she accomplishes this through community service and involvement; sometimes the Top Dog mentors other real estate professionals on their own career path.

Mentoring is a tool used to guide and develop someone else's career. If you focus on the seven principles of personal and professional power and coach your protégé on the New Ideal, then both of you will gain immeasurably. You have an abundance of wisdom and experience to share, and an attitude of gratitude to go with it. Your protégé has enthusiasm and fresh ideas to share with you. The synergy between mentor and protégé is an awe-inspiring process that feeds both mentor and protégé great riches and reward. For some Top Dogs, the process of mentoring is their way to express gratitude for things gone well.

The Least You Need to Know

- ◆ The successful small business is a mix of entrepreneurial, managerial, technical, and *Personal and Professional Power*.

- ◆ With as-needed technology support, you can keep pace with technology and not have to master it yourself.

- ◆ There are many options concerning an assistant, like full time or part time, licensed or unlicensed, local or virtual.

- ◆ Technology can stomp personalized service out of your business if you don't keep it in check.

- ◆ A spiritual practice can vitalize your business with humanitarian values.

Chapter 22

Staging Your Listings

In This Chapter

- ◆ A look at what a stager does
- ◆ An explanation of curb appeal
- ◆ A lesson in exterior staging
- ◆ A quick course in interior staging
- ◆ A view of why staging is cost effective for you

Another step some Top Dogs take is to stage their listings. They see every single listing as an opportunity to top the market. They analyze the properties they list and have them professionally staged before they are presented to their market. These Top Dogs pay for their own staging, making it part of their listing package. They see it as a cost of doing business and a powerful market advantage. Let's take a closer look at staging and why it has become an important process utilized by some Top Dogs.

The Stage for Home Staging

But first, let's set the stage for the need for home staging. How many times have you visited a property to give a listing presentation and have been greeted by a disorganized mess? The house was fine, its location was excellent, but it was in need of some tender loving care. You wanted to banish the clutter, freshen up the wear and tear, spruce up the landscaping, and give it a brighter overall look. You toyed with the idea of bringing over a cleaning team, suggesting that your clients have a yard sale, or better yet, just rolling in the moving truck early and taking most if it away. But your hands were tied. You serviced the listing as best you could and the property sold for lower than fair market value and took longer to sell.

> **The Inside Scoop**
>
> Do a search on the Internet for "home staging", and then confine the search to your locale. You should find a number of home stagers and a description of their services.

You might occasionally get the courage to suggest staging to clients, but the sellers balk at the idea. Here's how it went with Mark, a typical listing agent. Mark told his clients: "Mr. and Mrs. B, I think we should have your home staged. We find that staged properties sell sooner and for higher prices." Mr. and Mrs. B ask, "How much does it cost?" Mark responds, "It varies, but about $1,500." The Bs respond, "What do they do?" Mark tells them, "They clear out and freshen things up. They give your home a facelift of sorts."

Mr. and Mrs. B respond with, "We have lived here for ten years and we think we did a beautiful job decorating our home. Now you want us to pay $1,500 to have someone undo our decorating. Regardless, we're moving. This isn't the time to redecorate. Moving is expensive. We're already paying you a sales commission, and now you want us to pay more. You know that listing agreement we just signed, the one that's in your folder? Well, we've reconsidered. Honey, call that nice agent we met the other day. We have a listing for him."

Staging Is a Sensitive Subject

Historically, home staging was the privilege of the wealthy. Staging wasn't really something within the province of the everyday homeowner. Times have changed. Staging has emerged as a respected method of increasing the value of a home for sale and reducing the time it stays on the market.

> **FYI!**
>
> Nationwide, the typical homebuyer household consists of a married couple aged 36 with a household income of $71,300. This is the homebuyer staging should be geared toward.

It's not just the cluttered property that staging benefits. The staging process can enhance even the most pristine home, increasing its market appeal and value. In California, where staging is most often used, properties can sell for 5–10 percent more than their non-staged competition. Yet even in California only a small portion of listings in the highest priced areas are staged. In most other areas of the country, staging hasn't caught on at all. If staging is so effective, why aren't more agents using it to sell homes?

For the most part, agents have been unsuccessful in making staging a part of their listing protocol. When they try to incorporate staging into their practices, they receive the response that Mark did. The problem is that home staging carries with it a highly inflammatory potential. The sensitive subject of staging requires just the right ingredients of political correctness and a whole lot of luck to tell an owner who's been living in his home for ten years and has fixed it up to be his dream home that it needs to be redecorated and spruced up.

If you're lucky enough to get past that conversation, you have an uphill battle convincing this seller, who has already agreed to pay you a hardy sales commission, that he should now spend a hefty sum to have his property undecorated. It doesn't go over well.

Agents are understandably hesitant to raise the issue of staging with their clients, afraid they will lose their listings. It takes an assertive and confident person to convincingly assert the position as a real estate expert that staging is an essential step to be taken to produce the best sale price in the soonest amount of time. Most agents have not been able to take this step. Moreover, it is difficult to deviate from the proven and highly successful process of home sales. Change is invariably met with opposition and the real estate sales process is no exception. If it's working, and working well, why change it?

 FYI!

In 2002, the average time on the market nationwide was four weeks, down from seven weeks in the 1990s. Average appreciation across the country for 2002 was 6.8 percent. In the higher priced areas of the country where staging is used more frequently, appreciation is much higher and the time on the market is shorter.

Convincing Clients to Stage

Staging is a sensitive subject at best, especially when you are asking your clients to shell out hard bucks to pay for it. But there is an easier way to accomplish this objective. You can have your listing staged with the blessing of your client. In fact, not only will you have your client's blessing, you will be assured of getting their listing and their many referrals in the future.

The first hurdle is to emphasize that the staging you propose has nothing to do with the seller's decorating choices. It is just a marketing process you feel brings sellers more money than they would otherwise receive. The second hurdle is to pay for the staging yourself.

This is how this Top Dog handles the same situation. The Top Dog starts with: "Mr. and Mrs. B, I believe in getting top dollar for the properties that I list, so much so that I provide staging as a part of my listing services. It costs about $1,500, but I am such a believer in it, that I pick up the cost. Staging has a proven track record of bringing a higher price and a quicker sale than a property that is not staged." Mr. and Mrs. B respond with, "We appreciate it. How can we help?" The Top Dog answers, "The stager will be asking your permission to take a number of steps that result in making homes appeal to a wide range of buyers. Just your cooperation would be appreciated."

Mr. and Mrs. B respond, "Oh sure, whatever we can do. Thanks so much for your help. Will we pay you back when the property sells?" The Top Dog response is, "No, this is part of the service I provide at my cost." Mr. and Mrs. B (to their sphere of influence of 250 people), "Top Dog paid to have our home staged, and it sold in 15 days for more than the house down the street. The home staging process really worked, and Top Dog didn't even allow us to reimburse him. He paid $1,500 out of his pocket, increased our sales price, and reduced its time on the market." Bs' sphere of influence: "What was Top Dog's name and number?" Mr. and Mrs. B, "Better yet, go to his website where the services he provides to sellers are listed, and you can view other properties for sale. It also includes a picture of his family."

> **Caution**
>
> Make sure the designer you hire has extensive staging experience. Staging is a highly specialized service entailing specific proven steps that make a home more appealing to your typical homebuyer.

What Is Staging?

Staging a home for sale is a two-step process. Step one is to improve the home's curb appeal. Step two is to enhance its interior appeal. Home staging is a type of psychological artistry. Nobody was trained for it. There's no licensing for it. Although stagers employ some elements of interior design, they may not be licensed interior designers. Some in the staging field break down the process further by defining *home styling* as reorganizing and redesigning the home's *existing* elements and decor while *home staging* involves bringing in *new* elements and decor. For purposes of this book, we will just call the process *home staging*.

The intent of staging is to create a favorable first impression from the first vision of the property at streetside to the inside entry and throughout the primary rooms through the skillful use of design procedures. Staging a home for sale is actually the opposite of interior design. Interior designers customize a home to the needs and style of its owner; staging is a *depersonalizing* process. The stager neutralizes the home to give it a look that is universally appealing. The process entails wiping the home clean, refreshing it, and furnishing it in a neutral manner so as to make it appeal to the widest possible audience of home buyers.

Home staging is an art form of sorts, which incorporates openness and light while dramatizing entry focal points. The professional stager who has experience staging homes for sale is able to create a home that does not look as if it belongs to someone else. Instead, it looks like a display in a designer showcase. The effect makes buyers want to call it their own. Let's take a closer look at each of these processes involved in home staging beginning with improving a home's curb appeal.

Adding Curb Appeal

Have you ever watched a show on Home & Garden TV called *Curb Appeal*? This excellent show depicts the process of creating curb appeal at its very best. It is no less than miraculous to watch these talented home stagers increase a home's curb appeal.

Exactly what is meant when someone says a home has good curb appeal? Curb appeal is real estate lingo for a house that looks so good on the outside that it says, "Come on in." First impressions are important when it comes to selling homes. Buyers thirsting for their perfect dream home must be greeted with curb appeal in order for a home to reach the top of its market. Curb appeal is an intangible quality that causes buyers to think emotionally instead of logically.

We've all been exposed to good curb appeal. You drive up to a home and you want to make it your own. It could be the grassy lawn, the English garden and arbor, or the meandering walkway. This home speaks to the potential buyer, who responds, "Yes. This is it. This is the home I have been dreaming of." This is that subtle quality called curb appeal. A home with curb appeal will get the attention of every potential buyer who sees it.

> **The Inside Scoop**
>
> The National Association of Realtors reports that good curb appeal is a major contributing factor in 49 percent of homes sold.

When your client bought this home it probably had good curb appeal. But over the course of a long ownership, people just naturally improve the inside of their homes while paying little attention to the outside. When it comes time to sell their home, an ideal opportunity to restore curb appeal comes knocking on the door. Giving a home curb appeal doesn't have to mean major retrofitting. There are eight basic steps home stagers follow:

1. **Landscaping.** Trim, mow, and clear away. Replace flower beds with fresh blooming flowers. Create a small English garden on the way up to the door with a profusion of flowering and wispy plants.

2. **The entryway.** Is the walkway appealing? If not, spruce it up, wash it, paint it, or replace it. If possible, make it meander gently as it delivers buyers to the front door. Do the porch, landing, or stairs need attention? Painting or surfacing can go a long way toward making the exterior entryway more appealing.

3. **The front door.** The front door is a major focal point. Painting or staining it just the right color to anchor entryway features to the house and yard works wonders to revitalize the exterior.

4. **Exterior paint.** Touch up the exterior trim and paint.

5. **Windows.** A good cleaning of all windows and screens will add sparkle to the entire home. Should some trim around the windows be added? Add shutters if they would complement the look. Would awnings enhance the look of the windows?

6. **Accessories.** How about an arbor? Would some wrought-iron accessories be a good addition? Is the fence in good shape or should it be repaired and painted? Would simple additions of roof rails, garden rails, or porch railings enhance the look?

7. **Sprucing up.** Open the front curtains and shutters. Replace the welcome mat with a classy decorative one. Clean out the garage and then keep the garage doors closed.

8. **Neighbors.** What do the neighboring properties look like? One thing stagers sometimes miss is the neighbors' yards. You want your neighbors' homes to look as nice as yours. Often, it is worth paying for a little staging on their properties, if they will agree.

Caution

Your stager should have workers who can follow a basic staging system for a reasonable cost. Be sure, however, that you and your stager agree about what is included in "basic staging."

The Inside Scoop

One method I have used successfully to make the neighborhood more attractive is to offer to spruce up the yards for the immediate neighbors. I have paid to have lawns mowed and debris hauled. I also use this as a door-knocking opportunity to meet the neighbors who have in turn ended up as my future clients. They are always impressed that I stage my listings and pay for this service.

Interior Staging

The following are the primary steps involved in interior staging:

1. **Cleaning, repairing, and painting.** A professional cleaning team deep-cleans every surface, window, floor, carpet, nook, and cranny. All odors are eliminated and air fresheners are placed at ideal locations. Cosmetic and functional repairs are made, such as caulking tubs, fixing drippy faucets, repairing sticking doors, and mending fences. A fresh coat of paint is applied to the entryway and primary rooms.

2. **Getting rid of clutter.** Many homes have many more furnishings than they should. One of the objectives of home staging is opening up the home, giving it an inviting, airy flow. This is done by reducing clutter, furnishings, and accessories. The stager will need your client's assistance in storing many of her furnishings and belongings. All it means is early boxing up or clearing out since they will be moving anyway. About half of contents of closets, shelves, and cabinets should be packed up and moved out of the home entirely. Space needs to be freed up so a buyer can get the feeling of spaciousness.

3. **Depersonalizing.** Your clients are asked to pack up family photographs and personal collections. Buyers need to envision themselves living in the home, and it is hard for them to do so when faced with the seller's personal items. Every room of the home needs to be neutralized to make it attractive to a wide range of buyers. Nothing should distract the buyer or bring his focus to the seller's belongings instead of the house itself.

 FYI!

If you don't already have a stager on your *Power Team*, find one and establish a package that will address basic staging as described in this chapter. It should not cost more than $1,500. There may be add-ons your stager suggests, and your client can decide whether they want to absorb the cost of items beyond the basic staging package.

4. **Open everything up** to increase the flow to the door, through the home and its yard. Furnishings are reorganized to maximize the feeling of space and comfort.

5. **Decorating and accessorizing.** Once the home is uncluttered, depersonalized, and opened up, the process of decorating takes place. Some of the owner's pieces are brought back in while some rental pieces are used for accessorizing and décor. Rental artwork is sometimes placed throughout, plants are often brought in, and decorative lighting is ideally situated. Stagers have sources to rent anything and everything.

6. **Highlighting focal points.** The stager highlights key features particularly in entry rooms, such as fireplaces, view windows, and doors. Sometimes new window treatments and mirrors are added for special effect.

7. **Maintaining.** The seller must commit to keeping the home spotless for the time it is on the market. They should leave the home each day believing it will be previewed by its potential buyer that day. They should keep the outside as well maintained as the inside. Fresh cut flowers are delivered and placed weekly in the home.

Home staging can be done on many different levels, from a thorough cleaning to a remodeling. The more done in the staging process, the better the opportunity to secure a faster sale and a higher sales price.

More advanced staging involving minor remodeling and re-landscaping should also be considered in conjunction with basic staging. High-end properties frequently justify this expense, which may increase an already high listing price significantly. Remodels are generally aesthetic in nature, like removing an inconvenient wall or redesigning an entryway. Landscaping changes may encompass modifying the flow of the garden or redesigning how the yard relates to the home. Only you and your stager can determine whether the market and the property justify the use of advanced staging. Just know that it is there for the asking.

Staging Is an Investment

Why would the Top Dog want to incur an expense that averages about $1,500 a pop? It doesn't sound like a good way to make money. The reason is that it sets the Top Dog apart from the rest and causes homeowners to want the Top Dog to make the same thing happen to their homes. The Top Dog gets a well-deserved reputation for selling homes faster and at higher prices. He also becomes known for being professional enough to know what steps to take and to believe in the results enough to pay for the work to make it happen.

Top Dogs recognize that it takes spending money to make money. This is the Top Dog's thinking. He looks at the time and money he spends to market his business. Sometimes he gets a return; often he doesn't. Most facets involve his time, like the time-intensive prospecting he once had to do. Staging is a direct investment in obtaining a listing and increasing the value of the listed property from which he will make a commission while reducing the time the home will be on the market. It takes none of his time, only that of his stager. He can't really think of a better investment in his business and a more guaranteed return on investment.

When you realize that the new market the Top Dog captures with his listing package allows him to reduce or even eliminate time and money spent prospecting, he's made the staging costs back in spades. But the Top Dog doesn't think in nickels and dimes. He knows that operating a profitable business means making investments. With his entrepreneurial state of mind, he recognizes that this is just another investment in a long line of many made to ensure that his business will thrive and stand out from the rest.

> ### The Inside Scoop
>
> The agent also knows that his expenses are deductible, and that his commission increases with the increase in selling price. His time is valuable, too, so if he can reduce the listing time, he reduces the effort required for additional open houses and reviewing unacceptable offers.

Also, understand that it doesn't have to cost $1500. If you practice in an area where values are below the median home price, have your stager customize a package that costs less but is still effective and impressive. You will know how to package staging within your marketplace to bring forth the very best result for both you and your client, even if its cost is only a few hundred dollars. It's more a matter of gaining client allegiance because you care enough to contribute to their well-being while at the same time enhancing the appeal of their home. This is certainly a winning combination.

When your stager performs her job, have her also prepare a list of add-ons she recommends and her price associated with each. Quite often, once sellers see the transformation brought about by basic staging, they are willing to go further and absorb the cost of additional work themselves. Sometimes sellers are willing to match the contribution you have made, making the staging result all that much more dramatic.

Some homes require more than the basic package to achieve an optimum staged looked. Since money is often an issue, especially when the seller is moving and often upgrading to a more expensive home, we have a system in place that allows the seller to pay at closing when the house sells. If the extra work is provided by our stager or one of our regular workers, they agree to defer payment until closing. In the unlikely event that the property does not close, the seller signs an agreement to pay within 30 days of expiration of the listing. If the contractor providing the add-on will not defer payment until closing, I advance the payment with my client's agreement to reimburse me.

The Least You Need to Know

- A stager is a professional whose business is to make a property appealing to buyers at sales time.

- Curb appeal is the first impression that every property you list should have.

- The interior of a home should look spacious and airy.

- Most homes have too much clutter and too much furniture and accessories.

- A properly staged home will typically sell quicker and for more money than a similar home without staging.

Chapter 23

Future Income Streams

In This Chapter

- ◆ What is a *Future Income Stream*?
- ◆ Why is real estate an excellent investment choice?
- ◆ How can you invest in real estate without investing money?
- ◆ How can you creatively put together real estate investments?
- ◆ How can you package your business for future sale?

Top Dogs focus on ways to earn income without spending too much time earning that income. Although commission earnings are far better than hourly earnings, they are still tied to your time. If you don't spend the time, you won't receive an income. The same is true for any fee-based service.

Top Dogs also focus on ways to earn profit free of taxation. This means investing in real estate. They have "intuitive antennas" that are always searching for ways to invest in real estate so they can earn profit and exchange out of their investment without being taxed. In this manner they stockpile earnings tax-free, and if they do cash out without reinvesting, they are taxed at the lower *capital gains tax rates* instead of *ordinary income tax rates*.

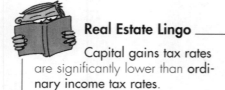

Real Estate Lingo

Capital gains tax rates are significantly lower than ordinary income tax rates.

If you start out your real estate career with the intention of creating *Future Income Streams*, you will have a future marked by financial abundance even if you are unable or unwilling to work. You will develop a frame of mind that continually probes for income stream opportunities. This chapter shows you how some Top Dogs accomplish this objective.

Creating Future Income Streams

There are four primary ways of creating *Future Income Streams* within the real estate sales field:

- Continually investing in real estate

- Turning your commissions into equity interests in clients' properties

- Facilitating stock market transitions to the real estate market

- Selling your business

Each of these is discussed in the following sections, but first, we take a look at your personality characteristics to see if you have an investor state of mind. Don't worry; if you don't, you are on your way to one right now.

The *Rich Dad* Books

I highly recommend Robert Kiyosaki's *Rich Dad* books, but most particularly *Cash-flow Quadrant*. He categorizes people as employees, self-employed, business owners, or investors depending on the way they generate income. Employees work for someone else and find security more important than money. The self-employed are their own bosses, rarely delegate, and generally work very hard with their earnings tied to their time. The business owner hires others to do the work while she navigates the ship. Business owners make money that is tied to their time far less than the self-employed.

The last category, and the one we all aspire to reach, is the investor group. This group makes money *with* money, irrespective of the time they put in. When you become an agent, you join the ranks of self-employed, but if you follow the steps in this chapter and in *Cashflow Quadrant*, you will join the right quadrant of the business owner and investor instead of settling into a life of the self-employed, always single-handedly taking the bull by the horns, commission by commission.

Investing in Real Estate Continually

As a real estate professional, you are exposed to deals every day of your life. You're continually in the right place at the right time. The question is, will you take advantage of your setting? Most agents do not.

Start investing in real estate whenever and wherever you can. We've seen the stock market collapse. Real estate has a reliable long-term rate of return, and with its preferred tax treatment, it really can't be beat. The demand for real estate will increase as investors transition from the stock market to the real estate market, especially when investors hear that retirement funds can be used to purchase real estate (addressed later in this chapter). Investment real estate has more tax advantages than any other investment. You receive investment income and appreciation, but your taxable bill diminishes as you take advantage of *depreciation*, *tax deductions*, *capital gains*, and *tax-free exchange* tax benefits.

> **Real Estate Lingo**
>
> **Depreciation** is the allocation of the cost of an improvement over the life of the asset in the form of a tax deduction. Other *tax deductions* for investment property are mortgage interest, property taxes, and insurance, to name a few. **Capital gains** tax treatment allows you to be taxed at minimum tax rates on sale while a **tax free exchange** defers any tax on gain at sale as long as you replace your investment property with another.

Take Commissions as Equity Interests

One way to create an income stream is to transform a potential commission to an interest in your client's property. If you are not a broker, you may not be able to apply this equity conversion to the company's portion of the commission, but you can for your own portion of the commission. In so doing, you also transform the tax laws relating to what you will earn, and you move from the quadrant of the self-employed to the quadrant of the investor.

Commissions are taxed as ordinary income whereas profits on long-term investment property ownership are taxed as capital gains. For

> **Caution**
>
> Check with your tax professional regarding criteria that must be met to avoid a finding of imputed income. Imputed income is income that would have been earned and taxed in a certain manner but was changed by an act of the Taxpayer.

example, $10,000 of the commission is your split. You and your client, the buyer, agree that you will convert your commission to an ownership interest in the property acquired. As a result, you start an automatic *Future Income Stream* because you will earn an agreed upon percentage of the property's appreciation and any income it may produce. This procedure is called equity sharing.

It works like this. Had you received your $10,000 commission, you would have earned $10,000 exactly and been taxed at ordinary income tax rates. You did not receive a commission; instead, you made an investment in real estate. As the owner of real estate, taxation is deferred until the real estate is sold later, at which time you have the option of exchanging tax-free into another investment property or paying tax at lower capital gains rates. The net result is you have reduced or deferred tax on earnings, set up *Future Income Streams*, and presumably will make a good tax deferred profit.

Not-so-Top Dogs do things differently. They are famous for not taking advantage of their ideal circumstances. Somebody asks them to keep their commission in a property, and they take offense, responding, "Don't you think I deserve to earn a living? Don't you think I have expenses to pay?" This is self-employed mentality speaking.

Top Dogs are different. They enter into the investor quadrant and take advantage of the opportunity to create *Future Income Streams*. The by-product of *Income Stream Mentality* is that you become financially sophisticated, and both you and your clients benefit from your expertise. You earn respect for your real estate acumen, acting as both agent and financial partner in your client's transactions.

> **FYI!**
>
> A recent survey by NAR indicates that 31 percent of agents have 100 percent commission arrangements with the offices they work for. They still pay fees, but not by commission split. For these agents, they are able to transform all of their commission to equity interests.

> **Caution**
>
> A potential conflict of interest arises when you become an owner with your client. Detailed, written disclosures are required along with a good measure of integrity.

The Inside Scoop

You may wonder how your investment in a client's home can be your *investment* property for tax purposes. Tax treatment depends on *your* tax treatment of your investment, not your co-owner's use of the property as his principal residence. Thus, your ownership interest qualifies as your investment property. For more information on this interesting strategy, go to www.msullivan.com and click on products.

Facilitating Stock Market Transition

Top Dogs are set up to take advantage of ideal economic conditions by specializing in emerging markets. In the current marketplace, the public can no longer count on the stock market as a means to make them rich, so real estate, with its enviable consistent record of performance and beneficial tax treatment, is more attractive than ever. In addition, with mortgage rates at all-time lows, real estate leverage is extremely advantageous.

These conditions provide the ideal setting for Top Dogs to facilitate investor transition from the stock market to the real estate market. Your average investor is highly motivated to invest in real estate, yet he does not have the know-how to tap the lucrative real estate investment pot. Top Dog steps in to create a ready marketplace to rescue investors from the stock market and transfer their investments to the real estate market. Top Dogs cater to investor needs by providing a seamless way for clients to cash out of the stock market and into the real estate market. They are able to fit the needs of the investor wanting to acquire an investment property on his own or just a small percentage of a property.

> **Caution**
>
> The Dow Industrials declined 6.2 percent in 2000, 7 percent in 2001, and 17 percent in 2002; whereas the NASDAQ declined 39 percent in 2000, 21 percent in 2001, and 31.5 percent in 2002. In 2002, the real estate market appreciated 6.8 percent nationwide.

Create Diversification Opportunities

Top Dogs create *stock-size* investments in real estate to satisfy the stock market investor's desire to easily diversify and buy-in with small contributions. Investors are accustomed to calling their stockbrokers and saying, "Buy me some Cisco or put me into something with fixed income." Who do they call now? How does your typical investor directly invest in real estate?

Enter stage left, the Top Dog specializing in stock market transition. Agents who can help clients invest in bite-sized percentages of property ownership are able to scoop up the business stockbrokers had in the 1990s. In fact, a number of stockbrokers have transitioned into real estate sales and are providing this very service, yet now it is under the umbrella of real estate and is called limited partnership interests instead of shares in Cisco. They acquire investment real estate in the name of a limited partnership or limited liability company and offer investors bite-size ownership percentages.

The Top Dog is the person an investor can now call and say, "Put $20,000 into a good appreciating real estate investment." The Top Dog has a client base of investors and is able to pool them together in real estate investments. In return, the Top Dog receives a percentage of ownership instead of a commission on purchase and again on sale. The following sections show you how this works.

Your Business Plan

Aside from consistent appreciation, real estate is more attractive than the stock market because real estate comes with a set of tax benefits that stock market investments do not enjoy. With real estate, investors can deduct payments made and pay no tax on gains. All you need to do is collect stock market weary investors, which is not a hard thing to do. Just put yourself in the middle of any group of thirty-somethings and up. Or stand on a corner with a sign that says, "Real estate investments, $20,000 each." They will come in droves.

Next find the properties into which you will pool your investors. The philosophy is that the investors supply the initial capital and make the payments while you convert your commission, put the deal together, manage the investment, and receive a commensurate ownership interest. You will also receive the listing at sale later, which can again become a commission conversion to tax-free equity. Stock market transition is an opportune market for the Top Dog who is willing to work creatively and with *Income Stream Mentality*.

The More the Merrier

You can make your investment pools as simple or extravagant as you desire. If you decide to put development projects together, you may want to add additional members to your investment team, and your *Power Team* members are the most likely candidates. The following are categories of professionals that may choose to contribute their time to a project in exchange for a portion of the appreciation at the end:

◆ Attorney for the contract work

◆ Developer for subdivision work

- ◆ Contractor for property improvement
- ◆ Engineer for property improvement
- ◆ Loan broker for contributing commissions earned on loans procured

When the professionals whose services are required to put a development project together contribute their time in exchange for equity, a development project has the best chance of success and profit. Top Dogs cultivate contacts with professionals with similar *Income Stream Mentality* and have ready teams to put together when a development opportunity comes along.

Use of a Business Entity

You can either use a business entity such as a limited partnership or limited liability company to hold title to these properties or you and your clients can go directly on title. The more investors participating in one property, the more inclined you will be to use a business entity. Lately we have seen a resurgence of *limited partnerships* that were so popular in the 1990s.

Before tax reform of the late 1990s, limited partnerships were a popular method of owning and operating real estate because they allowed limited partners to take tax losses for their investments and to enjoy limited liability. In those days the savvy agent became a general partner in a client's investment and earned a portion of the appreciation in return for his services in pooling investors and managing the investment.

With tax reform, the limited partnership no longer enjoys preferred tax treatment, yet the structure of the limited partnership is ideal for agent-facilitated real estate investing. Whether a limited partnership or limited liability company holds title or the agent and client go on title individually, the intent is the same—the agent takes an ownership interest in lieu of a real estate commission, just as the general partner of the limited partnership did.

> **Real Estate Lingo**
>
> A **limited partnership** consists of one or more general partners and limited partners and is often used as a real estate investment vehicle. Limited partners have no personal liability. This structure provides asset protection.

Qualified Retirement Fund Investment

Now that your imagination is working, you say, "This would be an incredible venture if investors could use their qualified retirement funds to buy real estate." Since you asked, the answer is, "Yes, they can." The one qualification is that if the property is subject to a loan, special rules apply. Retirement funds can be invested in co-owned real estate, as long as the retirement funds are safely segregated in its own ownership interest. The main considerations with retirement funds are as follows:

◆ Retirement funds must be transferred to a self-directed retirement account, which means hiring a custodian to take title on behalf of the account owner.

◆ If the property will have a loan, carefully follow the criteria for self-directed retirement accounts.

◆ Make sure the retirement account investor's interest is safely expressed as a separate but undivided percentage interest in the property if there is more than one owner of the property.

FYI!

When joining with others owning and operating real estate, liability is always a concern. As part of the service you provide to your investors, you may want to form a limited partnership (LP) or limited liability company (LLC) to hold title to the real estate and appoint yourself the managing member and the investors as passive members. The LLC is similar to the limited partnership but the LLC provides a better shield from liability. With one of these entities in place, you will have the best vehicle to appreciate your new investment, rent it out, and shield yourself and your investors from liability. Have an attorney set up the first company. After that, just follow the same format.

It may sound as if this type of service is beyond your expertise. It actually sounds a lot more difficult than it is. It just takes registration of the LP or an LLC with the Secretary of State and an operating agreement in which you allocate percentage interests according to the contributions each member makes. If you want to forgo the LP or LLC in favor of one less step, owners can hold title as tenants in common, subject to an Equity Sharing Agreement identifying each owner's ownership interest and obligations. The equity-sharing format affords no protection from liability, however. See www.msullivan. com, products, for tools on these subjects.

One very popular way of using retirement funds in real estate is to acquire a retirement home. Until your client reaches retirement age, he is not able to use the home for personal or family use, not even for the typical vacation home personal use period. Thus, he rents it out and income is paid to his retirement account. At retirement age, the retirement home is distributed to him. As facilitator of these transactions, we help our clients move their retirement funds to appreciating and tax-preferred real estate, we help them choose their retirement homes, and we manage or facilitate rental of it until they retire.

If we had as many real estate investment brokers as we have stockbrokers, taxpayers would understand that their retirement funds can purchase real estate instead of dwindling in the stock market. Since it is not in the best interest of stockbrokers or retirement fund managers, taxpayers are unaware that their retirement funds can purchase real estate with the assistance of an account custodian, whose role is very similar to that of the *exchange intermediary*.

To find these custodians, search on the Internet under "self-directed retirement account custodian," and you will find a variety of capable firms that have long good-standing histories. The custodianship process is simple. The client's retirement funds are signed over to the custodianship of the self-directed account manager. Then the account manager takes title to the designated real estate in the name of the retirement account. There is a fee for this service, just as your stock broker received a fee for her service.

> **Real Estate Lingo**
>
> An **exchange intermediary** facilitates an exchange of real estate under IRC section 1031.

> **The Inside Scoop**
>
> For example, go to www.pensco.com. This site provides detailed information relating to purchases of real estate with self-directed accounts. They also respond to e-mail inquiry and are knowledgeable and helpful.

Selling Your Business

An important place to look for an income stream is right in your own backyard. Well, not exactly your backyard, but in your business. Every business owner looks to his business for *current* income streams. Every successful entrepreneur looks to her business for *Future Income Streams*. The entrepreneur's mindset is to plan for the future *now* by setting up her business knowing she will sell it when the time is right.

Knowing that you are building something that will live on indefinitely, the administration of your business becomes less mundane and may even border on exciting. Your marketing talent comes to life on behalf of your client's properties, and your business also becomes beneficiary of your active imagination. You dream up names to call certain tasks. You begin to assign logos and mottos to your business. You see it as a thriving enterprise because you know it is your nest egg. It is not just a humdrum place where you earn a living until you're 60, and then it's gone. It is your golden egg that earns you a good living now and an early retirement later.

They Are Your Clients

I can hear you say, "How can I sell a business that has a broker attached to it?" You can. The clients are yours, not your broker's. The clients go wherever you go. If you or your successor leaves this real estate firm, your solid reputation and strong client base go with you.

Many agents obtain their broker's licenses when they reach a certain level of success. Some choose to go work on their own alone while some hire other agents to work for them. Some never leave the firm they're with because they are comfortable with the reputation or the support it provides. Whichever route you follow, your business and your clients are yours. When you sell your business, if you are with a firm and you feel the success of your business depends on staying with that firm, you will build in a contingency that the successful purchaser must place their license with the same firm.

> **Caution**
>
> Broker-associate contracts generally do not address ownership of the agent's client list, yet it is prudent to review this agreement with respect to this issue.

Be Entrepreneurial-Minded

Most people are not entrepreneurial-minded. They develop successful businesses and when they retire, the business does too. In other words, they stay in the second quadrant of the self-employed. For Top Dogs, the business lives on and provides an active income stream into the future. Even if your business is a professional service such as real estate, it is a highly marketable business opportunity if you plan it that way from the beginning.

When you retire, you can refer clients to your successor and make money from each referral. To do this, build into the purchase agreement a contingency period to approve of your buyer, so before you commit to a sale you know your successor will continue the business with a similar degree of success and integrity. Stay involved in the transition from yourself to the successful purchaser for a year or two. To ensure successful continuity of your business, it is in your best interest to allow the transition to take place over a well-measured period of time, so your clients and your successor will find a successful rhythm together.

Because your income stream depends on your successor's success, you want to do everything you can to ensure that the purchaser will be successful. Also, you want to leave your clients with someone who treats them well and will fill your shoes effectively in satisfying their real estate needs.

It might seem early to start thinking about selling your business if you're just starting it up. But *Income Stream Mentality* should become your state of mind early on, especially in the business formation stage. The time to ready your business for sale is now, not when the goodwill of your business has dwindled and you need to find an income stream. With this state of mind, every function of your business should be set up as a prototype that can be operated by the person or company to whom you sell your business. Everything should be turnkey. Your buyer turns the key and the business operates itself.

> **The Inside Scoop**
>
> The seller services provision of the Business Opportunity Purchase Agreement should detail as specifically as possible the extent of the seller's availability in terms of days and hours of days and the types of services the seller will render for the period of time agreed to.

Your Business Opportunity Checklist

Here is a checklist of points to consider as you set up your business with an eye toward selling it later:

♦ **Organize your client database and keep it organized**. You want to be able to show the extent of your client list and a history of your transactions. If you decide to sell ten years from now, you want to have organized and easily ascertainable records that will show all transactions and all clients. *Goodwill*, one of the most important business valuation factors, is based on how long a company has operated as shown by its records.

> **Real Estate Lingo**
>
> **Goodwill** is the value of the advantages that a business has developed as a result of intangibles such as business name, reputation, and length of operation.

♦ **Maintain good accounting records**. Part of a business opportunity valuation is to analyze the business's gross and net income and its expenses. Use a good computerized accounting program such as Quick Books or its equivalent and have computer printouts of all income and expense categories for each year of operation. Have your tax returns clearly labeled and organized for easy review by your purchaser. These records should be produced for at least three years prior to the sale of the business.

> **FYI!**
>
> Often only the prior three years of records are produced to the buyer. However, some buyers want to review longer periods, and the willing seller should be able to produce them.

♦ **Have systems in place**. Businesses have more value if the talent responsible for its success is not dependent on a single person, but instead depends on systems incorporated to increase profit. Follow the *Referral Stream System* and instruct your buyer in the use of it. The system will have been in place for a period of time showing a reliable rate of return, and all your buyer will need to do is to continue what you have done.

Your Future Income Stream systems, too, should have a proven track record, allowing your buyer to step into the income stream models you have built. Your website and its marketing features are another valuable component of your business. The more self-sustaining systems you incorporate into your business, the more value it will have without you. In fact, if you have sufficient systems in place, you should seriously consider franchising your company as opposed to selling it.

Real Estate Lingo

Franchising is the licensing of others to use your business name and/or business format in return for a fee.

♦ **Have competent personnel in place**. If you have a competent staff or assistant to work for your purchaser, your business will better retain its continuity while operation shifts from you to your purchaser.

♦ **Obtain a good lease**. If your business is at a leased location, obtain a favorable long-term, transferable lease before you sell your business. A long-term lease with options for renewal will guarantee the business's location for your purchaser, which will also increase your business's value. It is generally important for purchasers of real estate businesses to stay in the same location where the business operated.

♦ **Incorporate your business**. Consider incorporating your business if you have not already done so before the sale to your buyer. Incorporated businesses are considered more valuable and more transferable than unincorporated ones.

♦ **Take back a note**. Consider creative financing by taking back a note as part of the purchase price or receiving a percentage of the profits as they come in. Many times you can get a higher sales price and instill confidence in the buyer if you do so.

♦ **Offer your services**. Many people stay on with their business for a period of time, perhaps one to two years, to bolster buyer confidence and ease transition problems with your client base. An employment contract with you will benefit you and your purchaser.

- ◆ **Maintain documentation.** Make sure that you maintain good documentation on every transaction you handle. A buyer has more confidence in a business that is well documented and organized and can show its proven track record.

- ◆ **Organize and retain your bank statements.** You will need to prove your income and deposits so the buyer can confirm gross and net sales figures.

- ◆ **Monitor the financial ratio of income to expense so you can provide this information as part of your buyer package.**

- ◆ **When it is time to sell, hire a business broker to list your business.** This professional will prepare a business valuation and suggested listing price just as you would with a comparative market analysis. This valuation is understandably more in depth than the analysis for the sale of a home.

> **The Inside Scoop**
>
> If you are with another office when you sell your business, the broker will have your past files for a period of five to seven years after the closing of a transaction. Brokers will cooperate with you in making records available to your buyer.

The Least You Need to Know

- ◆ Your *Future Income Stream* is the key to your future earnings and gives you freedom from working sooner rather than later.

- ◆ As an agent, there are opportunities to create *Future Income Streams* all around you.

- ◆ You can allow your commission to be converted to an ownership interest in a property.

- ◆ You can put together investment deals and even use qualified retirement funds of investors to purchase income property and other real estate investments.

- ◆ Your business can be packaged for sale or for franchise with some careful planning.

Glossary

access easement   An access easement is the right to use someone else's property for access only.

adverse possession   The acquisition of property through prolonged and unauthorized use of someone else's property.

agency relationship   In real estate, this is a relationship where your client, the principal, is represented by you, the agent, to act on her behalf.

amortization   A process by which you gradually pay off a debt by making periodic payments to the lender.

appraiser   This person's job is to estimate the value of property as of a particular date.

arbitration, binding. A legal process that replaces the court system and the appeal process if the parties so agree in writing.

asset protection   The sheltering of assets from excessive taxation and personal liability by the use of irrevocable trusts, family limited partnerships, house trusts, and limited liability companies, to name a few.

bridge loan   A short-term loan made in expectation of a permanent, longer-term loan. Also know as a swing loan.

broker's open house   This is the property showing for the agent community as opposed to the open house, which is the showing for the public.

capital gains tax rates   The tax rate you pay when you profit on a long-term real estate investment. This rate is far lower than ordinary income tax rates.

capitalization rates   These represent the relationship between the value of the property and the income it produces.

CC&Rs   See covenants, conditions, and restrictions.

closing professional   The escrow agent or closing attorney (depending upon which handles transactions in your state). The closing professional serves as a neutral intermediary facilitating the transaction to closing.

closing statement (a.k.a. settlement statement)   A detailed accounting of buyer and seller debits and credits in the transaction. This is one of the last steps the closing professional performs in a transaction.

community property   A way of holding a title by married persons in states that have community property laws.

community property with right of survivorship   A way of holding a title by married persons in some states that have community property laws, which allows the surviving spouse to receive a deceased spouse's interest without probate.

comparables   Similar properties recently sold, which are located in the same proximity as the subject property.

comparative market analysis (CMA)   A summary of comparable properties in the area that are currently listed, in escrow, have expired, or have sold recently.

conditional contract   A contract that has conditions that make it nonbinding until the conditions are removed.

condominium   A property developed for concurrent ownership where each owner has a separate interest in a unit combined with an undivided interest in the common areas of the property.

contingencies   Conditions that are built into a purchase offer to make it conditional. The offer is conditional until such time as the contingencies are removed. The most common contingencies in the real estate transaction are loans, physical inspections, and reviews of title.

contingency release   A contingency is released either by satisfaction or waiver. There is a specified time period for this to happen.

cooperatives   The ownership of property by a corporation in which each resident owns a percentage share of the corporation, but does not hold title to the property.

counteroffer   A response to an offer that changes or adds terms, such as change in price or closing date.

covenants, conditions, and restrictions (CC&Rs)   Rules that govern how a property looks and/or is used. They are common with condominiums and multi-use properties, but also sometimes pertain to single-family homes.

deed of trust   A document used in some states while mortgages are used in others to secure a lender's interest in a property.

default   This occurs when you do not meet a legal obligation.

depreciation   Allocation of the cost of an improvement over the life of the asset in the form of a tax deduction.

dual agent   An agent who acts for both the seller and the buyer.

E&O insurance   *See* errors and omissions insurance.

easements   Rights to use the property of another person for a specific purpose. Easements are recorded on the title on both the property enjoying the right and the property burdened by the right.

eminent domain   The governmental right to take private property for public use as long as it fairly compensates the owner.

equity   The difference between the value of the property and the loans against it.

equity sharing   A real estate co-ownership strategy whereby one party, the occupier, lives in the property and pays its expenses, while the other party, the investor, puts up the down-payment funds. They share tax deductions and profit. Many other structures are also possible, but this is the most popular.

errors and omissions insurance (E&O insurance)   Insurance that covers you for any claim made against you for your real estate services.

escrow   The independent third party that holds the funds and distributes them according to buyer and seller instructions and processes and prepares the transaction documents. Depending upon your location, escrow is either an escrow company or a closing attorney.

exchange (also known as tax-free exchanges and § 1031 exchange)   Tax-free exchanges, which are also know as 1031 exchanges, allow tax on profits to be deferred for real estate owners selling investment, rental, business, or vacation real estate and investing in other real estate.

exchange intermediary   A professional who facilitates an exchange of real estate property under IRC § 1031.

exclusive right to sell listing agreement   A type of listing agreement between an owner and agent that pays the agent a commission even if the property is sold by someone else during the listing term.

extrovert   A person who directs much of his or her energy to the outer world of people and things. An overwhelming number of real estate sales agents fall into this category.

family limited partnership   A specially designed limited partnership, consisting of one or more general partners and one or more limited partners, which can provide asset protection from personal liability and discount valuation for estate tax purposes.

fee simple   The highest and most complete ownership one can have in a property.

feng shui   The ancient Chinese science of balancing the elements within the environment. *Feng shui* means "wind and water."

fiduciary duty   A requirement to act on behalf of your client with the utmost care, integrity, honesty, confidentiality, and loyalty.

floor time   The rotation of agents to respond to inquiries that come from advertisements and signs. These agents get the walk-in traffic and phone calls to the office when no particular agent is requested.

for sale by owner (FSBO)   A property put on market by an owner working without an agent.

foreclosure   To liquidate the property for payment of a debt secured by it.

franchising   The licensing of others to use your business name and/or business format in return for a fee.

goodwill   The value of the advantages that a business has developed as a result of intangibles such as business name, reputation, and length of operation.

grant deed   A deed that transfers title to a property and makes certain title guarantees.

handheld organizer   A minicomputer of sorts that fits in your hand and holds your contacts, MLS database, calendar, and e-mail.

home sale/purchase contingencies   Sellers accept offers contingent upon finding a new home. Buyers make offers contingent upon selling their home.

independent contractor   A worker with the right to direct and control the way he works, including the details of when, where, and how he does his job.

inspection contingency   The right for the buyer to perform inspections he feels necessary to discover the condition of the property. Often this period is 15 days in a fast market.

joint tenancy   A way co-owners hold title in nearly all states if they want a surviving co-owner to receive the deceased co-owner's interest without probate. The co-owners do not have to be married.

lease option   Allows the buyer to occupy the property with a right to buy it at a later date.

limited liability   A company that affords its members limited liability similar to a corporation and pass-through taxation similar to a sole-proprietorship or partnership. It can provide asset protection and discount valuation for estate tax purposes.

limited partnership   A partnership consisting of one or more general partners and limited partners, often used as an investment vehicle. Limited partners have no personal liability. This structure provides asset protection.

liquidated damages agreement   A provision in the purchase agreement where the seller retains the buyer's deposit if the buyer defaults on the purchase.

listing   A contract between broker and owner that gives the broker the right to sell or lease the property.

listing agent   The broker who acts for the seller according to the terms of the listing agreement.

listing agreement   The contract between the seller and broker, which outlines what the broker will do for the seller and how much the agent will be paid.

living trust   A written agreement that appoints a trustee to take charge of assets, thereby sidestepping the probate process at death.

loan approval   The full and final process whereby the lender approves of the loan and the property that will secure it.

loan contingency   The period during which the buyer obtains loan approval. The loan contingency often expires 30 days prior to closing.

lockbox   An attachment to a door that holds the key to that door. Agents have a key to the lockbox so that they can obtain the key to the property on site.

locked in loan   The status of a loan when the lender guarantees its rate and terms.

mechanics liens   Recorded liens that contractors and suppliers may record on a property if they have provided services or materials to the property.

mediation   A settlement process that precedes legal proceedings and is often agreed to in the purchase agreement.

metes and bounds   A method of identifying a parcel by reference to its boundaries and its shape.

mortgage   Used in some states, while deeds of trust are used in others to secure a lender's interest in a property.

multiple listing service   A database of properties listed for sale and rent within a certain locale.

net proceeds sheet A document that helps sellers understand what their closing costs will be and how much they will net from the sale.

open house An open house is a set date and time when a home for sale is opened to interested buyers to tour.

option agreement The right of a buyer to buy a property at a later specified time and price.

passive loss Loss in excess of income on a rental property.

personal property Anything on the land that is moveable.

physical inspection contingency See inspection contingency.

preapproval The lender takes all the confirmation steps it would for full loan approval with the exception of appraisal of the property (since the property has not yet been located).

prequalification A lender takes the potential buyers' application and prequalifies them for a loan based on the information provided, but undertakes no confirmation of the buyer's information, as it does in preapproval.

property profile The report a title company provides that includes a property's title vesting, loan, tax information, legal description, and information on surrounding properties.

prorations The division of a property's expenses between the buyer and seller as of the property's transfer date.

quitclaim deed A deed that transfers any interest someone has in a property, and contains no warranty of good title.

real property The land, its rights, and anything attached to it.

recording The act of entering instruments affecting title to a property in the public record.

referral fee A fee paid for referral of a client.

section I conditions, pest control report Conditions that have existing damage.

section II conditions, pest control report Conditions that do not have existing damage, but if not corrected in the future, they could lead to damage.

self-directed retirement account custodian A fiduciary who holds retirement funds for a client to be invested pursuant to the client's instructions. These accounts are most commonly used for real estate investments.

self-employment tax   Social security and Medicare tax paid by self-employed taxpayers on the net income from their trade or business.

seller financing   When the seller agrees to make a loan to a buyer.

seller-only services   The single agency representation of the seller only.

selling agent   The agent who brings in the successful buyer.

set back   A requirement that is established by zoning law or agreement between neighbors as to how far an improvement may be situated from a certain marker.

settlement statement   Also known as a closing statement, this is a detailed accounting of buyer and seller debits and credits in the transaction.

sphere of influence   The first group you will market to, which should be heavily weighted with current contacts but also include people from the past.

stager   A designer or decorator versed in staging properties for sale.

staging   A specialized service entailing specific proven steps that make a home for sale more appealing to your typical homebuyer.

survivorship   A right whereby a co-owner automatically receives full title without the need for probate when a co-owner dies.

tenants by the entirety   The way husband and wife hold title in 27 states if they want the surviving spouse to receive the deceased spouse's interest without probate. It is similar to joint tenancy used in other states.

tenants in common   A way for co-owners to own property together without survivorship rights. Their interests pass to their heirs, not to one another when they die.

title company   A company that performs a title search to make sure all rights and obligations affecting a property are set forth in one report for the buyer's review.

title insurance   A policy guaranteeing that title is clear and the property is legally owned by the seller.

title report   The report issued by a title company or closing attorney reporting the condition of title to a property as disclosed by a search of the public record.

transaction timeline   A timeline that details the dates by which the steps in a transaction must be taken.

trust account   A bank account that holds funds that clients have entrusted to an agent to be used on the client's behalf.

virtual assistant   A support professional providing administrative, creative, or technical services on a contractual basis.

virtual tour   A 360 degree depiction of a property as if it were photographed with a video camera.

warranty deed   A deed that transfers title and guarantees that title is free and clear.

zoning   A governmental regulation regarding the use of a property. For instance, a property may be zoned for use as a single family residence.

Index

C

D